INSIDE THE GESTAPO

Facsimile version reprinted by

Progressive Press
PO Box 126
Joshua Tree, Calif. 92252
ProgressivePress.com

July 2008

Limited edition.

Pending search for copyright holders.

Classification codes:

HIS014000   HISTORY / Europe / Germany

POL042030   POLITICAL SCIENCE / Political Ideologies
/ Fascism & Totalitarianism

HIS027100   HISTORY / Military / World War II

TRU001000   TRUE CRIME / Espionage

Inside The Gestapo
Hitler's Shadow Over the World

★

HANSJÜRGEN KOEHLER

PALLAS PUBLISHING CO. LTD.
12 *Henrietta Street, London, W.C.*2

FIRST EDITION - JANUARY 1940
SECOND EDITION - JANUARY 1940
THIRD EDITION - MARCH 1940
FOURTH EDITION - MAY   1940

Made and Printed in Great Britain at
The Mayflower Press, Plymouth. William Brendon & Son ,Ltd.

Contents

★

5

INTRODUCTION

★

I AM A HAUNTED MAN.

When, on a sunny September morning, I entered the free country of Switzerland, I was amazed at my own good luck. I still am. People have been kidnapped and killed for possessing infinitely less knowledge than that which I carried out of Nazi Germany in my head and in my secret notes. I feel like a man who is carrying dynamite in his pocket with a lighted fuse attached. Or like a little boy walking in a jungle where fangs and claws lurk in ambush for his blood.

It must be a minor miracle that I am still alive to write this book and recount my story. To the best of my knowledge I am the only man who has escaped from Germany to tell a tale—and who really had a tale to tell. At least such a tale, of bloodshed and violence, of intrigue and cunning, of secret executions and briberies; of courage and cowardice and the whole gamut of human baseness and human greatness.

A fair-sized library could be collected from the books written on Hitler's Germany. Many of them are accurate; still more are full of misinformation and distortion of facts. Hate hinders clear sight and confuses the issue just as much as do undue admiration and misguided loyalty. I shall try and avoid both. I do not hate the masters of to-day's Germany. In my humble way I have shared in their power. I left their circle voluntarily; and up to now they had done me no harm. I think that, except for a few cold and scheming intellects like that of Reinhard Heydrich, they are to be pitied. History has proved the axiom that violence ends in violence and dictators seldom die in their beds.

Nor do I admire them. Most of them are much too human, these leaders of Nazidom, with all the human frailties and even some of the saving graces. They think that they are guiding events and shaping destinies; whereas all the time circumstances are forcing them into new, desperate gambles. This is the tragedy of dictators and their satellites; they can never turn back: they can never halt. Every success must be surpassed, every result outdone by some more audacious coup, more bluff, more threats—till they reach the pinnacle and have to face the abyss on the other side.

A thick pane of glass shields me from the icy wind which ruffles the surface of virgin snow on the mountain-side. The radiators fill the room with a caressing warmth; in Germany most people are huddled around a stove trying to get a little heat out of synthetic fuel. There is a shortage of firewood in Germany and coal is used to stoke the furnaces of factories working day and night—making guns, guns, ever more guns, which are more important than butter. There is fruit on my table—in Berlin and Vienna people are queuing up for a pound of frozen apples or sprouting potatoes. One Sunday every month every family in the Reich has a " one-dish lunch "— but there are hundreds of thousands whose lunch is one dish all through the year. If they are not actually starving, they are certainly not overfed. And how could it be different when farmers are taken from their ploughs to build forts and gardeners from their gardens to erect dams? In Upper Silesia they tried to grumble—and three hundred of them were arrested by the Gestapo.

But the Germans are a hardy race—they can stand privation and suffering longer than most of the nations in Europe. This they proved during the last years of the Great War; they proved it again during the terrible period of inflation when the Mark made a nose-dive and people had to carry billions to pay their tram fare. It is for their souls, their immortal spirits that I tremble.

I used to know a Berlin family. The father was a retired naval officer, still connected with a large shipping firm. His wife was a doctor. They had three children, fair-haired little angels, two girls and a boy. They were Aryans—not even the most painstaking research could find a single drop of Jewish blood in their veins. They had expected much of

Nazism; a new national consciousness, sweeping economic reforms, a higher standard of living. They were disappointed —at least the father was. One night, in the privacy of their dining-room, he voiced his opinions. Two days later he was arrested and taken to a concentration camp, where he is still waiting for a release which may never come. His fair-haired little daughter, his pet and spoiled darling, had denounced him. She was twelve and had had almost five years of undiluted Nazi training. She "thought it her duty" to denounce anyone who dared to speak against the Fuehrer and criticize his god-like acts.

Episodes like this happen every day. The Gestapo has its voluntary or involuntary agents in every household. Sometimes it is a trusted servant, grown grey with the family service; the janitor of the block of flats; tram conductor or the attendant in the park. Germany has become a country of suspicious glances, of whispers and surreptitious movements. Even those who are high up in the governing machine are afraid. Many of them had fallen, many had been "purged" or "eliminated." Nobody is safe from slander or intrigue. And the spiritual effects of such a system may be worse than its physical ones.

Every dictatorship has its main characteristic, determined by the qualities of the people who live under it. In Nazidom the leading spirit is Prussianism and Hitler's reign differs from that in other totalitarian states by being so horribly systematic. There are perennial jokes about the German passion for order, discipline, and system in everything. These qualities have been put to rather grim uses in contemporary Germany. The persecution of both Jews and Gentiles has been organized on a businesslike basis, with severe efficiency. Nobody can escape it—sooner or later he is overtaken and robbed of his possessions or his life . . . or both. The same strict logic is shown in the organization of the Gestapo which can be called the most efficient, the most formidable secret police organization in the world. While the British Intelligence Service may have more money, the French Deuxième Bureau more imagination, the Russian G.P.U. more fanatics at its disposal— there is no hidden cranny of German life into which the tentacles of the Gestapo do not probe; there is no country in the world, be it never so distant or so unimportant, in which the Gestapo has not its agents. Hitler's shadow falls over the world—and the projector of this shadow is the German Secret State Police.

Some of the chapters of this book may read like a cheap thriller. But never has Oscar Wilde's paradox of life imitating art been so true as it is nowadays. Has not the German State built up its religion on a paganism which hardly even existed outside books and Wagner's operas? Are not the roots of the Fascist State of Italy embedded in a pseudo-Roman civilization which has very little to do with the Rome of Cæsar and Augustus? Modern statesmen are even fonder of quoting poetry and shaping their ideas according to doubtful philosophers than were their colleagues of the eighteenth century. If life is sometimes stranger than fiction, neither life nor fiction can be blamed.

To my best knowledge every word of what I have written down is true and according to the facts. I have been connected with the Gestapo in some capacity or other almost from the time of its inception. I have served in the Saar and in Berlin; I have worked in close association with its leaders.

The object of this book is not to offer " sensational revelations " or to add to the literature of vituperation which is glutting the bookstalls of every capital. Nor is it a confession. I would like to state the facts and let the reader draw his own conclusions. I do not think that Messrs. Hitler, Goering, Goebbels, Himmler and the others will have a single sleepless night after reading or hearing about this book, but it may help towards understanding of the strange phenomenon of Nazi Germany and its most horrible weapon, the Gestapo.

I said that I am a haunted man. I may be signing my own death warrant by the publication of this book—and if at the moment this sounds melodramatic, ample reason will be found for the statement in the later chapters. I am not condemning my would-be murderers, for if I did so I would be condemning myself. For a great many years I have been taking part in their schemes and have been their accomplice. Much of what I have done I loathe to consider now ; of many things I have deeply repented. But sometimes it has been fun and sometimes adventure of the best kind in the world. When a man takes his life into his hands and throws it into the lap of the gods, he cannot complain if he meets a violent end.

To those who have arrived at a cross-road and attempt to look back ; to those who have failed and tried again ; to those who believe in justice and a brighter future of Mankind—in short, to the idealists, I dedicate this book, the inside story of the Gestapo which is also a chart to the tortuous channels of Nazi Germany.

AROSA,
1939.

CHAPTER I

★

THE BIRTH OF THE GESTAPO

THE POTSDAMERSTRASSE IS ONE of the main thoroughfares of Berlin's West End. Squat and ugly blocks of flats flank it, the twin glittering tracks of tramways mark it.

On the night of the 30th January, 1933, all lights of a flat in the house at the corner of the Potsdamer and Luetzow-strasse were ablaze. Behind the heavily curtained windows men were coming and going, taking their orders from a slim man with soldierly bearing who wore the brown shirt of an S.A. leader. Kurt Daluege, in his private flat which he rented as a member of the Prussian Landtag, was organizing the raids against the Communists in the North and East of Berlin. Heavy trucks, armoured cars screeched on the wet pavement; machine-guns and hand-grenades were being stored; and dozens of streets awoke to tortured desperate life. Adolf Hitler had become Chancellor of the German Reich and his henchmen were exacting a terrible reckoning with those who did not share their convictions. Men, women, and children were rounded up, taken to the cellars of the Field Police in the General Pape Strasse, or simply executed on the spot. The raiders were especially keen on discovering and destroying the secret printing works of Communist publications. Sometimes they found only a miserable duplicating machine in the cellar of a poverty-stricken worker's flat; sometimes they wrecked linotypes and the full equipment of an up-to-date printer. All through the night the wheels raced, the brakes screeched.

The Gestapo had commenced its work.

The man who created the German Secret State Police has

many other titles and offices. Field-Marshal Hermann Goering had originally conceived the structure of the Gestapo as an enlargement of his own bodyguard. It is neither to his shame nor to his credit that the spirits he liberated—like the magician's apprentice of Goethe—have become almost stronger than their creator. Once at least the leaders of the Gestapo deliberately jeopardized Goering's life—as will be seen later— and the Prime Minister of Prussia, Air Minister of Germany, Chief Forester of the Reich, to mention only a few of the portly gentleman's titles, has lost a great deal of his influence over the Secret State Police.

It was not so at the time when I first came into contact with the dreaded organization. Hitler had just become Chancellor; Goering was appointed Minister of the Interior for Prussia. This was a key position and Goering used it to its full extent. He had two men to help him in creating a deadly weapon for the Nazi Party, apart from the already existing S.A. and S.S. men—Chief Government Councillor Diels of the Prussian Ministry of the Interior and the professional soldier, Kurt Daluege. Diels has relapsed into complete obscurity—but Police General Daluege is still an important personality in the Gestapo.

Councillor Diels was a very ambitious man. His ambition was like a devouring flame—he sacrificed everything to it. He married the daughter of a rich industrialist, a member of Germany's " iron and concrete aristocracy." His marriage opened doors to him which would otherwise have remained closed to such a comparatively junior civil servant. During the short chancellorships of Papen-Bracht and General Schleicher he gained considerable influence. During this time he met Hermann Goering, " Hitler's diplomat," and became an intimate of Papen. This did not hinder him from playing the informer for Adolf Hitler and supplying the Nazi leaders with data on every movement of their opponents or allies. When Hitler met Papen secretly in the house of Schroeder, the banker, it was Diels who had arranged the principal details and who acted as intermediary between the parties. This was the momentous meeting which led to Hitler's chancellorship. . . . In those critical last days of 1932 Diels had his finger in every political pie, and took good care to have a door open into every direction.

He was a " rising young man " under Severing, the Social Democrat Minister of the Interior, being a department leader of the Political Branch. When Papen and Bracht ruled, he committed his first serious blunder—and became the laughing-stock of Germany. In his zeal to earn publicity and promotion he gave his worthy attention to the matter of—bathing dresses. Never have these prosaic or enticing garments been regulated so fully ; their length, material, circumference and every other detail was laid down in solemn paragraphs by the solicitous Herr Diels. The police edict was laughed out of existence, but not even ridicule could kill this man. He continued his intrigues under Schleicher and when the great day dawned, he became leader of the Secret State Police under Hermann Goering.

Alas, the ambitions of Herr Diels were not fulfilled. To-day he is a man who counts for very little. He lost his important job and became head of the local government of Cologne. Even this position he could not hold. His wife objected, probably to his attitude towards bathing dresses—or, perhaps, to the girls they contained—and divorced him. Herr Diels has joined those " has beens " who are on the board of the armament factories. Not that he should be pitied. He provided against a rainy day by putting away a very gratifying sum in a Swiss private bank. But even this is perhaps scanty compensation for an ambitious man. . . .

However, when the " old man," Paul von Hindenburg, relented and the " Bohemian corporal " became Reich Chancellor of Germany, Herr Diels was very much in evidence. Hitler was Chancellor but Papen still hoped to rule him. The Nazis needed a bogy to frighten Germany into complete submission. The bogy-man was conveniently provided by Communism and the process later led to the mysterious Reichstag Fire.

Now Herr Diels knew all about Communists and Social Democrats in Germany. A Social Democrat had been his chief ; in his various political peregrinations he had met the leading lights of both parties. He " reassured " his new masters that they had nothing to fear. These men were harmless. It was true that several million people had voted at the last presidential election for Thaelmann, the Communist candidate—but they were either in hiding or . . . had joined the Nazi Party.

It was a rather bitter joke during the Austrian Chancellorship of Dolfuss that party loyalties were always governed by the stomach. According to an anecdote four members of the Austrian Heimwehr—a conservative and patriotic organization —were walking two and two through the Prater.

" I say," said one Heimwehr man to the other, pointing to the pair in front of them, " do these two Communists know that we are Nazis ? "

It was rather like that in the first days or even weeks of Hitler's chancellorship. Loyalties were still undecided and " just to be on the safe side,"(Herr Diels advised Hermann Goering to organize a Political Police which would possess extraordinary executive powers and would have as its sole task the combatting of " Communism and Marxism and other subversive influences." This was the birth of the Gestapo.

I have said that loyalties were divided at this time ; hence it was rather difficult to find the personnel for such a police organization.

" We need men who will be blind and deaf and dumb when we want them to be so," Hermann Goering told Diels. " We want automatons—but they must shoot straight."

Diels overcame the difficulty by recruiting the criminal investigators and policemen of the Department 1.A. in the Berlin Police H.Q. Their leader was an honest and simple man—Criminal Commissioner Heller, who was promoted to the rank of Criminal Councillor. This, of course, was only a nucleus, but it proved a very useful one.

The next step was to find headquarters. This, again, offered no serious difficulty. The Communists had a central building, the Karl Liebknecht House, comfortably equipped. Even if it had been wrecked a little in the " first flush of enthusiasm " the damage could easily be repaired. It was re-named Horst Wessel House and Heller set up his headquarters there. Not for long, however, for some weeks later Diels took possession of the building of the former Labour Courts. To-day, this forbidding house in the Prinz Albrechtstrasse of Berlin's South West is called Gestapo Building.

The Police in most countries of the world is an executive organ for law and justice, more or less under the direction of State Attorneys. The Gestapo would not dream of submitting to such authority. As a matter of fact, it became the supreme local authority in Prussia. It was only later that branches were organized in the provinces. Herr Diels' domain remained solely Prussia; in the other parts of Germany, Heinrich Himmler, Reichs Fuehrer of the S.S., reigned supreme over the police. It was Himmler and his faithful satellite, Heydrich, who finally ousted Diels from his position and obtained control of the Gestapo.

When Hitler came to power, hell was let loose in Germany —but especially in that sluggish, yet lovable city, Berlin. Every little S.S. or S.A. leader used the unexpected opportunity to pursue his private feuds. People were killed, kidnapped or flogged who had nothing to do with politics, who were not even Jews. No man on earth can boast of complete freedom from enemies. He may have trodden on a pet corn of someone, or spoken harshly to the janitor's son who kept him waiting when he wanted to get into the house. Even less active offences sufficed to constitute serious danger. The fact that a man had a suit of better cut or a more elegant motor car made him a target for revenge.

Jew-baiting and Jew hunts went on all the time. I was walking one day in the Friedrichstrasse when some young S.S. men cornered a well-dressed, swarthy, black-haired gentleman carrying an attaché case. They took him under a doorway and proceeded to manhandle him. In vain did he protest that he was the secretary of a South American legation and certainly no Jew. When I interfered, the young hooligans favoured me with scowls. There was no other way—the gentleman in question had to prove that he did not possess the physical propensities of a Jew—and even then he did not get an apology. " Accidents happen, old man," one of the S.S. youths said and they went on their way blithely. The swarthy young man

B

straightened his tie, shrugged his shoulders and went on. He knew, as well as I or his attackers did, that a diplomatic protest would be duly filed—and forgotten.

About the end of the second year of the Nazi regime, a little pamphlet was circulated both in Germany and abroad. Its title page depicted a highly romantic castle on the Rhine and it bore the legend : " Come to Romantic Germany ! " The next two pages contained only the ominous words : " . . . and you will be treated like this." " Like this " was detailed in the rest of the pamphlet ; a careful selection of atrocities committed against foreigners. Every item was supported by full data of places and names. A most amusing document, though hardly effective as " Come to Germany " propaganda.

Such cases were most frequent in the first weeks of the Nazi regime and were especially prevalent in Berlin. The Gestapo was founded not least for the combating of such " independent actions," to create order and discipline in chaos, to originate a system, so beloved to all Prussians. Formally it began its work only at the end of March, 1933, after all other existing authorities had miserably failed to check the hordes. " A German is hard to rouse, but when he is roused, hell's fury is nothing compared with his," a famous general once said, and during the first three months of the fateful year 1933 this dictum was certainly proved true. Even the Gestapo did not succeed in fulfilling its task at the outset. Hermann Goering had to use his trusted bodyguard, the so-called Field Police, to stop the senseless murder and torture. Only through the Field Police was the Gestapo installed as the highest authority in Prussia.

This Field Police was later disbanded and most of its members absorbed by the Traffic Police. Its leaders were Captain Weiss and a former Major Schneider of the infamous Ejrhardt Brigade. It would be utterly false to think that these were " ordinary policemen." They were simply another branch of hooligan whom Goering kept under an iron discipline, and who were able to command respect even in the members of the S.A. and S.S. But when Goering, or one of his henchmen, ordered the arrest of some opponent, he had to be prepared for torture and death, just as if the S.A. or S.S.

had arrested him. The walls of the cellars in the grim building of the Field Police which was in the General Pape Street were thick and whatever happened there must be shrouded in darkness. Those nights in the underground passages and rooms constitute the grimmest chapters in the reign of the Nazis. There was only one slight difference between being tortured by the S.A., S.S. or the Field Police, the victims of the latter could not be taken to the General Pape Street without the knowledge of Hermann Goering or Herr Diels.

In order to avoid too strong resentment in the S.S. and S.A., the Gestapo gave them free rein in the " management " of concentration camps. Whatever they did in these horrible places, they could do without fear of punishment. Sometimes when necessary to stage a tragi-comedy of " shot while trying to escape," the Gestapo even obligingly helped the guards of the concentration camps.

" They are only well-known Marxist pigs," Herr Diels told me once. " The best they deserve is death—painful death. . . ."

He had good reason to change his opinion when, on and after the 30th June, 1934, well-known Nazis were delivered into concentration camps—Nazis who had been guilty of the bad judgment to back Ernst Roehm instead of Hermann Goering. But at that time Herr Diels was no longer responsible for the Gestapo. . . .

Nominally Vice-Chancellor von Papen was responsible for everything in Prussia. In fact, Hermann Goering, the " provisional Minister of Interior," would never dream of taking orders from him. Not that von Papen ever tried to do such a thing. Goering had his henchmen. Herr Diels was only one of them. The other was much more important and was lucky to retain his position up to the present day. Together with the new Prussian Minister of Interior S.S. Group Leader Kurt Daluege entered the building of the Ministry.

Kurt Daluege had volunteered in the Great War and fought through it. Afterwards he became a chief lieutenant in the " Black Reichswehr," that strange army which facilitated Hitler's coming to power. As a guerrilla fighter he was among those who stormed the Annaberg in Upper Silesia, fighting a terrible battle with the Polish insurgents.

But every guerrilla war must end and Kurt Daluege had to find a job. It was considerably less romantic than sniping Poles or storming enemy machine-gun nests. He became book-keeper of the City Scavenger Department in Berlin. He joined the Nazi Party and was one of its first deputies in the Prussian Landtag.

To-day, Kurt Daluege is a staid, settled family man and a Police General. He earned his high position by suppressing the bloody Stennes Putsch at the command of Dr. Goebbels who, at that time, was Gau Leader of Berlin. When Stennes was blackballed and Ernst Roehm became the Chief of Staff of the S.A. Daluege became commandant of the newly founded S.S. in Berlin. Not a very intelligent, but a diligent and tenacious man, he earned the respect of the Reichswehr and the sympathy of Goering. Soon after the Nazis came to power he became a Police General—the Reichswehr had to be con-sulted about such an appointment—and is to-day the chief of the uniformed police of Germany. Nominally he is even the deputy of Heinrich Himmler, although there is not much love lost between the two.

Daluege was dependable ; when Goering wanted something to be done, Daluege did the dirty work. Two days after Hitler was appointed Chancellor, on the 1st February, 1933, Kurt Daluege was called by Hermann Goering into the Prus-sian Ministry of Interior to " reorganize " the Prussian police and was appointed " Commissioner for special purposes." He brought an efficient aide-de-camp in the person of Captain Gourdet, who was later supplanted by Police Captain Schlange.

Daluege's appointment caused considerable resentment. Here was a man who had had no police experience, suddenly he received powers possessed by nobody apart from Hermann Goering. Intrigues started, poisonous tongues wagged. Daluege bided his time.

The leader of the law department in the Ministry of Interior was the newly appointed Councillor Luetgenbrunn. A cunning fox, Luetgenbrunn used his position and connections to extort immense amounts from clients he professed to defend.

He was one of Daluege's most dangerous enemies, but he broke his own neck—by his greed. The Nazi leaders did not mind graft so long as it was not public. But Luetgenbrunn's crookedness became public through the infamous Nordwolle trial. For some time he was even imprisoned—but he never came up for trial. He had to give up his position and to promise never to practise law—but his huge fortune was left intact. Nor did his intrigues against Daluege have any success. Daluege was a soldier, disciplined, silent, blindly loyal—and such a man had always more weight with Goering and even Hitler than an " intellectual." Goering had been sincere when he said that the word " culture " made him loosen his gun. Luetgenbrunn and many of his colleagues had too much " culture " for the liking of the former Air Force captain. . . .

But Luetgenbrunn was only small fry. Daluege had another rival, almost from the hour of his appointment. It may sound strange that the mystic, dreamy philosopher of the Nazi movement, the Baltic German Alfred Rosenberg, should have the ambition of becoming the head of the Gestapo. And yet this was the case. Goering had outwitted Rosenberg, and he felt his influence waning. It was Goering's prestige, Goering's connections which created the way for Hitler to Papen and Hindenburg ; he had an unquestionable share in the appointment to Chancellor of the Reich. Therefore, Rosenberg was planning revenge. The best way, he thought, would be to discredit Daluege and thereby discredit Goering himself. Let us add at once that he failed in his intrigue. Whether good or bad, he was too much of a philosopher to be a merciless and cunning intriguer. His judgment was also faulty, or he would not have chosen as his accomplice that curious rascal, Harald Siebert.

Siebert had been an intimate and friend of Rosenberg even at the time when the former was " officially " working for the Social Democrats, Noske, Scheidemann and Severing. He also came from the Baltic. Being an agent of the Social Democrats did not deter him from spying on behalf of the Communists, Heckert and Kippenberger. As a " journalist " he was an expert in forging political news and documents. There was hardly any political pie in pre-Nazi Germany in which he had not a finger. Hardly an intelligence service to which he had not sold himself at one time or the other—be it the Russian G.P.U., the Black Reichswehr or the party centres in post-war Germany. During the war he was intelligence officer for a Russian army corps—fighting against Germany. He had an associate, Ernst Doeffinger, who kept a news office in Berlin and who was Siebert's agent when he wanted to sell something to the French Deuxième Bureau. To-day both of them are loyal Nazis, although they do not belong to the Party. Times change and loyalties change with them. . . .

Alfred Rosenberg gave to Harald Siebert the task of manufacturing some " proof " which would lead to the fall of Kurt Daluege. But for once, the cunning and skilful Siebert slipped up. He concocted a long, impudent and stupid document accusing Daluege of anti-Nazi practices, and especially censoring his association with a doubtful individual named Ary Marr. Marr had spent a considerable part of his life in prison as a swindler and confidence trickster ; he had at least eight or ten criminal sentences in his more than questionable past. It must sound rather fantastic that the " philosopher " Rosenberg, who had little inkling of realities and who is still counted as a man of unimpeachable honesty, could believe in the effectiveness of such a silly accusation. His honesty did not prevent him from associating with such rascals as Siebert ; and he must have sincerely believed that Goering and Hitler would drop Daluege when they read the accusation.

The only connection between Daluege and Marr consisted of an offer of the latter to supply incriminating material against certain high state officials from the pre-Nazi period. Daluege, himself, did not know of this offer which was made to his aide-de-camp, Gourdet. But when he found out about Marr's record, he ordered his arrest and had him placed in a concentration camp, while Gourdet was transferred. But the false accusation returned like a boomerang to Siebert, and his friend Doeffinger. It was Marr who had denounced them before he himself was arrested. They were taken immediately to the torture chambers in the General Pape Strasse and spent there some extremely uncomfortable days. Only days— because Rosenberg felt a certain obligation towards his fellowintriguers and they were transferred to Munich, which meant their complete liberation. Heinrich Himmler and Reinhard Heydrich, who reigned in the Bavarian capital, hated their Prussian rivals; whoever was an enemy of the latter, became their friend. Harald Siebert remained in Munich, taking good care not to cross Daluege's path again; he soon gained the personal favour of Heydrich for whom he is still working. But the days and nights in the barracks of the Field Police must have been terrible even for such a hardened man—for Harald Siebert had tried to commit suicide by severing an artery. . . .

"Everyone against everyone"—this was the motto in the first weeks of the Nazi regime and so it has remained with very little change through the long, eventful years since January, 1933./ Such schemes and intrigues as Rosenberg's were not at all uncommon; Party leaders who appeared arm-in-arm in public, their faces wreathed in smiles, snarled at each other when they left the limelight and would have cheerfully stabbed each other in the back.

But Kurt Daluege felt safe under the wings of the all-powerful Goering. He was officially appointed a Director of the Ministry of Interior. He saw himself already as the chief of the Prussian Police—when, unexpectedly, another rival appeared. It was Goering himself who had selected Herr Diels, and Daluege had to endure with hardly veiled fury the little, modest Councillor becoming the leader of the newly founded Political Police, the Gestapo. It did not exactly help matters that in this capacity Diels was not responsible to Daluege, but only directly to Goering! Everybody knew that the Gestapo was, and would be, the most important organization in Prussia. Goering had made it evident in the long conferences which he held in his office at the Ministry of Interior. I had the honour of taking part in some of these discussions. Goering loved them. He, as so many of his colleagues, was drunk with the sense of his new power and liked to air his deviously acquired information and roughshod wisdom; hardly a day but he spent hours lecturing to his subordinates; enthroned like a demi-god in his huge arm-chair, he held forth on various matters. Nothing was too trivial to escape his attention ; and his vassals had to listen with well-simulated rapture.

Herr Diels had sat all through these conferences, unobtrusive, quiet as a mouse. His Nazi colleagues paid him scant attention. Nobody thought it important that after the conferences were finished, Herr Diels was always recalled and had long private conversations with the mighty chief. He was an expert, to be used and discarded according to necessity. Most of the others were newcomers who knew comparatively little about the material with which they had to cope. Herr Diels was known as the possessor of an immense knowledge of things and persons. But everybody was more than astonished when this little man became suddenly the master of the Political Police.

Divers considerations influenced Goering in his choice. In the first place, he knew Diels much better than anyone could suspect—and Diels knew *him* sufficiently well to exercise a little gentle blackmailing pressure in his " modest " demands. This also was the reason why Goering ridded himself of the blackmailer when he felt himself safe enough. Then again, Daluege would not have been the man to handle such a delicate and dangerous organization as the Gestapo. Diels was a clever and intelligent man with an agile mind ; hardly a situation could arise with which his cunning could not cope. As he had not been a member of the Nazi Party before Hitler's coming to power, he could never dare to try and supplant his lord and master. Goering could not have found a more willing and, at the same time, more intelligent instrument.

Thus, Herr Diels became suddenly an equal of Kurt Daluege. At Goering's command their field of activity was strictly divided. Even so, a certain co-operation was necessary. There never was much love lost between Diels and Daluege. " The old fighter " Daluege met the " March Victim " Diels with suspicion, a polite but aloof coldness. " March Victims " were those who had become members of the National Socialist Party only in February or March, 1933—those cautious men who changed their loyalties after the event and not before it. Diels, of course, belonged to the latter group.

The clever and cautious man was strangely misguided in

his choice of friends. After being repeatedly snubbed by Daluege, he became intimate with the young Berlin S.A. leader, Karl Ernst—the famous Karl Ernst whose name is connected with the mysterious document purporting to be the real story of the Reichstag Fire—the man who was shot during the purge of the 30th June, 1934. Ernst's execution weakened Diels' position considerably and in the end the leaders of the S.S. succeeded in ousting him from his position. It was not Daluege's doing—he could not do anything against Goering's collaborator—but the action of two others who ultimately became the masters of the Gestapo. Dark-haired, grim, Heinrich Himmler and ambitious, merciless Reinhard Heydrich were the fatal opponents of Herr Diels and these two became the lords, not only of the Gestapo, but of the whole German police. It was Himmler and Heydrich who shaped the Gestapo to become such a deadly weapon in the hands of Germany's new overlords. . . .

CHAPTER II

★

THE MASTERS OF THE GESTAPO

"NEVER UNDER ANY CIRCUMSTANCES," Reinhard Heydrich told me, " are any women or children related to prisoners to be admitted to our Chief. It is our full responsibility that he should not be brought in contact with them." Then he added, with a queer little smile : " Heinrich is a sensitive soul."

I was more than a little surprised. Heinrich Himmler, Chief of the German Police, master of the dreaded S.S. in the whole Reich, did not impress one as a particularly sensitive or sentimental being. He was a Nazi of long standing ; he had become an intimate of Hitler during the exciting days of the misfired Putsch in Munich, 1923. He has a forbidding, rather unpleasant face and the fact that he wears pince-nez makes him look like a school inspector suffering from severe, chronic indigestion.

His rise in the Party was connected with the fact that he was Gregor Strasser's secretary—he worked for the man whose children had Hitler for their godfather and whom Hitler had had executed. Strasser had been the organizing leader of the Nazi Party. Compared to the excellent propagandist, Himmler's mental qualities could not be called very brilliant. But he always had known how to hide this fact behind a front of flattering and nauseating servility in the presence of his Fuehrer. Also, he was incredibly unscrupulous ; he could be blind and deaf and dumb whenever there was an unpleasant task to do. He made himself practically indispensable—if there is such a thing as a human being whom Hitler considers indispensable.

Himmler has another talent which—strange as it may

seem—has made him a special favourite of Adolf Hitler. He is an excellent raconteur, and has an inexhaustible fund of funny stories. The melancholy and moody Fuehrer appreciated that his chief of the S.S. was also an amusing clown who entertained him whenever things seemed to be particularly gloomy.

It is rather ironical that Himmler is considered by all his friends, and also by Hitler, as "extremely honest," and "rather sensitive." No doubt he is a pedant and a prig whom the smallest speck of dust, a slightly tarnished button, can send flying off into a terrible rage. I have seen him show signs of the deepest distress on seeing an inkstand or a file out of the usual military precision on his desk. His subordinates often tremble when they spill a drop of ink, or if some papers slip from their hands.

It is also true that Himmler is "rather sensitive." At least, he is addicted to tears and easily touched by any misery which he sees with his own eyes : hence the reason of Heydrich's strange order. If Himmler had been allowed to see an imploring woman, a weeping child, he might have ordered the release of a husband or a father from a concentration camp or "protective custody." Therefore, Heydrich and his associates guarded him carefully from such calamity and Himmler was never allowed to see any petitioner.

Heydrich succeeded in creating a reputation for Himmler, making him out to be a tyrant and a "man of iron," whereas, in truth, he was a sadistic weakling and an unscrupulous sycophant. His suave flattery, his cunning sense of intrigue have made him more dangerous than any strong "go-getter" could be. How formidable an enemy he can be is an experience which even such an important person as Hermann Goering could not avoid.

Himmler has one pet aversion : the General Staff of the Reichswehr. He hates "the reactionary generals" with all the passion of his thwarted soul. The reason for this antagonism is not far to seek. The Reichswehr always refused to have anything to do with Herr Heinrich Himmler. In the beginning the Chief of the German Police tried his usual method of flattery and subtle innuendo ; but Major-General Fritsch and his staff remained adamant. Himmler sent letters and messages; he chose intermediaries who, he hoped, would have some influence with the General Staff; he called in person—all in vain, he was not appointed a member of this exclusive coterie. He would have been entitled to receive the rank of a Major-General as the Reich Fuehrer of the S.S. and chief of the "Black Division." His failure was the more galling as Hierl, the chief of the Reich Labour Service, and Huehnlein, the chief of the Nazi Culture Chamber, had attained this rank. Thus Himmler, with secret gnashing of his teeth, had to endure Kurt Daluege, his underling, becoming a commanding general, fully acknowledged by the Reichswehr, while he still lacked any military title.

Himmler is the personal friend of Hitler; the Fuehrer gives him unlimited powers in every police activity. But he will never be able to go beyond this activity. His field is strictly limited—and even if he is tempted by richer pastures, he can never trespass. Hitler's friends can never become Hitler's rivals.

Himmler's deputies are as different from each other as two human beings can be. Kurt Daluege, of whom I have given a thumb-nail sketch in Chapter I, is at the head of the whole German uniformed police, a friend of the Reich Minister of Interior, Dr. Frick and Hermann Goering. Although an important and well-established personality in the Party, he never had any influence on the Political Police—the Gestapo.

The all-powerful police executive of the Third Reich is neither Himmler nor Daluege—his name is Reinhard Heydrich. Without him, Himmler would be just a senseless dummy; without him Daluege's uniformed police could not withstand the terrific pressure of hidden discontent and foreign disapproval. He is the man who moves everything—behind the scenes, yet with unchanging dexterity—he is the Power Behind the Throne, pulling the strings and following his own dark aims.

Heydrich is young and intelligent. Officially a Group Leader of the S.S. and chief of the Security Police, he is also the head of the S.S. Security Service, a special branch for the use of the Reich Fuehrer of the S.S. and the master of the

Berlin Gestapo. In short, he is the brutal, despotic and merci-less master of the Nazi Police; a go-getter, whose hard certainty of aim knows no deviation. Some may call him a genius; he is certainly clever enough never to press in the foreground. He uses Himmler cleverly as his intermediary whenever he wants something from Hitler. He knows very well how the Fuehrer trusts the grim man in the pince-nez and, therefore, leaves him all the honours, gives him full opportunity to sate his vanity. Although he is hot-blooded and impetuous himself, he remains soberly, coldly calculating in the background and knows that the power he coveted is already his. Cruelty and sudden rage are just as severely disciplined in his make-up as his untiring activity. He not only watches over every movement of his political opponents, but has his spies in the offices of his subordinates and closest collaborators. There is no better complement and no more formidable one than Himmler's and Heydrich's, the prattler and the worker, the cunning weakling and the brutal man of action, the " sensitive " intriguer and the merciless go-getter. Both of them need each other, therefore it is an ideal partner-ship. Together they represent a symbol of unscrupulous terrorism, horrible for all real or alleged opponents, whether personal or political. Himmler shines while Heydrich works. Himmler betrays loyalties and friends, Heydrich annihilates them. Together they have caused immeasurable suffering, misery, and death. Their methods are too little known both in Germany and abroad—their means and ways, the institu-tions and organizations which they use to satisfy their endless lust for power, to protect the Hitler regime. There can be very little doubt about the harm they did and do to Germany and her suffering population. They have certainly debased all that can be called humanity and culture.

If these are strong words, I shall try my best to prove how well-founded they are. I have worked with those two men and felt their influence; it is still haunting my dreams. I have seen them in a close-up as very few others have. The tasks they gave me betrayed their diabolical cunning and ruth-lessness. Nations and individuals, families and groups suffered by them and still suffer. I was their weapon and implement as long as I could stand it. I think I am what Americans call " hard-boiled," but in the end even I revolted. And that is the reason why I had to leave Germany and why I am sitting here in this quiet Swiss hotel trying to put down in cold, unromantic type all the horror through which I lived.

Heydrich's power is much more founded on the Security Service of the Reich Fuehrer S.S. (shortened SD.RFSS.) than on the Gestapo—yet the SD.RFSS. is a much too elastic and fluid organization to be described in detail. Its departments, leaders, and organization change from month to month while the Gestapo has been stabilized into a system. I have been in close contact with most of the departments and branches ; I have known their leaders and most of their personnel. Since I left Germany I have been in touch with some of them through the subterranean grape-vine system and I know that almost all of them are still in their positions. To my best knowledge the following organization's plan is still accurate and in use :

SECRET STATE POLICE OFFICE (DAS GEHEIME STAATSPOLIZEI AMT)

Centre of the German Political Police. Headquarters : Berlin SW. Prinz Albrechtstrasse.

CHIEF OF THE GERMAN POLICE :
Reich Fuehrer of the S.S. Heinrich Himmler.

I

Chief of the Uniformed Police :
Police General Kurt Daluege, at the same time Deputy Chief of the German Police.

II

Chief of the Security Police :
S.S. Group Leader Reinhard Heydrich, at the same time Chief of the Security Service of the S.S. Reich Fuehrer (SD.RFSS.) and head of the Gestapo in Berlin.

Deputy Chief of the Gestapo :
S.S. Chief Leader (Oberfuehrer) Dr. Werner Best, Ministry Directory and President of the Committee for Police Law in the " Academy of German Law." As Deputy Chief he is at

the same time Chief of the Main Department III of the Gestapo
and a prominent member of the SD.RFSS.

I had known Dr. Best ever since my youthful days at the
university. He had been a fellow-student and well known as
a leader of Nationalist students. After finishing my university
years, I went abroad for a long period ; but I had belonged to
the sadly famed O.C., the Organization Consul. We were
young ragamuffins who simply could not resign ourselves to
the fact of Germany's defeat and were unable to find our
places in the post-war times. So it was easy to understand that
we formed this half-baked organization, led by rascals and
adventurers, without a clear-cut aim or a serious goal. It
soon became just as ill-famed as senseless. I felt just as
uncomfortable in it as I disliked the rowdyism of Dr. Best's
" gang " at the university. But when I met him, some years
later, shortly before I entered the Security Service of the
S.S. Reich Fuehrer, his roughneck manners had vanished ;
he was polished and suave, even helpful. He encouraged me
in my plans, which included the joining of the French Deuxième
Bureau to gather information for the Gestapo. He gave me a
letter of introduction to Himmler and Heydrich who at that
time were still at Munich and so he became my sponsor when
I joined the SD.RFSS. His was an extremely important
position in the Gestapo and his influence is still increasing.
He is just as unscrupulous and merciless as his chief, Heydrich,
but he manages to hide these qualities behind an immaculate
front of a man-about-town.

The Gestapo has three main departments which work in
close co-operation yet possess an individual authority.

Department I consists of administration, financial matters,
supervision of the so-called Stapo Posts (State Police Local
Posts) in the Reich and manages all staff affairs.

These Stapo Posts are the executive organs of the Gestapo.
As Heydrich told me once, the Gestapo was the heart of the
police executive in Germany, while these posts were the fine
veins and arteries covering the whole body of the German
people. In every county of Prussia, in every police district of
the other German countries there is such an independent

"Stapo Service Post." They do not belong under the authority of the local police chief or police director; they are connected directly with the Berlin Gestapo. Even in administration they are belonging to the Gestapo's circle of power. All of them have their subordinate posts, the so-called Stapo Posts. In every city, even in every large-sized village, there is such an organization. No field of activity, no hidden cranny of national life can remain unobserved, uncovered by these posts. They are placed mostly in the local police headquarters, but during the last years Heydrich had tried everything to separate them even in such respect.

Berlin itself has its own Stapo Service Post which has its seat in the Berlin Police Headquarters at the Alexanderplatz. This Post is the real executive centre for the Political Police in Greater Berlin, while the Gestapo strives more and more to become the highest central authority for the whole Political Police, leaving the local activities to the individual Stapo Posts. This, of course, does not mean that if there is some particularly difficult or complicated task to be done the Gestapo does not take a decisive part in its fulfilment. Although it may sound like blasphemy to the British, the Gestapo can be compared to Scotland Yard and the Stapo Posts to the local police stations, with the important difference that the Gestapo does not wait to be " called in." It takes the initiative whenever it thinks advisable.

All supplies, uniforms, etc., are bought and distributed through Department I of the Gestapo, and every expense or purchase has to be approved by it for the local Stapo Posts.

Besides the sub-departments already mentioned Department I of the Gestapo has another important branch—the so-called " Protective Custody." Nobody knows against whom or what the unfortunates are to be protected—but protected they are, even if it costs their lives. This branch registers all those in protective custody in the different concentration camps. Here is the notorious register of all the people who are or have been in protective custody, with fingerprints, photographs, report of conduct, etc. But this branch has nothing to say about release, punishment or transfer of the prisoners, it is only an administrative organ for the political Departments Numbers II and III in the Gestapo.

Department I has no individual chief, the leaders of the different branches are under the authority of the " Adjutancy Heydrich," which gives its directions and commands.

Reinhard Heydrich's chief aide-de-camp is the Police Captain Pomme, at the same time chief of the Adjutancy. Heydrich has other aides, among them a Chief Lieutenant of the Land Police, an S.S. Storm Leader (Sturmbannfuehrer), two S.S. Chief Storm Leaders (Obersturmfuehrer), and a staff of clerks of the secret archive. But Pomme is in charge.

Captain Pomme is about forty, a tall, broad-shouldered man with close-cropped dark hair, parted on the side. His face is round, his eyes dark, his bearing is the typical stiff one of an old-fashioned Prussian officer. He has a hard, commanding manner of speech, he behaves very politely, even amiably, to strangers. He is married and lives very simply, almost modestly. I knew him as a humane, honest man, very " moderate." In spite of his important post he has no influence whatsoever on Heydrich's actions or the steps taken by the Gestapo. His task is to keep the contacts of the Gestapo with the different State Ministries, and in the first place to the Prussian Prime Minister and Special Commissioner of the Four Year Plan, Hermann Goering. It was Goering who forced Heydrich to employ Pomme. He wanted to have a confidential observer within the mysterious precincts of the Gestapo. But Heydrich outwitted the Field-Marshal with brilliant cunning. Pomme's work is mostly representing Heydrich at different functions, dealing with matters of etiquette—what little etiquette there is left in the Third Reich—so that he has very little opportunity or time for the observation or influencing of the Political Police.

Heydrich's " Adjutancy " supervises the secret archive of the Gestapo. It also manages the Museum of Political Criminals and rules over the guard of the Gestapo Headquarters. This guard is relieved weekly and consists of different groups of the S.S. Police Troops (SS-Polizei-Verfuegungstruppen). Just to be on the safe side, the Adjutancy has its own arsenal, several light and two heavy machine-guns, quick-firing auto-

c

matics, hand-grenades, carbines, etc. Heydrich does not want to be caught napping—not that he ever is.

Department II of the Gestapo has also no chief of its own, but the leaders of the different sub-departments are responsible to Heydrich. Every morning between nine and ten they have to make their reports and accept their instructions. This department covers all the currents and movements of legal and illegal politics within the Third Reich—and covers them so well that no private opinion of any individual can remain hidden for any length of time. I have had comparatively little contact with this department, although I knew its sub-department leaders. They have evolved a system which is practically "foolproof."

SUB-DEPARTMENT A deals with Communists and Social Democrats, also with the different small left-wing parties and their members. Leader: SS. Flag Leader (SS-Standarten-fuehrer) Mueller II, officially a Criminal Councillor. This gentleman had served under Heydrich at Munich with the Bavarian Political Police and was an old member of the SD.RFSS. His task was to watch over the former Communists and Social Democrats, to arrest anyone who could be considered of harbouring such dangerous opinions.

SUB-DEPARTMENT B covers illegal trade unions and illegal organizations in factories, etc. (Sub-department A combated such organizations o u t s i d e the enterprises.) Its leader is Criminal Councillor (Kriminal-Regierungsrat) Reinhold Heller. Heller had been an important personality in the Department I.A. of the Berlin Police Headquarters. After Herr Diels left the Gestapo, he lost all his influence and importance. He had hoped to become Department Chief one day, he received promises—but they only remained promises. Heydrich even took away more than half of his authority.

SUB-DEPARTMENT C supervises associations, clubs and economic unions (including the German Labour Front). These are all legal organizations—but even they have to be watched. Its leader is S.S. Storm Fuehrer (Sturmbannfuehrer) Flechtner, also a Criminal Councillor. Flechtner (I confess that I am not quite sure about the right spelling of his name)

THE MASTERS OF THE GESTAPO   35

has also been one of Heydrich's henchmen in Munich and an old member of the SD.RFSS. He has the distinction of being a Nazi " Martyr " ; in 1930 he had to leave his post at the Bavarian police because he belonged to the Party.

SUB-DEPARTMENT D is for " reaction and Church." (Former Centrum Party, Stahlhelm, Catholics and Protestants.) Special Commissioner Huber is an S.S. Chief Storm Leader (Obersturmbannfuehrer) and also an old member of the SD.RFSS. He, too, comes from Munich ; during the massacre of the 30th June, 1934, he played an important part. He is one of Heydrich's favourites and is considered to be a very " efficient " man.

SUB-DEPARTMENT E : Freemasons and religious sects. Leader : Councillor (Regierungsrat) Dr. Hasselbach, formerly in the Ministry of Interior. The good doctor has nothing to do with the persecution of Catholics, etc. He tried to save as many people as he could—and had lost Heydrich's favour in consequence. A mild little man.

SUB-DEPARTMENT F : National Socialist Party and Homosexuality. There is a certain unconscious irony in lumping these two things together ; but Himmler and Heydrich are too thick-skinned for irony. This sub-department is conducted by Criminal Councillor S.S. Chief Storm Leader (Obersturmbannfuehrer) Meissinger. Meissinger, a Bavarian, is also Heydrich's special favourite and has served with the Bavarian Political Police in Munich. His is one of the most important sub-departments. He has to supervise all activities and members of the Nazi Party, the S.A., the Labour Service and all sub-organizations of the Nazi Party (except the German Labour Front) ; and he has also to combat homosexuals and Jews—as far as no criminal delicts are involved which would refer the matter to any other department.

Each of these sub-departments used a number and letter which are changed from time to time.

Apart from the main departments of the Gestapo there are two special branches which can be called even more important.

The first of them is the Special Commissariat for special purposes (Sonderkommissariat zur besonderen Verwendung)

—i.e. for the special purposes of Reinhard Heydrich. Only he can dispose of these men and they are responsible only to him. This branch has a day-and-night service and a highly specialized task : any attempts against the life of Nazi leaders, assassinations, suspicious persons, loiterers, alleged plots, belong to its field of activity. It must be ready to travel a hundred miles at a moment's notice or to kill a hundred people if necessary. But as soon as arrests have been made its duty ends ; the further work is done by the different departments.

An important side-line of this special branch is the " Postal Supervision." This innocuous name hides postal censorship —systematic and complete like every part of the Gestapo machine. Incoming letters are opened with a thin steam jet compressed under high pressure ; they are read quickly, their contents noted in a few words in a ledger which has different columns corresponding to the different departments. It would be an exaggeration to say that every letter arriving in and being sent from Germany is being censored ; but if there is the slightest doubt as to the conduct of addressee or sender, " Postal Supervision " starts its work. Many an unsuspecting foreigner has caused untold suffering to a German friend of his because he aired his views a little incautiously in a letter ; many an innocent German regretted his rashness in putting to paper what was better left unsaid.

After being censored, the letter is closed again with two quick strokes of a brush and the next delivery can take it away. The addressee seldom knows that his letter has been opened. Only the initiates notice the brush-strokes on the flap of the envelope ; as they are made in a hurry, they differ from the regular adhesive paste. In especially important cases, or if there is a special instruction from one of the departments, letters with incriminating contents are immediately copied and a photostat is made of them. There is a huge apparatus devised by the Siemens Company which copies in two minutes six letters. About three or four photostats are made of every letter.

The " Special Commissariat for special purposes " is a purely political guard which does not conduct any criminal investigations nor does it question those arrested by its

members. Reinhard Heydrich disposes of its services directly ;
indirectly it is connected with the different departments for
which it manages the " Postal Supervision."   Of course the
same commissariat is responsible for the tapping of wires and
recording of telephone conversations.   How well it works is
shown by the case of " Prince Auwi " (Prince August Wilhelm
of Hohenzollern).   The Prince who had joined early the Nazi
Party and was one of its show pieces committed the indis-
cretion of being a friend of Karl Ernst, the young S.A. Leader
executed on the 30th June, 1934.   The same day he was summoned to Goering, who glowered at him and advised him to
take a holiday in Switzerland.   Goering also asked the Prince
what sort of telephone conversation he had with Ernst who,
a few days ago, had started on his honeymoon.   The Prince
truthfully replied that Ernst only wanted to say good-bye to
him ; whereat Goering answered with heavy sarcasm : " Lucky
for you that for once you told the truth."   Then he flipped open
a secret drawer containing a gramophone and started a record
which reproduced the telephone talk from beginning to end.
The Prince was flabbergasted and only too glad to get out of
Germany—and the " Postal Supervision " scored a new
triumph.

This department is conducted by S.S. Chief Storm Leader
(Hauptsturmfuehrer) Wippert, a young, ambitious man who
demands strict discipline of his men and does not stand for
any excesses.

On the fourth floor of the Gestapo building there is another
special branch, the notorious " SD.RFSS. Alarm Command "
which is at the exclusive disposal of Reinhard Heydrich. This
group is composed of the members of the Berlin Special
Service of the S.S. Reich Fuehrer.   If there is a band of terrorists, the Alarm Command can be called that with full justice.
They have many a murder on their consciences ; they are the
executioners of the S.S. Special Service.   The terrible " Feme
Sentences " are carried out by them.   It is a most convenient
weapon for Heydrich who gets rid, through them, of his
accomplices who know too much, former collaborators, personal enemies and opponents.   It is a highly formidable group

of assassins, under an iron discipline and with as few scruples as a pack of ravenous wolves. Many excesses and atrocities which are ascribed to the Gestapo have been committed by this " Alarm Command."

" Heydrich's Killers," as they are sometimes called, are commanded by S.S. Flag Leader (Standartenfuehrer) Sohst. A tall, slim and well-dressed man, he is a typical Prussian officer. A northern German, he has an oval face, eyes and eyebrows of a light colour, fair, close-cropped hair parted on the side, narrow lips. He is a cynic and a grim jester. A notorious member of the SD.RFSS., he has been warned several times on account of his cruelty and unnecessary excesses ; twice he was even suspended temporarily. Sohst fought through the war and has a great many decorations, well earned ; but after the war he could not find his place in the changed world and remained a killer and torturer. It is rather strange that such a man should have one overwhelming hobby ; pottering in a workshop, trying to invent electrical and radio devices. He is hated and feared even among his S.S. comrades.

The " Alarm Command " does not mean a continuous service although some sort of night service has been installed. Under normal circumstances these men are used but seldom, so that sometimes they spend days idling around. It boils down to being a private police troop of Reinhard Heydrich, and as such much more dangerous and formidable than any official state executive.

Department III of the Gestapo deals with high treason and counter-espionage. The work of this department is so secret and important that it is strictly separated even within the Gestapo building from the other branches. It is situated on the first floor of the house, it has a special guard, iron grilles, special locks to guard it from intruders. It has a single exit ; every visitor is escorted every yard of his way and never left alone. Films and highly coloured penny thrillers may tell of the thrilling escapades of some secret agent who manages to explore such a fastness—but it is practically impossible for any unauthorised person to get into Department III of the Gestapo and leave again—alive.

Chief of the Department is Dr. Werner Best, at the same time Deputy Chief of the whole Gestapo.

Dr. Best has taken over this department a little more than three years ago. Up to the summer, 1935, Chief Government Councillor and S.S. Flag Leader (Oberregierungsrat and S.S. Standartenfuehrer) Dr. Patschowski was responsible for high treason and counter-espionage affairs. Dr. Patschowski, a man in his late thirties, is a tall, stiff, but not fat, man with thick, black hair, parted in the middle; he has dark and penetrating eyes, a little rasping, unpleasant voice with a Silesian accent, an overbearing manner; a brutal and egotistic man. Patschowski had started his work in Breslau; he organized Department III under the leadership of Dr. Diels. He was the secret intimate of Heydrich and Himmler who, at that time, were still at Munich; he had a substantial part in engineering Diels' fall.

But the leaders of the Gestapo have short memories and very little sense of gratitude. Patschowski, although an accomplished intriguer, was no match for the cunning of Dr. Best. In the end he lost Heydrich's favour and had to resign. To-day he is working as Special Commissioner of the Gestapo on a secret mission. His territory is Upper Silesia, where he conducts the Gestapo operations against Poland and—up to a short time ago—against Czechoslovakia. He is also supposed to be a chief of the South East department of the RD.RFSS. (also mostly covering Upper Silesian territory) and to organize the espionage department in connection with the Ministry of War (Chief Department V. Admiral Canaris). His centre of operations is Breslau, but Patschowski spends most of his time around Beuthen in Upper Silesia.

Government Councillor (Regierungsrat) Damzog is deputy chief of Department III. Patschowski brought him with himself from Breslau in 1933–34. Damzog, a sturdy, almost fat man of middle stature, has thinning fair hair, a broad peasant face, eyes of light colour. He is about 45–50, comes from an old civil servant family, and is known as an honest, dependable man.

Of course there are several sub-departments in this, perhaps the most important, department of the Gestapo. They are organized according to the territory they are covering.

Sub-Department EAST deals with Poland, Russia, Czecho-slovakia, Hungary, Roumania, and all Balkan States; also with the Far East. Its leader is Criminal Councillor Kubitzki, an old, experienced criminologist. He accompanied Pats-chowski and Damzog from Breslau and is an expert for all Eastern countries. He is of middle stature, on the smallish side, slim, always clean shaven, bespectacled; his nose is sharp, his face hawk-like, with a completely bald dome and unpleasant frog's eyes. He can be about 42–45.

In Sub-Department East Poland, Czechoslovakia, Hungary, and the Balkans are dealt with by Criminal Commissioner Dr. Riedel, a young, very correct man. Dr. Riedel is tall and slim, bears himself a little loosely, with bent shoulders; he has a smooth, expressionless face; fair hair parted in the middle and eyes of light colour. He is about 30.

Russia and the Far East are covered in this sub-department by Criminal Commissioner Fenner, a Baltic German. Fenner, of middle stature, slim, very swarthy, always well-dressed, looking like a Southerner or Mexican, has worked his way up from the lowest rung of the ladder. He is alleged to have worked for the Ochrana during his student days in Russia, and is considered to be the great G.P.U. expert of the Gestapo. He has greying, thick hair, is smooth-shaven and about 45–50.

Sub-Department WEST in Department III handles France, Belgium, Holland, Luxembourg, England, and Scotland (but not Ireland). Its chief is Criminal Councillor Gross (or Groos ? Grohs ?), an old and experienced man just like Kubitzki; he hails from Cologne and was called by Patschowski to Berlin. He is of middle stature, rather plump and very bad hearing; his hair is fair and thinning, his eyes lively and light of colour, his face smooth-shaven. He looks very alert and quick-witted; his age is between 45 and 50. It is said that during the Occupation of the Rhineland he had taken a decisive part in the passive resistance against the French and the English. Within Sub-Department West France has a special Com-missioner called Dr. Fischer. Dr. Fischer was also active in the time of the Rhineland Occupation against the French and English; later he became a police inspector and came with his superior Criminal Councillor Gross to Berlin. He is known as an expert in the affairs of the Deuxième Bureau. A small, slim, slight man with reddish, close-cropped hair, light, penetrating eyes, smooth-shaven, with remarkably white teeth, narrow lips. His age is about 40–42.

Sub-Department WEST Belgium, Luxembourg, Holland, and England are also covered by Dr. Fischer, but there are special experts attached to his staff for each of these countries.

Sub-Department SOUTH is only recently established. Up to 1935–36 Spain, Italy, North Africa, including Egypt and the Sudan—and before the *Anschluss*, Austria—were covered by the Bavarian Political Police in Munich. About a year ago this department was transferred to Berlin.

Sub-Department OVERSEAS was incorporated in the Political Police of Hamburg, but has recently also been transferred to the Berlin Gestapo.

Sub-Department Coast handles all the countries of the East Sea, including the Baltic States and Ireland. Its leader is Criminal Commissioner Manns (or Manz—Mahns?) He comes from Stettin, and is little respected or liked by his colleagues. He is tall, very broad-shouldered, with a broad, rounded face, thick hair, light-coloured eyes, with the typical gait of a sailor. His age is about 35–40.

Sub-Department ECONOMIC ESPIONAGE covers only such offences where the betrayal of military secrets is not involved. This department is extremely important, because it has active as well as passive duties. About its active work I shall speak later. Its leader, Dr. Hans Schmidt, has been a leader of Department " I " (Information) of the SD.RFSS. Main Branch EAST (Berlin), which is the most important department in any such organization. Dr. Schmidt is considered as the probable successor of Damzog, the deputy chief of Department III of the Gestapo. Schmidt is of average height, slim, with close-cropped hair and dark eyes, a narrow face. A deep cut —a memory of the students' duels so popular in pre-war Germany—disfigures him, making his lips twisted.

These men are, of course, only the leaders of the different departments, sub-departments, and special branches. They all have their staff of picked executives, criminal assistants and clerks. These are in part old, well-experienced criminologists—a great many former police sergeants—and partly young, new S.S. men who want to attain the rank of a lower civil servant or aspire to become a Criminal Commissioner. Sometimes members of the SD.RFSS. are appointed temporarily in Department III to be trained and educated before they are sent abroad or to the frontier. The employees of the Gestapo never know what the duration and purpose of such an appointment is. Only the chiefs of the main Departments, who are also prominent members of the SD.RFSS., are familiar with such important details.

This is the organization of the Gestapo, Hitler's most formidable weapon. Hundreds of thousands curse it all over the world; everybody fears it and very few know about its system and work. I have seen it functioning and have been one of those who move its wheels and start its deathly machinery whirring. No fantastic spy story could do justice to its scope; but I hope that my factual description will give an idea of its importance and power.

CHAPTER III

★

"HE MUST BE KIDNAPPED . . ."

SEVEN MEN WERE SITTING around a table in the Hotel
Excelsior at Frankfurt-on-the-Main. They were discussing in
a calm and matter-of-fact way how to kidnap a man, smuggle
him over the frontier, and deliver him to certain death.

It was in the first days of May, 1933. The weeks after the
Reichstag elections and the Reichstag Fire had been an anxious
period for the National Socialist reign. The newspapers and
weeklies of the German exiles both abroad and in the Saar
District caused much worry among the "*higher-ups*" (high
officials). In the rooms of the Gestapo and the Prussian
Ministry of Interior high officials were sitting and devising
ways and means to get rid of this "pest."

The Reichstag Fire had been badly staged and badly
prepared. Although its details were still wreathed in mystery
and the notorious Karl Ernst document was hardly an answer
to all the questions, so much is certain that there had been no
carefully nurtured plan. It was simply cutting the Gordian
knot, an impudent, common practical joke. In the last
minute it had been chosen as a solution, lacking anything
better. The "Fuehrer" himself, his unpleasant associates
(Papen and Co.), the electors, and the population had to be
convinced that there was a " Communist danger," although it
was completely non-existent. Goebbels had fathered the idea.
He had left a conference in the company of Goering ; during
this discussion Adolf Hitler had scolded them like boys who
were caught smoking—finishing up with a well-acted scene
of uncontrolled fury. Goebbels conceived the idea—and the
same night Goering sent for his two " comrades," Count

Helldorf, at that time Group Leader of the Berlin S.A., and the S.A. Chief Leader, Karl Ernst. It was so comfortable to look through the window of the Reichstag President's Palace where Goering was installed—at the building of the Reichstag opposite, and to discuss the rather naïve details of the plan.

For two days Hermann Goering did not show up in his Ministry at the Unter den Linden. When he appeared again there was gossip about a large-scale Communist plot which their great chief foiled by personal measures. The whole police apparatus was held ready for several days, till at last the " signal " came in the shape of the flames enveloping the dome of the Reichstag. It was a signal to destroy everybody who could be called a Communist or Marxist.

So much is certain that neither Kurt Daluege nor Herr Diels, nor any official of the Ministry of the Interior, nor the Police, knew anything about the real culprits before the 27th February, 1933. They were all commanded by Goering to search for the criminal among the Communists and then obeyed the orders. Those entrusted with the investigation had to notice after the first questioning that " something was wrong ! " All of them had to choose between losing their position and freedom or—against their conviction or personal knowledge—to fix the guilt on a Communist. An intelligent man like Dr. Diels could solve the puzzle very quickly. And when the clumsy, honest Criminal Councillor Heller telephoned to Diels, asking him what he should do with the Communist Torgler who was rounded up with such surprising speed, he received the rough answer : " You must do your duty, keep that in mind ! " And Heller suddenly knew what " his duty " was and arrested Torgler.

The Reichstag Fire was badly engineered, but both Goering and Goebbels had the necessary talent to send clumsy and often contradictory lies out into the world ; they also knew that they had to keep " mum " even in the circle of their best friends. To-day they have reached the state which they share with so many brilliant swindlers and liars : they believe in their own falsehoods. Herr Hitler, who has so often talked himself into ecstasy that he is always seeing the Communist bogy-man, against whom he wants to defend Germany and the whole of Europe, never troubled about the truth. The " truth " had to be created especially for him and his Party. Thus Messrs. Goering and Goebbels have attained their goal : they have secured the dictatorial powers for their Fuehrer, have made safe their own positions and paved the way for a long Nazi reign in Germany.

All this may be slightly beside the point ; but in those spring months of 1933 Hitler and his associates still felt " wobbly " enough to be annoyed and even troubled by the vituperative attacks of the German and foreign press abroad. There was another problem : these damned scribblers were so confoundedly well informed. Information even reached them from the close circle around old Paul von Hindenburg. The Saar District was still under international supervision, it did not belong to Nazi Germany. The refugees who lived there must have had agents who helped them not only to gain information—but to get money ! Germans living in Germany were financing, to some extent, the attacks against Germany's present rulers. This was unbearable, this was abominable ! Something had to be done. And in the first place there was the man who caused the greatest worry to the Gestapo—the Communist, Willi Muenzenberg.

It was on his account that we met at the Hotel Excelsior. Muenzenberg had been one of the most talented and versatile of the leaders of the KPD, the German Communist Party. He worked as a journalist ; founded the I.A.H. (International Workers' Help) and interested prominent non-Communists in his organization, which was supposed to stand above all parties.

He was founder and proprietor of the " unpolitical " newspapers such as *Die Welt am Abend*, or *Berlin am Morgen*, and also conducted a large publishing firm, the " Neuer Deutchser Verlag." In the circles of the Communist Party he was known as a " red newspaper-Hugenberg " ; he was compared with the formerly powerful magnate who controlled dozens of newspapers and the whole German film industry. Apart from Hans Kippenberger, the chief of the G.P.U. in Germany, he was the only dangerous opponent for the new regime shortly after its coming to power.

Just like Kippenberger, Muenzenberg had left Germany just in time—during the early days of March, 1933—not waiting till his Reichstag membership had been annulled and his immunity taken away. Beyond the frontiers of the Reich he founded new dailies, bought magazines and publishing firms, appointed skilful editors, acquired excellent news material, and forced them into a united front against the Third Reich. He reviled the terrorism, appealed to the conscience of the world, pointed out the weaknesses and failings of the new rulers. That he failed in his beginning, was not his fault, but that of his own comrades and Party-leaders who thought theories more important than realities, and who spent their time in endless discussion instead of action.

Since April, 1933, I had been working for the Gestapo in the Saar District, and sent my reports to my old friend Heller, and at the same time to Daluege, although, by that time, he had nothing to do with the Political Police. I worked as a special agent without depending on the ordinary or secret police. My only helpmate was a former fellow-officer and personal friend of Heller in Saarbruecken, whose mother-in-law owned a simple restaurant there. My first assignment was to discover Muenzenberg's connections in the Saar District.

We had expected Dr. Diels to attend the conference at the Hotel Excelsior. But in his place Criminal Councillor Heller turned out as his plenipotentiary. The chief of the Political Police at the Police Headquarters of Frankfurt-on-Main was also present. As representative of the Political Police in the Pfalz Captain Buchmann arrived from Ludwigshafen. Heller was accompanied by a special agent of Goering, a man called Huerten, and a small, unimportant criminal assistant who had a forged passport bearing the name Hirsch and who looked a Jew. Apart from myself and these five only Heller's friend and war-comrade, whom I had brought from Saarbruecken, was present, and from that day he acted officially as my secretary.

" He must be kidnapped," said Heller, and we all nodded.

" He " was, of course, Willi Muenzenberg, the Communist and the arch-enemy of Nazidom. We started to debate the ways and means. The Frankfurt leader of the Political Police was reproached because Muenzenberg was alleged to have visited Frankfurt ; but this man had nothing to do with the kidnapping plan.

Captain Buchmann, a small, wiry man with a sharp birdlike face, was a real expert in kidnapping. During the French occupation of the Pfalz, he had become well-known through his daring exploits ; the Reichswehr held him in high esteem as well-versed both in espionage and counter-espionage. But he had also a great many Social Democrat friends and, therefore, was not very popular with the Nazis. They employed him because they needed him ; and now he wanted to prove what an excellent man he was, how well he could serve his new masters. His position was not at all safe ; he hoped to consolidate it by the daring kidnapping of the hated Muenzenberg. Unfortunately his plan miscarried ; but even so, he managed to hold his post till 1935, as a faithful collaborator of Reich Commissioner Buerckel. He broke his neck when it became known that he belonged to a German National Free Mason Lodge. Later, when I became Buerckel's special agent in the Saar District, I found further opportunity to collaborate with him.

Huerten, Goering's confidant, was a curious creature. He had been a theatrical producer who had several times been bankrupt. In March, 1933, he became an assistant manager at the biggest official theatre ticket agency of Berlin. Goering used him to spin all sorts of cunning webs in the German theatrical life. He talked more than would have been healthy for anyone. He maintained that he knew Muenzenberg personally. To follow his fate—friend Huerten was taken into custody at the end of 1933 by Goering's Field Police and was never seen again. He talked too much—and dared to mention Goering's relations with a well-known German actress. This was too much for the future Field-Marshal, and Huerten vanished, without leaving a trace.

The plan which was presented at the Hotel Excelsior was rather complicated. Muenzenberg's place of residence was to be ascertained; should he visit the Saar District, he was to be followed; the kidnappers would wait till he entered a restaurant or some other public place; he was to be called under some pretext to the lavatory and from there dragged by waiting Gestapo men (using, if necessary, some drug) to a swift car and then carried across the frontier. If possible, all this should happen in Saarbruecken, where the border was very near. Captain Buchmann would take care that the prisoner should be transported without fuss or noise to Berlin. If the kidnapping in a restaurant should fail, an attempt would be made when Muenzenberg drove from Saarbruecken to the aerodrome situated outside the city.

This rather romantic and somewhat childish plan was rather dangerous for Muenzenberg. How well such a plan could succeed was proved in 1935 when the journalist Jakobs was kidnapped in Basle and taken to Loerrach. But Muenzenberg was much too careful, suspicious, and clever to fall into such a trap or give his enemies an opportunity to capture him.

" Hirsch," Heller's assistant, went to Paris to get information about Muenzenberg's future movements. There he behaved so stupidly that his bragging was published twenty-four hours later in the German refugee paper *Pariser Tageblatt*. He chose a well-known refugee café to air his " inside knowledge " of Nazi Germany. The article in the refugee daily accused " Hirsch "—with full justification—of being an agent pro-vocateur and a spy of the Gestapo. He had to leave France in a hurry to avoid being arrested by the French authorities. In consequence of his stupidity he lost his job in the Gestapo and was happy to land in the unimportant Press Bureau of the Berlin Police Headquarters.

Before " Hirsch " (whose real name was either Lautenbach or Lauterbacher) went to Paris, Heller and Buchmann hurried to Loerrach on the Swiss–German border. They had received a telephone message alleging that Muenzenberg had arrived in Basle. " Hirsch " and Huerten went to Basle; after spending three days in chasing Muenzenberg's shadow (he was several hundred miles away) " Hirsch " travelled to Paris, while Buchmann and Heller returned to Germany. Huerten enjoyed himself for some time at the Gestapo's cost in

Switzerland. Heller's friend and myself had gone back to
Saarbruecken directly from Frankfurt-on-Main.

It was a badly laid booby trap which just did not come off.
Yet it showed what the Gestapo was capable of planning,
and very often of realizing.

I felt rather relieved that I had nothing to do with the plan
or its attempted execution and returned to the Saar District
with a new zest for my not very easy job.

CHAPTER IV

★

MUDDLE IN THE SAAR

THE SAAR DISTRICT, THAT rich and beautiful slice of the Reich, was a thorn in Germany's flesh. In 1919 it was placed under the League of Nations. The Treaty of Versailles set up a committee of five persons to govern it—for fifteen years, when a plebiscite would be held and the Saar was either to retain its position or be joined to France or Germany. Results and circumstances of the plebiscite are too well known for me to attempt a description; but at the time when I was sent there, the issue was still undecided. The Third Reich would have received a mortal blow had not the Saar been returned to its bosom—therefore, it is quite comprehensible why the Nazi leaders concentrated all their power of propaganda, terrorism, and subterfuge to attain their end.

Three different factors aided them in their beginning—much more than their own actions. First, the almost unbelievable attitude of the Communists; second, the faulty policy of the French; and third, the discord within the " middle-class " parties.

In May, 1933, I talked with a leading functionary of the Communists of the Saar. He told me that they were no separationists; they were fighting for the German proletariat. They would prefer to go into a concentration camp rather than betray their comrades beyond the present frontier. . . . Well, if God wants to destroy someone, He makes him blind. These were the same Communists who had said that Hitler's coming to power did not mean the defeat of the proletariat —on the contrary, the collapse of the capitalistic system would come all the earlier on account of it. Only at the beginning of 1934 did the Communists realize what a fatal mistake they had committed in advocating the return to Germany—but by that time it was much too late, their followers had dwindled away.

Max Braun, the intelligent but much too honest leader of the Social Democrats in the Saar, strove in vain to form a united front with the Communists against the Third Reich. His comrades of the left reviled him as a " social-fascist " and " bourgeois "—carrying on their campaign of vilification with even more heat and zeal than any Nazi propaganda centre could have done. The French, who would have had ample reason for Braun's support, committed one blunder after the other, and soon lost all interest, because it seemed impossible to annex the Saar to France. The Nazis found it easy to depict Max Braun as a paid puppet of the French and a traitor to the German people, thereby wholly discrediting him.

The fulcrum of the political balance in the Saar was the Catholic Centrum Party, the strongest unit of the middle-class. Their attitude decided the fate of the whole district. During the time of the French occupation, the Catholics in the Rhineland, the Saar, and Mosel, were reputed to be Francophiles and separatists. Now when von Papen was discussing the terms of a concordat with Adolf Hitler, the Catholic clergy of the Saar tried to pave the way to an agreement by becoming strongly German. This was the easier to understand as they came under the Reich. The Bishop of Trier had a special reason to try and force his flock in the Saar to a co-operation with Nazi Germany. The " Holy Rock of Trier " was the centre of Trier's holy year and the good Bishop expected millions of pilgrims. Adolf Hitler had only to raise his little finger and these pilgrims would have to stay at home. But as the Bishop behaved himself, the Nazis did not raise any objection—and gained the Saar District by it.

The French did very little to prevent this. Their blunders were glaring. The Frenchman Hamburger, who was the Minister of Police in the Saar Government, could not get any help from his own countrymen. He was unable to recruit faithful and trusted police executives either for his Political

Police or his gendarmerie. It was of little use that two or three really efficient police inspectors left the Third Reich and took employment under Hamburger—almost single-handed they could do nothing.

Up to 1918, when the Saar was severed from the Reich, the district had belonged in its greater part to Prussia; a smaller territory was under the authority to the Bavarian Rhinepfalz. The mater of the latter and President of the Bavarian Government since Hitler's coming to power, was the Gau Leader Buerckel (to-day Governor of Austria) whose seat was at the nearby Neustadt on the Haardt. Prussia's overlord was Hermann Goering, enthroned in far-away Berlin. The representative of the Nazi regime in the Saar District was Reich Commissioner von Papen. Three different authorities clashed, therefore—all the three had the same aim, but used highly divergent ways and mea s.

Up to 1933 Buerckel had been the Gau Leader of the Nazi Party in the Saar. When Hitler became Chancellor he had to resign this post; according to the statutes governing the disputed district, no German or French civil servant could be a Party leader in the Saar. The National Socialist Party was locally a purely Saar District institution—although this was only a matter of form and they worked in close contact with the Party centres in the Reich.

Buerckel had to be replaced by someone who had no official connection with the new German Government. A young, inexperienced man called Spaniol was chosen. He was such an unpleasant rowdy that soon he became extremely unpopular among all non-Nazis, and especially the members of the Centrum Party and Stahlhelm. But Goering liked and valued him, he pushed him forward; he did everything to support Spaniol against Franz von Papen and Buerckel.

The fight of Prussia versus Pfalz began behind the scenes. On one side the apparently all-powerful Goering in Berlin; on the other, the small, unobtrusive Buerckel in Neustadt on the Haardt. But Goering was too far away; he had little time to give personal attention to the Saar problems, nor did he know much about them. And his middleman, young Spaniol, committed new blunders every day. For Buerckel, the influencing of the Saar policy was a highly important matter. He was fully acquainted with all the details, persons and connections; he watched soberly all the stupidities and blunders of his successor. He had a well organized net of spies and informers scattered over the district and kept in touch with the smallest events there.

Buerckel had been a schoolmaster and had learned how to tame and discipline bad little boys. Spaniol was a bad little boy—even if he could swagger in a highly decorative Nazi uniform. Buerckel recognized that he was not a dangerous opponent. The nearer the time of the plebiscite, the more pressing did the problem of the Saar become for Hitler's regime. Buerckel knew that the young Gau Leader would break his own neck by his escapades and haughtiness. So he quietly collected all necessary material against him—till there was no possible existence for him or for the whole Nazi Party in the Saar.

I have known Buerckel as well as anyone could know him; I have worked in close co-operation with him and seen his methods, preferences, and dislikes. To-day, as Governor of Austria (although nobody can tell how long he will hold this precarious and not at all enviable position) he is an even more important figure in the Nazi constellation than he was five years ago.

His origin was very humble; his home country, the Pfalz with its wine-growing peasants, is a very poor district. In spite of all his low cunning and often reprehensible schemes, Buerckel has a certain amount of impressive greatness in his nature. He always emphasized his personal modesty and unobtrusiveness. He strictly forbade his collaborators to give him any of his numerous titles; he remained the simple " Herr Buerckel." He is deeply hated by all his opponents and his political enemies; they have good reason for this hate, as Buerckel has often cheated and trapped them, sometimes with surprisingly simple peasant tricks. But he is loved by his associates for whom he would do anything. He demands the utmost efficiency and quick results, but he also knows how to get comfortable positions for his favourites. To-day, all over the Saar his beloved Pfalz men are in clover;

probably they are well established now in Vienna. He likes to play the part of a simple, sober man, although he is a Gau Leader, an S.A. Chief Group Leader, an S.S. Group Leader, President of the Bavarian Government and Reich Commissioner. He does not like to appear in public, is neither a good orator nor a good propagandist. But he is something which may explain all his success : an unscrupulous fanatic who calculates coldly, weighs all the pros and cons soberly and is willing to use any means to vanquish a political opponent. In his moral conception he shares the ideas of all Nazi leaders : there is no honour if the Party's well being is at stake ; promises do not count, agreements are of no validity. This is the morality of political fanatics and this morality becomes really dangerous when they possess the necessary executive power, as do Buerckel and the Nazis to-day.

Buerckel acted the part of the helpful friend and seemed to join forces with the impetuous Spaniol against their common enemy, the " Papist Papen." All true Nazis hated the Reich Minister and Reich Commissioner of the Saar. Through his discussions of a possible concordat Papen was held in high esteem—at least up to 1934—by the Catholic clergy. Up to the 30th June, 1934, he was the great white hope of all so-called reactionaries and Centrum politicians ; he seemed to guarantee a moderate National Socialist home policy. No wonder that he was hated by the members of the Party.

I could fill a long book about all Herr von Papen's double-crossing, about his treachery, his breach of trust, his highly questionable intrigues and schemes, both before and after the Nazis were installed as rulers of Germany. In later chapters I shall have to tell about the part he played in the downfall of Austria. But here I want to explain his role as Commissioner of the Reich Government in the Saar.

Papen is the proprietor of the firm Villeroy & Boch, whose central offices are in Dresden, but most important factories in the Saar District, namely in Mettlach and Merzig. The family estate of the Papens is Wallerfangen near Sarrlouis, and Papen's wife (née Boch) is known as the patroness of large Catholic endowments in the Saar. The family spends a considerable part of every year on the estate ; so it was very easy for Baron Franz to create the best possible relations with all important circles of the Saar. He seemed to be predestined to fill the position of a Saar Commissioner.

The clergy in the Saar was under the authority of two bishops. In the territory which belonged formerly to Prussia, it was the Bishop of Trier ; in the land which had been a part of the Bavarian Pfalz, the Bishop of Speyer. Papen conferred with them, had long talks with the Centrum politicians abroad and advised them urgently to dissolve the Party. He failed, miserably. The Gestapo had conducted a systematic war against priests in the Reich ; their brothers in the Saar had become highly suspicious of the Nazi intentions. In spite of Papen's discussions and endeavours for a concordat with Rome, they would not listen to his advice. Part of the Saar clergy even sent a deputation to Rome asking for a bishop to be appointed for their territory. They not only wanted to get away from the German Reich, but also from the German bishops.

His Holiness sent a special envoy to the Saar to study the situation and gather first-hand information. This was bad news for Herr von Papen, bad news for the Nazis and the Gestapo. But, by the time the Pope's envoy arrived in the Saar, by the time he prepared his report and returned to Rome, events had followed each other with such rapidity that nothing could be done and Buerckel had taken over the management of the Saar affairs.

It was during this critical period that I met Buerckel, and began a close co-operation with him.

The discussion about Willi Muenzenberg's kidnapping had taken place in the beginning of May, 1933. A few days later I had returned to Saarbruecken where I was notified about the failure of the plan.

The Gestapo was not very much interested in the activity of the Saar Communists.

The Social Democrats under the leadership of Max Braun were much more dangerous. Political refugees from the Reich were repulsed by the Communists' policy, and if they did not join Max Braun, they gathered around another man—the former separatist and Marxist, Max Walz.

Max Walz was a political failure and Party vagabond. He had tried his luck with the Communists and Social Democrats ; at the time when I met him he did not belong to any party. He used the general political insecurity and restlessness of the Saar to approach the French and offer his services ; at the same time he formed contacts with all more or less prominent political exiles who came from Germany to the Saar. These people knew very little about Maz Walz ; they were happy to find a helpful friend. In most cases they had not the slightest idea that in reality he was a small, badly paid and not very efficient French secret agent who remitted all confessions, informations, etc., to the " Deuxième Bureau " in Saargemuend or Forbach—selling it on strictly C.O.D. terms.

Max Braun was much too clever to attack Walz in his newspapers or to warn people against him who were not his Party comrades. On the contrary ; he used Walz repeatedly as intermediary to the unimportant French frontier clerks of the " Commissariat special " in Forbach or Saargemuend. Max Braun's personal connections were much more important, led to much higher personalities—straight to Paul Boncour, at that time French Foreign Secretary, and to the leader of the French Socialists, the later Minister President Léon Blum.

The Gestapo was naturally keenly interested in Max Walz and the people who surrounded him. My task was to gather all available information—by hook or by crook, by force, if necessary, but preferably by simple cunning. Now, in order to gain Walz's confidence, I had to pose as a political refugee. The trouble was that I could not be a German Communist or Social Democrat. The two Party centres were so well organized and fully informed that I should soon have been unmasked. But I was quite familiar with the circumstances, leaders and theories of Western Marxism and so I acted a—Trotzkiist. A Gestapo agent as a Trotzkiist—I felt there was some grim humour in such a masquerade. As a Trotzkiist I went to the Saar and made the acquaintance of Max Walz at the Café

Excelsior, the favourite hunting ground of all political exiles.

As a poor, persecuted Trotzkiist, I soon gained Walz's full confidence. What this "full confidence" meant I did not quite know—but it served me well enough to get an introduction to M. Bernheim. M. Bernheim was a Frenchman who lived in Forbach, France, and managed the bureau of the "Commissariat special," the branch office of the French Secret Service. Walz sent me to him to get a refugee legitimation, the so-called *carte d'identité pour refugiés politiques*. He even advised me to take up my domicile beyond the French frontier —such a prominent Trotzkiist must be careful or the agents of the Gestapo might kidnap him one day—and I soon moved to Forbach, partly to show Max Walz how much I valued his advice; and partly because I found it convenient to have a new base for my operations. I travelled every day on the tram to Saarbruecken. Of course, I knew perfectly well that Max Walz did not care a jot about my personal security. He wanted to have me in a spot where the French could watch me all the time. Even if I were a Trotzkiist, he had no other proof for my political beliefs than my unsupported word, and he preferred to be careful. It was in Forbach that, after a painstaking investigation (which, however, was not painstaking enough) the "Deuxième Bureau" approached me and I became a French spy—while all the time I was in the employ of the Gestapo.

The longer I worked in the Saar, the more frequent and detailed had my reports to the Gestapo to be. But the contact and co-operation with Berlin became worse and worse. There was a branch of the Gestapo in Trier, close to the frontier. But Trier and Saarbruecken are quite a distance apart; also I refused—having my own good reasons—to work with Trier. There a few dull-witted people were sitting; they thought it their most important task to keep a complete file of petty criminals, smugglers and such-like. I not only had to deliver reports which had to be sent on; I was expecting instructions all the time. Besides asking and giving information, I had to receive replies to questions, and in many cases had to know the attitude of my superiors towards my propositions before

I could undertake anything. All this was clumsy, uncertain, even unsafe. Often I had to wait very long for an answer; precious time was lost and my position repeatedly endangered. Berlin and the Gestapo was far away; Herr Diels and his collaborators had a great many other, more urgent and important, troubles—the Saar was treated as a step-child, at least for the time being.

In the end, I was weary of all these difficulties. Carefully shedding my Trotzkiist disguise and burying my forged passport, I went to Berlin and had long discussions with Diels' deputy, Dr. Folk. But although he promised everything, as soon as I returned, the old carelessness and the dangerous delays were continued.

I had only one confederate and collaborator in Saarbruecken, Criminal Councillor Heller's friend and former fellow-officer; he helped me unselfishly, self-sacrificingly, being at my disposal day and night. As he was the manager of his mother-in-law's restaurant, which had a rather variegated clientele, I could come and go safely. I composed my reports in his back room, and he took care of their being sent on. I think I was a sort of idol to him—the good man had only a modest share of brains—and he would have gone through fire and water for me. Sometimes he almost did.

With my knowledge and approval, he had recruited two very reliable and discreet men. One of them had a motor cycle; the other travelled by train. These two took my reports and posted them beyond the frontier, on German soil. We chose these two simple people on purpose, because as independent, small artisans, they had often business in the Reich and could travel unobtrusively to and fro. One of them was a member of the Nazi Party in the Saar, but neither had been seriously involved in politics. Both of them were horrified by Spaniol's brutal methods. There was no danger that they would betray my presence in the Saar to the young devil; that, of course, would have been very unpleasant, as my hidden activities would have become impossible.

My two couriers knew neither my name nor anything about my appearance. I had gone to the Café Kiefer and observed them from a nearby table. They were sitting with my friend and secretary and had no idea that they were watched. I observed them carefully and then approved their appointment. They did their work smoothly, without any hitch. They never tried to open the letters they had to post; they never asked any questions; probably they knew that they would never get any answer. They knew that they were serving a Gestapo man, as Heller had instructed Captain Buchmann to receive and, as far as possible, train the two men when they spent some time in Ludwigshafen. No doubt they thought themselves extremely important, and their self-assurance increased visibly. It must have been such a romantic affair for them—while, for me, it was a job which had to be done and done well. Neither the French nor the Gestapo gave any quarter to the agent who failed.

I had been living for some time in Forbach when Max Walz called me aside one day in the Café Excelsior.

"I have good news for you," he said, and I waited expectantly. "An important Trotzkiist has arrived in Saarbruecken. Here's his address. I'm sure you'll be happy to meet such a distinguished comrade."

I took the slip of paper with rather mixed feelings. What if it was a man who knew me . . . or who knew the German Trotzkiists well enough to unmask a fake one? But when I looked at the name, I was rather reassured. The "eminent Trotzkiist" was the almost completely deaf Karl Groehl who had, until a short time ago, been a member of the Communist Party (Trotzki employed him as an informer). Only after Hitler's coming to power had the Communists of Basle unmasked him as a Trotzkiist and expelled him from the Party. At least that was what Groehl said, although I had no other proof than his word. Anyhow, he presented some documents which showed that he was in direct contact and a well-established personal relation with Trotzki who was living in France at that time. Trotzki could have hardly chosen a less suitable emissary to send to the Saar—but here he was, all set to study the political situation and report to his exiled chief.

Groehl had been the business manager of Muenzenberg's

publishing house in Berlin. During the Ruhr revolts he was one of the most active inciters of workers and had spent considerable time in different German prisons where he contracted an incurable ailment of the air. The Komintern invited him to Russia where he made several visits ; once he stayed at the famous Russian health resorts on the Black Sea. After Hitler came, he fled with Muenzenberg to Basle, where for some time he managed a publishing firm and organized the smuggling of Communistic pamphlets to Germany. He proved a good organizer—but he was a bad Communist, and so lost his job.

I called on him in Saarbruecken and had several long talks with him. After a lengthy preamble he proposed that we should start a regular Trotzkiist group in the Saar. I had been very anxious lest Groehl should find out about my double role ; but now my anxiety was more than allayed. Not only was I found a *bona fide* Trotzkiist, but I was to become a group-leader of the Trotzkiists in the Saar. Surely a fine career for a Gestapo agent ! Groehl also mentioned that we should publish a newspaper—a rather high-falutin' name for a number of mimeographed sheets fastened together—but, luckily, I was able to dissuade him from such an enterprise. We were to combat, in the first place, the Communists in the Saar and their stubborn propaganda for an *Anschluss* with the Reich. There were only a handful of Trotzkiists in the district, but a great many " unattached " left-wingers could be found, especially as the Trotzkiists strived for a close co-operation with the Social Democrats and " all honest leaders of workers." At that time Trotzki's idea of a " Fourth Internationale " was still alive.

The backbone of the proposed Trotzkiist group would have been Max Walz and his associates. Walz became a fast friend of Groehl's. The Party centre of the Trotzkiists was established in Max Walz's offices. There is no need to think of a suite of sumptuous rooms and comfortable arm-chairs in front of tidy roll-top desks. The rooms of Max Walz were in a tenement-house of Saarbruecken which also served as an asylum and information bureau for homeless, bewildered refugees from the Reich. But soon the exiles were replaced by a rather motley crowd, looking for a hide-out—and finding it under Max Walz's wings.

Karl Groehl spent only a few weeks in Saarbruecken, but he returned later for short visits. He was always grumbling and complaining, he always " knew better," but he was not unintelligent. He was well versed in political theory and history ; yet he could be childish and naïve if someone knew how to tickle his vanity. Through his deafness he was severely handicapped in his contact with people. He had a very faulty judgment of humanity ; his initial suspicion always dissolving into exaggerated trust. His travelling and modest living expenses were covered by Leo Trotzki himself.

Groehl's arrival and the organization of a Trotzkiist groups in the Saar served my purpose excellently. Now Groehl had more or less vouched for my convictions, and for my being a " genuine " Trotzkiist. I discussed a " united front " with Max Braun himself ; he not only received me several times, but I had free access to the editorial offices of his papers, the *Freiheit* (Liberty) and *Volkstimme* (Voice of the People). I was also admitted to the Trade Union House of the Social Democrats in Saarbruecken. At the same time I formed useful contacts in the boarding-house of a former Social Democrat Reichstag member, Mrs. Zukatsch, in the Bahnhofstrasse at Saarbruecken. Here I found a mixed company and gathered a wealth of precious information. I knew everything about the connections, ideas, and plans of prominent Saar politicians. I knew when the former German Police Officer, Macht, fled from the Reich and joined M. Heimburger's police forces—before the public or the Nazi Party had any information about it. Criminal Commissioner Lehnert, who had fled from the Rhineland, bragged to me about his heroic exploits and the contacts which he still possessed both with the Third Reich and the French authorities. Here I met Emil Kirschmann, a former German civil servant who had held a very high position and lived under the strictest incognito. Kirschmann had a great many friends among high and highest officials in Germany who had still retained their posts. His trusted secretary, Hannah, wife of a former City

Councillor and Social Democrat of Frankfurt, even told me all about the dealings of her adored " Emil " with the French Government. She persuaded me to visit the new police executive Macht at his office and to ask for a regular Saar passport. Macht, who was the chief of the Saar's Political Police, a miniature Gestapo, was " very sorry," but had to refuse my request, as it was not his department. But he gave me an introduction to Mr. Bernheim in Forbach, to whom Max Walz had sent me. Commissioner Lehnert had found a job, too, with the Saar Police, and overwhelmed me with his confidences. Sometimes I became quite uncomfortable, thinking how all these people trusted me, how they considered me as " one of us," and what a danger it would mean if they discovered my real identity.

I clung grimly to my part as a political refugee. This necessitated my living very modestly, almost in complete poverty ; otherwise I would soon have become suspicious. I did not stay all the time in Saarbruecken ; as a pedlar of household implements, pencils, and office supplies, I wandered through the whole Saar District ; I visited the Trade Union Bureaux and Marxist Party centres in Voelklingen, Saarlouis, and Homburg, knocked at the doors of the rectories in Lisdorf and Wallerfangen, offered my merchandise to the monasteries in Mettlach and in the smallest, most secluded villages. Thus I was always well informed about the general mood of the population, and my reports to Berlin were always true pictures of the situation.

The Gestapo in Berlin was still working badly. They were interested in my work, in the politics of the Saar—but they used few of my proposals and did not consider them if they contained any political advice. Diels was Goering's favourite. Therefore it was easy to understand that he did not like it when I warned him against the foolish blunders Goering's other favourite, Gau Leader Spaniol, was committing day by day. When I criticized Herr von Papen, he was even less enthusiastic. But I had sense enough to wrap my criticism in reports of what people were saying or doing—never offering them as my own opinion. On the other hand he always refused to consider my advice or suggestions.

I was rather tired of this lack of co-operation. I changed my garb again; the poverty-ridden Trotzkiist vanished and a prosperous wine merchant crossed the frontier of the Saar. Instead of Berlin I went to Ludwigshafen and described my difficulties to Captain Buchmann whom I met through our mutual friend Heller. Buchmann was an expert in such work and understood all my troubles.

" I'll take you to Buerckel," he told me. " He is the man for you."

Together we travelled to Neustradt an der Haardt.

Buerckel received me at once and I spent three hours in his room, giving a detailed report. He listened earnestly to my warnings and anxieties; then he told me to put them into writing. I stayed three days with him and drew up my report, which was preceded by other long discussions, in Captain Buchmann's office at the Police Headquarters in Ludwigshafen.

On the fourth day I met Buerckel at Mannheim and together we travelled to Berlin. Buchmann was to follow in the evening with the aide de camp of the S.S. Group (Standarte) No. 10, S.S. Storm Leader (Sturmbann-fuehrer) George Kemmet, one of Buerckel's intimates.

We agreed to meet next morning at eleven in the Secretariat of Dr. Ley, leader of the Nazi Party's Organization Branch and of the German Labour Front. At that time this office was in the Prussian Herrenhaus, a most distinguished building in the Leipzigerstrasse. Ley and Buerckel were always good friends; they had met through Buerckel's bosom friend and comrade, Klaus Selzner, who is Dr. Ley's right hand and practically the real leader of the German Labour Front. All three of them—Ley, Buerckel, and Selzner—like a glass of good wine; but while Buerckel and Selzner work like navvies, Dr. Ley is hardly such a diligent man.

In the report which I composed for Buerckel I demanded that the Nazi Party in the Saar District should be dissolved at once; after that a united front of all honest nationalists should be formed.

" You must be frank and without any reticence," Buerckel

had told me and I followed his instructions. I gave details about the foolish and dangerous activities of Spaniol and Herr von Papen. I explained how difficult it was to co-operate with a negligent Gestapo in Berlin. Buerckel promised me full immunity if my chiefs should object to my criticism.

When Kemmet and Buchmann arrived in Berlin, Buerckel told us to wait for twenty-four hours as he might need us. But neither of us was invited to the discussion which Buerckel had with Rudolf Hess, Dr. Ley, and Heinrich Himmler who had just arrived from Munich. Then Buerckel and Hess went to see Hitler and in twenty-four hours the decision was made which was later approved by a short cabinet meeting of the Reich Government—the Nazi Party in the Saar would be dissolved and Spaniol would be recalled.

Of course I cannot pride myself on being the author of such a momentous decision ; but I certainly appeared in Buerckel's office at an opportune moment. My material came in very handy and was a strong support for Buerckel's demand. He hated Spaniol and wanted to have a free hand in the Saar. This he attained ; the " German Front " (Deutsche Front) was formed in the Saar and was joined by the Centrum, the German Nationalists and the Stahlhelm.

Hitler himself appointed Buerckel as leader of this " German Front." So that the Saar statutes should not be violated and the Saar Government should be satisfied, there was a nominal leader, the petty civil servant Piro from Homburg ; but he was not taken seriously by anybody, not even by the people of the Stahlhelm and the Centrum. Buerckel remained in Neustadt and Papen was kept in his position of Saar Commissioner till the spring, 1934—but Buerckel did not worry about him. Papen had to be retained for the sake of the Centrum and the Stahlhelm whose organizations were also being disbanded. When it was all done and the " German Front " had swallowed and digested everything, Herr von Papen could vanish and was replaced officially by Buerckel as Hitler's and the Reich Government's Special Commissioner. It was Buerckel who did all the hard work to secure the success of the plebiscite—and it was Buerckel who triumphed.

During my days in Berlin I had the opportunity of meeting Dr. Ley and Rudolf Hess. Very few people know what great influence these two have over Hitler. It was through Dr. Ley and Hess that Buerckel attained his high appointments.

Rudolf Hess is " Hitler's Deputy." He appears but seldom in public, although he directs the whole apparatus of the Nazi Party. But he is also a chronic invalid, a very sick man. He lost half his lung in the war and is kept alive only by constant medical care, spending half the year in a sanatorium for T.B. In spite of the veto of the doctors and the advice of his well-meaning friends he persists in his burning ambition to deliver speeches. After every public oration he spends weeks in a nursing-home, mortally ill. Although he is an invalid—or perhaps just on this account as he had sacrificed himself so selflessly before the great triumph of his Fuehrer—Rudolf Hess has an almost unlimited influence over Adolf Hitler. Goering and Goebbels fight for his favour and his friendship. His ambitious wife, however, an Armenian girl, counts herself unlucky because, on account of her husband's illness, she is unable to play the rival to Frau Goering, the former actress Emmi Sonneman or Frau Goebbels, the divorced Mrs. Friedlaender. But there are compensations for such misfortune. . . .

As for myself, I was transferred at once to the Ludwigshafen Police Headquarters. The Gestapo raised no objection. I was, however, not under the authority of Police Director Artz, but directly under Buerckel, who had been in the meantime appointed President of the Bavarian Government for the Pfalz and become a high civil servant. I continued my work in the Saar ; the only difference was that I sent my reports to Buerckel instead of to Berlin. Our co-operation was very close from the first day, also smooth and almost on the basis of a friendship. When he was appointed officially a Commissioner of the Saar, I became a " special agent of Reich Commissioner Buerckel," with all the necessary powers.

E

Afterwards, when I was transferred again to Berlin, I retained this post.

Buerckel was a good chief, and it was extremely interesting to work for him. He was always just to his subordinates and helped them wherever he could. His backing gave me the courage and strength to go on with my dangerous job.

CHAPTER V

"HANSI" AND "RING"

I HAD BECOME A USEFUL agent of Buerckel's—less through my activities as a pseudo-Trotzkiist than through my pedlar's work in the role of a penniless refugee. Wandering from rectory to rectory, from one monastery to the other, I knew every change and shade in the attitude of the Roman Catholic clergy and the important people of the Centrum. I knew very well that in consequence of Spaniol's stupidity they would not hear about a co-operation with the Nazis; but I also knew that with a certain amount of tact and diplomacy they could be won over to the Third Reich just as the Stalhelm could be made to "join up." Buerckel was clever enough to realize the advantages which a *pro forma* dissolving of the Party and a "national united front in the Saar" would offer.

From the day when I started my work for Buerckel, it became not only much more intensive, but also on a much larger scale and more important.

In Berlin I had met the S.S. Chief Storm Leader (Obersturmfuehrer) Lurker. This Lurker organized in Zweibruecken, close to the Saar frontier, a sort of information bureau. He employed a host of petty spies and informers who worked mostly in Saarbruecken. It was rather a curious comedy that Lurker—who knew only that I was working for the Gestapo, without being familiar with my name and circumstances—warned me against myself as an "extremely dangerous Trotzkiist." After I had been transferred to Ludwigshafen I belonged to the same unit of the S.S. as Lurker. But the good man must be still unaware that his comrade in the S.S. and the "dangerous Trotzkiist" was the same person. I permitted myself the pleasure of asking him repeatedly for information about this formidable fellow. . . .

But Lurker's activity was no joke. It represented a serious danger to any systematic work. And yet even Buerckel let him continue, although he constantly referred to him as " that nitwit," if no worse. There were special reasons for Lurker's privileged position and for the fact that he was never reproached for his stupidity, but even consulted now and then. Lurker had been Adolf Hitler's and Rudolf Hess's prison guard in Landsberg. During the time Hitler spent in the fortress, Lurker was won over body and soul to the comparatively unknown Munich agitator. He procured all sorts of privileges and comforts for Hitler and Hess ; as soon as the Nazi Party was founded, he joined it enthusiastically and enrolled in the S.S. Later he was transferred to Zweibruecken, and when Hitler became Chancellor, received a year's leave with full pay. As he had become an Obersturmfuehrer in the S.S., he concluded that he had great talent for secret police work, and Buerckel may consider himself lucky that Lurker did not choose a more dangerous field of activity. He was an under-sized, bow-legged man, with shifty eyes ; his manner was sycophantic and unpleasant. And yet everybody knew him ; Hess, Goebbels, Buerckel, and even Hitler shook him by the hand ; still, nobody took his work seriously or wanted to have anything to do with him. Lurker had probably reached the height of his career. He is not only stupid but indolent and lazy and would never dream of doing any serious work. . . .

Buerckel despised him ; two other new " comrades " of mine, Schmelcher and Kemmet, hated him. Schmelcher was a Flag-Leader (Standartenfuehrer) of the Ludwigshafen S.S. ; a highly decorative man with his scarred, terrifying face. He wore the Order of Blood, which meant that he was one of the oldest Nazis in Germany ; but he also was lazy, indolent, and had very little ambition. His wife, a former chambermaid, was just the contrary ; her ambitious scheming drove Schmelcher up the rungs of the ladder. To-day he is Police President of Saarbruecken and his wife a social leader. Such is the " new aristocracy " of the Third Reich. But Schmelcher had one sterling quality ; he could be silent, and I had never any complaint to make about his discretion, although a great many curious Saar politicians visited Buerckel's office where Schmelcher also worked. He was the leader of the Ludwigs-hafen S.S. and his aide-de-camp, Georg Kemmet, shared his taciturnity.

Lurker had one useful man in his employ who did not like his chief. He was only an amateur and a beginner in secret service work, but he improved almost week by week. His name was Oskar Pfarr, a Saarbruecken jeweller and goldsmith.

On the recommendation of my friend and secretary, who still worked as manager of his mother-in-law's restaurant, I took Oskar Pfarr into my service; at the same time I employed a former member of the Stahlhelm, a bookkeeper of the Roech-ling Bank in Saarbruecken, who rejoiced in the highly decora-tive name of Narcissus Quindt. Both of them, Pfarr and Quindt, are probably still working as spies against the French in the Saar District. These two, with my faithful secretary, became my closest collaborators.

Narcissus Quindt became my banker and cashier. He paid salaries and rewards to all agents, spies, and occasional informers whom I employed. Oskar Pfarr acted as my deputy in dealing with all agents who still did not know my name; nor did they ever meet me. Thus my secretary had less to do, and my sphere of activity could be greatly enlarged. Soon our work did not cover the Saar District alone; we spun our net to include Metz, Strasbourg, and even Luxembourg. The simple task of gathering political information in the Saar slowly became a regular active military espionage against France.

Both Quindt and Pfarr had to have a pseudonym or code name by which they were known to me and to their subordin-ates. Quindt became "Hansi" and Pfarr "Ring." The trouble with these two was misguided zeal; often I had to restrain them from committing a foolish blunder, especially Pfarr. I had more difficulty with Pfarr's wife, who was small and very plump. She wanted her husband to become a civil servant—if possible a very high one—and her verbosity and bragging were often very dangerous. Her husband was a peasant boy, a tall, strapping fellow, but his formless and jealous wife had him well in hand. Quindt also had his differences with Pfarr and Mrs. Pfarr ; in such cases I had to be the judge. Quindt was just as ambitious as Pfarr, but he was more intelligent and cultured ; he was, however, less tenacious. They were very dissimilar friends, but with my hard-working secretary they formed an excellent team.

Our information service was soon so well established that for instance Max Braun could never take a trip without being accompanied by one of Pfarr's men. All the committees and deputations which the Social Democrats or the followers of Max Walz sent to Geneva or Paris had an " invisible " member in the person of one of our agents. Most of the committee members were silly or incautious enough to discuss the success or failure on their way home in their compartments or in the dining car. Often they quarrelled, and that was an excellent opportunity for our observer to get all the necessary data. As " Trotzkiist," I also had occasion to look at almost all documents, memoranda, petitions, and other material ; not only in the office of Max Walz, but also at Max Braun's.

M. Bernheim, the French Intelligence Officer at Forbach, came often to Saarbruecken. Every time he was followed by our agents ; almost every conference he had with his agent, an innkeeper and cinema proprietor, was reported to me verbatim. The two French agents had no idea that the innkeeper's own son-in-law had turned a well-paid informer ; to maintain the reputation of being an anti-Nazi, he used every opportunity to abuse National Socialism, and sometimes even had a brawl with S.A. men.

I still lived at Forbach and was constantly controlled by the French authorities. Even if I spent the day in Saarbruecken, I returned for the night to Forbach. If I stayed away for several days, I had a convenient alibi in my pedlar's business. I never carried a large amount of money ; I even incurred small debts on purpose. This lent colour to my role of political refugee and lessened the danger of my being unmasked.

After the French had watched me for some time, they summoned me one day to the Commissariat Special at the

Forbach railway station where they questioned me for several hours, although I quickly observed that no account of the proceedings was kept. At the end of all this an amiable, dark-haired little gentleman told me that he wanted to see me privately. When we were left alone, he declared in very bad German that "his firm" would be willing to offer me employment. I knew very well that this "firm" was the "Deuxième Bureau," the official French Intelligence Service. This was an opportunity of which I had never dreamt. The amiable little gentleman—no doubt a French Intelligence Officer—seemed to be convinced that I was the "real goods," a genuine refugee, and gave me some weeks to consider his offer. He thought that my fears and confusion were due to some "nationalistic inhibitions" while I could hardly wait in my impatience to return to my associates and report to Buerckel. With some patience and a good portion of impudence, I attained my goal and arrived safely in Neustadt on the Haardt. I visited Buerckel and explained my plans.

Buerckel was not very enthusiastic. He seemed to be sceptical about the results I would achieve—and in the last analysis he was right. He flatly refused to decide what I was to do ; he told me that I would have to apply to the Munich Political Police which was the secret service authority in the Pfalz. The chief of this police was Himmler, at that time still intriguing for the post at Berlin. The man I had to see was Reinhard Heydrich, Himmler's deputy and chief of the Security Service of the S.S. Reich Fuehrer, that formidable body known by the initials—SD.RFSS.

Captain Buchmann of Ludwigshafen advised me first to see Dr. Best who, in Stuttgart, was just organizing the new Special Service South-West. The Pfalz and later the Saar belonged to this branch. It was through Dr. Best that I became fully acquainted with the SD.RFSS, whose most authoritative member in espionage matters I later became.

Georg Kemmet, who worked with Captain Buchmann, offered to accompany me. As aide-de-camp of the S.S.-Standarte X, he was in constant touch with the Security Service without being a member of it. Dr. Best was already an important factor in this secret body.

There were three brand new Mercedes cars in Ludwigshafen, although its Police Headquarters were not at all on the large scale. The organizing talent of Germany's new rulers found an important outlet in acquiring as many luxury cars for every police executive as they could lay hands on. The origin of such cars was less important than the horse-power and the state of the upholstery. . . .

According to Buerckel's instructions I had to go to Munich. But first I drove with Kemmet to Stuttgart to see Dr. Best. Kemmet was present during the first official talk I had with Dr. Best; the latter displayed almost fascinating amiability. He enjoyed playing the part of the host and showing me the new achievements and branches of his department, the modern filing system, and the radio. He had established himself in the former Palace of the Crown Prince at Stuttgart.

Dr. Best even found it worth while to win the sympathy of honest Georg Kemmet, who felt no less flattered than myself. Kemmet saw himself already as the future leader of the Special Service in the Pfalz which Best was just organizing. Later he was deeply disappointed in his hopes and had to endure the bitter chagrin of seeing others, younger, more efficient men, preceding him on the rungs of the Nazi ladder; but at that time he was still hopeful.

Not that Georg Kemmet was an old man. He had fought through the war as sergeant, and in 1933 was about 45. For many years he had been a simple and efficient foreman in the I.G. Paint Factory at Ludwigshafen. Buerckel used him to prepare all sorts of bombs, fuses, and fireworks. He became involved in a legal process which caused a great sensation and was dismissed from his post. For two bitter years he remained unemployed, till Hitler came and filled the fleshpots for him and his family. He had always been a sort of bodyguard to Buerckel; the latter advanced him to the comparatively high rank of an S.S. Sturmbannfuehrer and aide-de-camp of the S.S. Group X. Buerckel's gratitude was not only for the bombs and other toys Kemmet had faithfully prepared, the brave man had even had his head broken in defence of his master. Buerckel had become embroiled in a fight at the Sausage Market of Duerckheim; Kemmet shielded him with his body, although his skull was badly smashed with a wine bottle. Such fights were common during the Duerckheim Fair, there was nothing political about it, just high spirits. Kemmet was rather proud of his broken head which earned him the life-long protection of Buerckel.

But even Buerckel could not protect him from his own stupidity. In February-March, 1933, Kemmet himself spoiled all his own chances of real advancement within the Party. He—just as Buerckel—was considered rather " left wing " within the Party and the S.S.—he took the " Socialist " part of the Nazi programme much too seriously. After the Nazis came to power in 1933, Kemmet, as S.S. leader, occupied the building of the Social Democrat Trade Union members only demanding their word of honour that they would carry on for the Nazis. He wanted to publish the Social Democrat paper as a Nazi daily for Ludwigshafen.

The S.S. Standarte of Neustadt on the Haardt, of which Kemmet was the aide-de-camp, had a strong group of S.S. men in the proletarian town Ludwigshafen. This group was led by a man called Eicke. Eicke objected to the action of his " comrade " Kemmet and regarded him as a " Red " who was fraternizing with " these damned Social Democrats." As Kemmet was formally his superior, his protests had very little effect. Thereupon Eicke did not hesitate long—he collected his S.S. men and tried to eject Kemmet and his workers by force from the " Vorwaerts " building. A regular siege followed, and Kemmet was in a very tight corner ; but in the end, Captain Buchmann appeared (at the orders of Buerckel) and freed him from his plight.

Buerckel was furious—both with Kemmet's stupidity and Eicke's impudence. The latter had to leave the Pfalz at once ; till this very day he is afraid to show himself in Buerckel's domain. The S.S. command censured Kemmet sharply, but Buerckel managed to retain him as an aide-de-camp. However, he had lost the sympathy of his superiors and probably also all chance of advancement.

Eicke fled to Munich where he was received with open arms by Heydrich. The latter and Himmler appointed him to organize the first official concentration camp in Dachau, near Munich, and became its first commandant; he also received the rank of S.S. Flag-Leader (Standartenfuehrer). Heydrich and Himmler seemed to find in him a kindred spirit; he rose to be an inspector of all official concentration camps in the Third Reich and an S.S. Group Leader.

But Eicke is the sort of man who bites the hand which feeds him. He tried to scheme against Heydrich; fortunately for him he noticed in time that the leader of the Gestapo was a much more formidable opponent than he had thought. In order to regain Heydrich's favour and to save his own skin, Eicke organized a troop of terrorists and executioners; the nucleus of this troop are his beloved " Dachauers," consisting mostly of Bavarians and Austrians, but also some Württemberg men. This troop was enlarged to the so-called S.S. Death's Head Battalions and are to-day the guards of all concentration camps. They act as executioners, and almost all of them have several murders on their conscience. Eicke is still their commandant; as a former officer he has shown a remarkable talent for organization. He earned his first " stripes " in Dachau and gained a sad notoriety.

Eicke's Death's Head battalions, with their strong military training and discipline, are to-day an important unit of the S.S. Police Executives. Their technical equipment is faultless, their spirit blindly loyal. They represent a strength equalling almost a division of infantry. In case of war they would be under the authority of the General Staff. In peace-time they are managed by the Reich Ministry of the Interior, under the command of Heinrich Himmler.

I had little reason to come into contact with these terrorist troops. But about the end of my Gestapo career I was given an appointment which took me to a concentration camp, and there I had ample opportunity to watch them at their deathly work.

★

CHAPTER VI

HELL ON EARTH

"I AM SENDING YOU to a concentration camp."

I stared at Heydrich who was sitting in his office at the Gestapo looking at me with airy nonchalance.

Quickly I racked my brains. What had I done or said to incur Heydrich's wrath? I have served him loyally for almost five years although sometimes my very soul revolted against the things I was expected to do. Only my soul—because I found life very sweet, and had no intention of dying. I had been discreet and—at least so I thought—fairly efficient. Why this dramatic announcement—and why the most fearful punishment?

Heydrich smiled and seemed to enjoy my discomfort.

" Don't be afraid," he added with a slow drawl. " You haven't deserved to be sent there. On the whole both Heinrich and myself are satisfied with you. In fact, this is a special job—which means quick promotion if you succeed. Frankly I don't expect you will, as a great number of others have tried and failed. Sit down."

I accepted the invitation and Heydrich began to explain. It seemed that a man had used the ancient subterfuge of getting into jail to avoid a more dangerous and severe sentence. This man—whom I shall call Kronstadt—was the possessor of highly important military secrets which he offered to Germany. There was some haggling about the price and then Kronstadt changed his mind and said that he would take his offer to another, more magnanimous power.

The Gestapo had not the slightest intention of letting him do that and watched him day and night. And yet he shook off his watchers and vanished. He could not have left the country—all the frontier stations were watched and a special look out kept by Gestapo agents and S.S. men—but he seemed to have vanished from the earth. Now Heydrich suspected that he had chosen the lesser of two evils—and had been sent as a minor offender to a concentration camp. He probably wore a disguise (something more elaborate than a wig or a false beard) and even if he did not have an easy time, he was safe from the torture of the Gestapo.

" You have to find the man," Heydrich told me. " And you have to be a prisoner yourself. I shall give instructions to Eicke but I am afraid you'll have to endure some rough handling. It will be worth while : the reward is considerable. As a prisoner in ' protective custody ' you'll be able to mingle with the other prisoners and find Kronstadt—if he is there."

I did not relish the task but could not dream of saying so. One word from Heydrich—and everything I had attained in the past four years would have been lost.

" Which . . . which camp is it ? " I asked.

Heydrich smiled grimly.

" Buchenwald."

I felt a little faint. Buchenwald, the newest concentration camp, was near Weimar where Goethe and Schiller lived and worked. It was in a " beauty spot," but there was just three words to describe it properly. . . .

Hell on earth. . . .

My talk with Heydrich was on the 12th June, 1938. The next day I was " arrested " and taken to the Police Head-quarters in Berlin, Alexanderplatz. On this and the following day about four thousand Jews had also been arrested—almost fifteen thousand in the whole Reich. I have said that Nazidom was nothing if not systematical. During these two days all the Jews who had a criminal record were rounded up. Do not think this record meant any serious offence. If someone had been sentenced to a few days in jail because he violated some traffic regulation or was fined for keeping his shop open after regular hours—that constituted a criminal record. In reality this was a purely political measure. Goering considered the exodus of the Jews much too slow and wanted to speed it up. The fancy name they gave to these mass arrests was "preventive custody." Though what they wanted to prevent and why, nobody could tell—least of those who ordained the measure.

There I was—not a Jew, but still a prisoner—and I soon realized that my fears of being recognized by some friend of mine were groundless. There was a huge crowd in the Police Headquarters and they had very little time to waste on a prisoner. I was registered and then transferred during the night of the 14th–15th June to Buchenwald. First we were examined by a young, sleepy doctor who proclaimed that we were all in the very best physical condition, although there were quite a number of people over seventy and a few consumptive cases who had obviously only a very short time to live.

It was 2 a.m. when we arrived at the Anhalter Bahnhof. No ordinary passenger was admitted to the railway station; we were watched by policemen armed with carbines. Around 6 a.m. we were received by Eicke's Death's Head troops in Weimar. Hardly had we left the train, when they began to beat the prisoners—selecting those who looked Jewish. Using their rifle-butts, their boots, and fists, they drove the whole mass into a nearby building. I now saw that Heydrich had decidedly understated matters when he spoke about "some rough handling." Roedl, the commander of Buchenwald, received the prisoners with a speech:

"There are people among you," he said, "who have been in prison. That's nothing to what you'll experience here. You're in a concentration camp, which means that you are in hell. If you offer the slightest resistance to a command given by an S.S. man you'll be shot. We know only two kinds of punishment here: death or flogging."

This encouraging speech was received in deep silence. I saw grown strong men tremble; I saw a young boy clutching his head while the tears oozed between his fingers.

When we arrived at Buchenwald, we had to dodge a rain of blows and kicks. I was still nimble enough to dodge most of them, but several of my fellow-prisoners fell and even then were kicked. The entrance was guarded with machine-guns and decorated with the ironical slogan : " RIGHT OR WRONG—MY FATHERLAND ! "

Heydrich's careful instructions to the commander of the camp saved me the unpleasant humiliation of having my head shaved. Then we had to give up our civilian clothes and received the regulation uniform. There were certain marks denoting our category. " Politicals " had a red stripe, " sectarians " pink, " lazy idlers " black. I received a red stripe, as we thought that Kronstadt would be in the latter group.

The Jews had to sew a " David's star " on a black-yellow background on to their coats which denoted that they were " Jews afraid of work." Most of them were independent businessmen, a few workers, a dentist, and several lawyers. All of them received a number and were never called by name. Then we were taken to our quarters.

An an " Aryan " prisoner, one of six thousand, I was taken to a wooden hut. Each hut had one hundred and forty men. The Jews fared worse ; they were packed five hundred in a stable. There were no tables, chairs, or beds. They had to sleep huddled together on the bare floor ; there was no room to stretch their limbs. Each received two thin blankets. There was no place to wash ; only on the ninth day were they given eight washbowls—to be used by five hundred men. They had to fetch water from the pump which was about ten minutes' walk. Their worst plight was that they were supervised by six habitual criminals in each stable who were also prisoners but acted as " trusties." These men had full " executive " powers and maltreated the Jews as much as they liked.

Conditions were slightly better in the barracks of the " Aryans," although we " Politicals " could not boast of an exaggerated kindness in our treatment. For appearance's sake I had to endure a few blows and kicks ; and it was rather difficult to restrain myself. On the other hand my actual guards did not know anything about my dual role and would have immediately shot me had I retaliated.

Nor, of course, could the Jews do anything against their torturers. Had they struck these " trusties " it would have been considered mutiny and the punishment for that was death. One of them told me how an old man had been so beaten up during the daily work that he moaned and groaned during the night. The "trusty" thereupon began to rain blows on his face. Next morning the man was dead— mercifully released from suffering.

As soon as I had opportunity I began my careful investigations. Kronstadt was, according to the description furnished by Heydrich, a tall, broad-shouldered man with reddish hair. He had probably dyed his hair—but he had a scar on his left palm which he could hardly obliterate. It would have been rather foolish to go around the camp looking at people's palms; and Heydrich had told me that I had to do it unobtrusively. The S.S.—Eicke's men—must not know what I was doing; this was strictly Gestapo work. He did not disclose the reasons for this secrecy and why the Gestapo was not willing to collaborate in this case with its close associate the S.S. But you soon learned in Heydrich's service never to question his motives nor try to fathom his hidden reasons. So I decided to single out those prisoners whose physical qualities corresponded to Kronstadt's—I could watch out for the scar after I had narrowed down my circle of suspects.

We had very little to eat; but the Jews had even less. In the first two days they did not get a morsel of food; but they had to "exercise." Work began only after eight days; first the "formalities" had to be settled. Everybody among the Jews had to sign a declaration that he had been "afraid of work" and taken into preventive custody for this reason. The document stated that they made this declaration out of their own free will. A Breslau lawyer refused to sign it. The unfortunate man had to endure every kind of punishment Eicke's men could devise. After four days—a dying man, half conscious, whose body was bruised and beaten almost out of shape—he signed.

It was hard work but at last I had seen most of my fellow-prisoners. I kept a sort of rough log of them on the wall of the barracks; there were fifty-four people whose physical characteristics corresponded to the rather vague description of Kronstadt. So I had to watch fifty-four people—and find an opportunity to ascertain whether one of them had a scar on his left palm !

I was rather fortunate to escape any punishment for the time being. The S.S. men displayed great ingenuity in devising new methods. If someone drank water during working hours, he did not get any lunch, and on Sundays, during the free period, he had to stand at attention for four hours under S.S. guard. The rest of the punishments were mostly beating and flogging. If a man was caught smoking during working hours, he was publicly flogged. Every afternoon at parade the numbers of these unlucky people were called out—and always there was quite a crowd of them. The victims were fastened to a frame and received twenty-five strokes. An S.S. man clapped a cloth over their mouth to stifle their screams. Old people who were unable to do their work swiftly enough were also "chastised" in the same way. After the flogging there was an inspection of the scars and wounds to see whether the punishment had been "thorough" enough. Apart from flogging, a favourite punishment was the "bunker," solitary confinement. A great many prisoners never left it alive. Day by day we heard the screams and groans of the maltreated prisoners behind the barred windows. A "gentler" method was to tie a man to a tree by his arms and to force him to run swiftly round it. If he was not quick enough, a few kicks soon speeded up his movements. . . .

Another method of "tree-tying" often proved fatal. The victim was tied so tightly that his circulation more or less stopped. He had to stay for hours in such a position ; nor was this barbaric punishment an exception, it happened only too often.

I had succeeded in eliminating all but twelve of my suspects. The others had no scar on their left palm—or they had special marks which were definitely missing from Kronstadt's description. After eight days I was made a "trusty" and detailed to guard the Jewish prisoners during their working hours.

Reveille for them was at 3.30 a.m. From 4.30 to 5.30 there

was the morning parade, then the march to work. Work
started a little before 6 a.m. ; there was no pause till noon.
Then they rested for half an hour and got a cup of thin coffee
without milk or sugar. Work was then continued till 3.45
p.m. At 4 p.m. there was another parade, usually lasting till
5.30. Dinner was at half-past five, then work till eight ; then
supper, and at 9 p.m. lights out. On Sundays work went on
from six till four. There were no holidays in the camp, not
even Christmas (as older prisoners told us). The weather
was unimportant—people, young and old, healthy and ailing,
had to work on even if there was a hailstorm or frost.

I was appointed foreman of a Jewish working group.
Without being a sentimental or soft-hearted man, I did
everything to lighten their plight—but I could not do much.
They were working in a quarry and had to carry the blocks
of stone to a road about a mile away which was also being
built by prisoners. Some of these blocks were so heavy that
several people had to lift them so that one man could stagger
away under the load. The road rose steeply and for the
last five hundred yards the S.S. men drove the prisoners
mercilessly—they had to run with that terrible load. They
were not permitted to drink or to rest for a moment. By the
afternoon of the first day I spent with this group, thirty men
out of a hundred had collapsed. And among them two died
during the night. . . .

Another kind of work was the transport of huge tree-
trunks. These too had to be carried at a swift trot and some
of the prisoners were crushed under a particularly heavy
trunk ; especially when an exceptionally inventive S.S. man
demanded " physical jerks " to be done during the transport.
Homo homini lupus ; truly I saw that man was man's worst
enemy. We of the Gestapo had seldom such " dirty " work
to do ; few of us were sadists. But all Eicke's men seemed
to be just that. . . .

Only five of my suspects remained. But these were working
in a different part of the camp and were thus difficult to
approach. I began to feel the strain. I had hardly any sleep,
and even if I did no strenuous work, the bad food and the

F

lack of rest began to undermine my health. I felt that I had to finish my task sooner or later—sooner if possible, if I wanted to get out alive from this "hell on earth." I even began to suspect Heydrich of having wanted to get rid of me and of having invented this mythical Kronstadt to get me into a concentration camp. But he could have done it so much more simply—why this roundabout way?

The food was really terrible. We got a litre of soup for lunch; but the Jewish prisoners got only $\frac{1}{2}$ litre and 250 grammes of bread (we got 625 grammes). It was forbidden to send food from outside; although money could be sent. But for most families this was practically impossible; having lost their bread-winner through his arrest, they could hardly exist themselves. Also there were always deductions and the rest was paid in rates of 5 marks a week. Not much could be bought for that in the camp shop, which charged fabulous prices. Often there was nothing left except a little custard. . . .

Among "Aryans" and Jews alike the death-roll mounted. In my hut we had one dead man almost every day. In the first four weeks 80 Jews out of 2000 died; in another week 30. These figures were carefully suppressed. . . .

I tried my best to continue my investigations and in the end had only two suspects remaining. If these should fail . . . all I had endured and suffered was in vain.

The camp was surrounded by barbed wire; at night this wire was charged with electricity. Outside—but very close to the wire—S.S. posts were placed with machine-guns in their iron-turreted watchtowers. The prisoners were forbidden to go near the wire, but the new arrivals were not told about it. The S.S. guards up in their towers liked to have their little jokes. They commanded a newcomer to step up to the wire. If the man obeyed the command, the guard took careful aim and fired. This was a very frequent case. Sometimes half-crazed prisoners who could not stand the "hell on earth" any longer, rushed up to the wire and the guards fired at once—although they knew quite well that these were men in despair and not people trying to escape. . . .

Most deaths occurred however in the quarry. Here they had also a chain of guards which could not be approached. Often an old or weak man had to hoist a block of stone which he was unable to drag along. The S.S. men forced him to lift it again and again. Of course the prisoner in question was left behind by the others. After a while they would hear a shot. The S.S. man had driven his man near the chain of guards who shot him " while trying to escape." Such murders also happened almost every day.

There was a particularly tragic case, that of young Erich Loewenberg, who was hardly twenty-two. This young boy —a singer in a synagogue—was driven by a guard under a lorry which killed him. Others again had a heart attack. Coffins had to be made by the prisoners themselves—never knowing whether it would be their own or not. The bodies were taken to the Weimar crematorium and there burned. The family was notified by a simple postcard, on which— consummate irony—they had to pay postage.

Many perished because there was no medical care. During the first weeks no Jew could get any medicine, and later the doctor refused to give place to Jewish patients in the primitive hospital. Once he kicked a man out as a " malingerer "— two hours later the man was dead. . . .

There were 8000 people in Buchenwald, 2000 Jews and 6000 " Aryans." But the S.S. plans to enlarge it to a capacity of 25,000 men—the biggest concentration camp in the whole of Germany.

These eight thousand were divided into different groups. First came the " political " prisoners, as for instance the Communist Reichstag members, Neubauer, Saefkow, Gezchke, Woitinski, etc., who for five years had been dragged from one camp to the other. The well-known Berlin barrister Hans Litten was also among them; during my months in Buchenwald he broke his leg in the quarry, although it was freshly healed from an earlier fracture. Besides these " politicals " there were a number of poor devils who had abused the Fuehrer and were denounced. *After* they had served their prison sentence they had been taken into protective custody—for an indefinite period. That was the really

terrible thing ; nobody knew how long his term would last
—it might be three months or it might be three years. . . .

Then there were the people " afraid of work " (Arbeits-
scheue). These were no tramps or touts—but mostly decent
men. I met a shopkeeper, for instance, who had sound
business training. He received a small dole after he went
bankrupt, but could find no position. One day he was told
that he could get work as a navvy. He refused. Thereupon
he was arrested by the Gestapo and taken to the concentration
camp.

The third group consisted of the " Bible students," a
religious sect, widespread in Germany, but forbidden by the
Gestapo because they deny the right of the State to wage
war or recruit soldiers. They were treated almost as badly
as the Jews.

The fourth kind of prisoners were the homosexuals or
those who had been branded as such by the Gestapo. During
the time I spent in Buchenwald there were no such people
in custody there.

The last group ; the habitual criminals. These were the
" trusties " of the camp, and had practically power over life
and death. They flattered the S.S. men in a nauseating way,
maltreating the prisoners whenever they could.

Nobody was released as long as there were traces of
beating and flogging on his body. The, doctors went to
work on him—but even so they could not avoid news of
brutalities becoming more or less public.

Then came two thunderbolts for me. The first was that
neither of my last two suspects answered to the description
of Kronstadt—neither of them had the significant scar. So
I had failed . . . and my quarry was not in Buchenwald.
Should I have to get acquainted with the other " sanatoriums "
of Standartenfuehrer Koch, the man who was responsible
beside Eicke for all the different concentration camps ?
Dachau, Woellersdorf, and the others . . . should I have
to visit them as a prisoner ? I shuddered.

The second surprise was even more staggering. I had
been seen giving some water to an old, sick Jewish prisoner

during working hours. I was denounced by a fellow " trusty " and sentenced to—flogging. . . .

This was a pretty kettle of fish. Heydrich had told me that under no circumstances should I betray my identity—he was giving instructions and these should shield me from any real trouble. On the other hand I was not going to endure the flogging. . . .

But I did. I, too, was fastened to the block and beaten till I fainted. Then they carted me off to the hospital and threw me on a cot.

When I opened my eyes the first thing I saw was a man's hand hanging over the edge of a bed. Its palm was open —and it had a scar. . . .

I turned my head and winced. My back was aching terribly. The man in the other bed had a long unkempt beard and a face lined by suffering. His hair was reddish.

It was Kronstadt.

Three weeks I spent in that primitive hospital, tended by not too gentle medical care, watching Kronstadt die. We became friends. Before he died he told me where he had hidden the documents Heydrich wanted so badly. He trusted me.

When I was discharged from hospital, I was also released from Buchenwald. I made my report to Heydrich who gave me full credit for the work I had done. Of course I could not dream that Kronstadt was in hospital, that he had been beaten to death. I stumbled on him—and I felt like a ghoul, having wrested the secret from the dying man.

But I had seen the " hell on earth " . . . and I think that this experience was an important factor in my decision to leave Germany and break my loyalty to its overlords.

As long as there are places like Buchenwald in the world, mankind cannot call itself civilized.

CHAPTER VII

★

THE HUNTED HUNTER

D R. BEST ENCOURAGED ME in my plan to join the French
Secret Service to try and ferret out as much information for
the Gestapo as possible. He promised me his full support
for my work in the Saar and for my plans for espionage in
France—and he kept his word.

I travelled on with Kemmet to Munich where I visited
Heydrich. He was deeply interested in my ideas and past
activities. I spent many hours in his private office discussing
the future. After three days we parted as friends, although
during our conferences we had often rather heated arguments
and I did not hesitate to give him my frank opinion on a great
many matters.

Heydrich had enrolled me personally in the secret Security
Service, took my oath, and introduced me to Himmler. As
a member of the notorious SD.RFSS. I was immediately
under Heydrich's authority and was able to continue my
work independently, without any red tape. From now on
I served two masters—Buerckel and Heydrich. But as
these two had nothing to do with each other (nor did
they want to co-operate) I had never any serious difficulty
endangering my activity. Buerckel was interested only in
the Saar—Heydrich was interested in espionage. Both of
them gave me a free hand, as they had approved my past
results.

On Buerckel's instructions I continued to play the part of
a Trotzkiist in the Saar and my well-founded organization
continued to function successfully. At Heydrich's command
I wandered through Alsace-Lorraine. My pedlar's disguise

stood me in good stead. I tried to collect information in the district of the Maginot Line.

The amiable little Frenchman in Forbach did not send for me again. But I knew that he was just biding his time.

I went to Strasbourg to meet a Gestapo agent. His name was Dr. Heines Mueller, a Dortmund lawyer and journalist. He had worked for a left-wing radical paper. After the Nazi debacle he saved his skin by becoming a Gestapo agent. He was well paid and quite useful.

His usefulness consisted chiefly in having a French fiancée, a very cultured young girl. She was an active member of the " Croix Rouge des Dames Françaises," and had a very good connection with the French General Staff. Dr. Mueller was a handsome young man and his fiancée very much in love with him. She was only too happy to put all this at this disposal. Of course she had no idea about the espionage activities of her " beloved," nor could she know that he misused his introductions to French generals and other military leaders.

Mueller told me in Strasbourg that I had to meet " Maurice " in Luxembourg. I had gone to Strasbourg to meet him there, but he was a cautious man. " Maurice " was an engineer who had been conducting some work near the French fortress Bitche. For a handsome consideration he was willing to sell these plans. Mueller contacted him and arranged for a meeting at the Café Alfa in Luxembourg City.

But before I was going to Luxembourg I had to find out something about a Jesuit Father called Feger or Freger. The Gestapo had received information that this priest was organizing the resistance of the Catholic clergy in the Saar against the German bishops in Trier and Speyer. According to this information Feger had influenced the Vatican to send a special envoy and to consider seriously the appointment of a bishop for the Saar District. In the meantime the Papal envoy had arrived in St. Ingbert ; we suspected Father Feger that he had been chosen to draw up a confidential report for Rome.

In vain I tried to be received by Father Feger as a poor

refugee and pedlar. He was much too wary to see anyone who had no personal introduction to him.

With Dr. Mueller I went to the Chancery of the Bishop of Strasbourg. I wanted to get a letter of recommendation for my pedlar's work; such a letter would have opened all the doors on which I was knocking in vain.

"I am sorry," the young priest who received us told me, "but we are not allowed to give any sort of business recommendations."

He was extremely polite but just as firm. Dr. Mueller, who acted as my sponsor, talked and talked, but the young man did not relent. At last he was called from the room. We had waited for this opportunity and quickly stamped a few blank sheets which we had prepared for such an emergency with the bishop's seal lying conveniently on the table.

As an experiment we composed a letter of introduction containing my name. I was cautious enough never to give it out of my hands, although I showed it everywhere. The same evening I was received by the Father Superior of the Strasbourg Jesuits. Skilfully I guided the conversation to the subject of Father Feger for whom I professed a great admiration. The Jesuits of Strasbourg numbered only half a dozen; they lived in a little house on the outskirts of the town; but they travelled all over Alsace-Lorraine and had a great fund of information. I more or less ascertained that the Gestapo had been wrong about Father Feger; he had nothing to do with the Papal envoy. His name had been probably mentioned by an agent who had incomplete details and chose Feger because the latter had been corresponding with Rome.

I had fulfilled my task on that point and thought that I was safe. But early next morning there was a knock at my door in the little hotel where I was living in my role of poor refugee.

I was awake and asked who it was. "The Sûreté," came the unpleasant answer. I told them that I would open the door in a minute—I was in bed and had to dress. Luckily they waited and I could destroy the forged letter of recommendation.

Very politely they asked me to accompany them to the Prefecture, the Strasbourg Police Headquarters.

At first I suspected Dr. Mueller of double-crossing me. He would have scored a bull by denouncing me to the French and would have received a fat reward. But soon I found out that I was unjust in my suspicions; nor were the Jesuits of the Chancery of the Bishop responsible for my arrest. My enemies were the Communists of Strasbourg, the General Secretariat of the French Communist Party. I had visited them as a pedlar, offering them pencils and india-rubbers for office use. I wanted to find out which leading German Communists were working there. Heydrich had told me that such information was especially important as lately, in connection with the approaching trial of the Reichstag Fire, a huge mass of illegal Communist pamphlets had been smuggled into Germany; most of it came from Strasbourg. But the comrades of Strasbourg were just as vigilant as their Saar Party-friends. Every attempt to get into one of their Party centres or become a member was foiled by their well-founded suspicions; they knew quite well how to defend themselves against spies and *agents provocateur*. It had happened that two of my own agents in Saarbruecken had been almost beaten to death when they tried to get into the local Party offices.

The Communists of Strasbourg probably considered me only as a small and unimportant agent, spy, or Gestapo-employee, but with the help of their excellent organization they informed the French police that I had been seen in Berlin and Frankfurt with Criminal Councillor Heller; there could be no doubt about my connections with the Gestapo.

Lucky for me that the French were less convinced about the efficiency of the Communist Intelligence Service than was I myself. They followed up the denunciation—"just in case"—but I managed to extricate myself from my highly uncomfortable position. I simply said that I was a Trotzkiist, a thing which the Communists hated, and that they were acting out of spiteful revenge.

But this was not so easy as it might sound. The French were real masters of interrogation. Even though I was in a very tight spot, I had to admire and envy them. As a matter of fact that questioning in Strasbourg taught me much which I was able to use later in my own work.

I was taken to a fair-sized room and given a comfortable chair. From the beginning to the end there were always five or six detectives around me who were partly relieved from time to time and partly supplemented. They plied me with questions, a rapid machine-gun fire of enquiries, denunciations, polite abuse, and frigid innuendo. Mostly these were only stupid, apparently unimportant remarks, returning again and again ; suddenly one man standing behind me burst in with a surprising and dangerous question, demanding instant reply ; they made ironical remarks about my appearance, my mental capacity, and so on ; they were like a swarm of particularly tenacious bumble-bees, buzzing, buzzing around me till I thought I was going mad. The whole thing was conducted by the *directeur général* of the Counter-Espionage in the Frontier District. I think his name must be Becker, and he was certainly an Alsatian.

I had to reconstruct every step of my wanderings as a pedlar on French territory. They had found very little money on me, and this was an extenuating circumstance. I could also prove that I was in debt to some extent. On the other hand, they had found some of the blank sheets stamped with the Bishop's seal ; I had no time to destroy all of them. This was a serious point against me and taxed all my powers of invention till I could present a creditable story.

I was in such a desperate position, I told them, that I had been tempted to stamp these sheets with the bishop's seal when it was lying there unguarded on the table. But, I continued, with a well-simulated frankness, I did not use them. My conscience would not let me. This made the honest French a little doubtful ; I don't think they gave much credit to my explanation. But anyhow, there was nothing actually *written* on those sheets, so I had probably not yet had opportunity to use them.

Then there was Dr. Mueller. What about him ? I said that I had met him in Strasbourg, that I did not know much about him, except that he, too, was a refugee from the Third Reich.

It would have been stupid and false to mix him up unnecessarily in the story with the bishop's seal.

They questioned me the whole day and then led me to the corridor. And there, to my great dismay, I saw Dr. Mueller who had also been arrested. While he was being questioned, I had to wait outside, under guard. But even the overcautious French committed the blunder of allowing Dr. Mueller to pass close by me. I whispered quickly :

" Admit nothing ; I take blame for seal story."

He nodded imperceptibly, and I felt very much relieved.

Dr. Mueller must have impressed the French greatly with his acquaintances in the French General Staff. He succeeded in clearing not only his own name, but mine too.

He was a cunning fellow, but even he met his Waterloo about a year later. To be just it was not his fault. An officer of the Reichswehr, who worked at the espionage department of Darmstadt, was stupid enough to go to the Saar District and take a note-book full of addresses and names of agents. He was caught, and all those who figured on his lists were arrested —among them Dr. Heines Mueller. The French Military Tribunal of Strasbourg sentenced him to a long term in prison.

But that was not until a year later. Now, Dr. Mueller was released after half an hour, and about an hour later they let me go. When I closed the front door of the Prefecture and was standing alone in the evening street, the tears began to run down my cheeks. I was completely exhausted ; I cried like a boy after his first caning. My nerves were all on edge and it took me some time to regain my composure.

I think that even the most hardened man could not stand the grilling à la French for any length of time. It all depended whether the questioner lost his patience first or his victim collapsed. Later, I confessed to Heydrich that it would have been only a matter of a few hours and I would have betrayed myself by a slip of the tongue. He looked at me strangely, as if I were slightly mad. But, of course, he had not gone through the same harassing experience. The French had taught me the tactics of " crumbling the defences." Any intelligent questioner could do very well without brutal methods and torture—if he had the tenacity and ingenuity to trap his victim.

A little chastened and without seeing Dr. Mueller again, I left Strasbourg and returned to Forbach. A few days later I went through Metz to Luxembourg. There, in the colourful Café Alfa, I met the French engineer " Maurice " and discussed his offer. He was a sly little man, this Maurice, but he was also sensible. Later, a Reichswehr officer bought the plans after I had settled all the details and examined their worth.

I left Luxembourg to return to Forbach.

In Thionville, on the French frontier, two French policemen came into my compartment and asked me to accompany them. I protested, but I could do nothing. I thought that my experience of Strasbourg would be repeated—but it was somewhat different. They took me to the " Commissariat Spécial," where I was again questioned and searched.

Now in Luxembourg I had bought a great many books and newspapers, all of them written and published by German refugees. Among them there was a copy of the *Neue Welt-buehne*, a well-edited and informative magazine which contained an interesting article about the latest military preparations in Germany with a wealth of technical detail. Instead of the name of the author there were three asterisks. I had been specially interested in this article and marked it with red pencil, underlining several passages in the text.

The inspector at the " Commissariat Spécial " who had most probably acted on instructions and had not selected my humble person at random from all the passengers, wanted to be especially " cunning."

He took the *Neue Weltbuehne*, pointed at the marked article, and said :

" *You* wrote this article ! "

" But, monsieur . . . " I protested, taken aback.

" Don't try to deny it ! I know ! Oh, we know much more than you suspect."

" But, monsieur, I really didn't. I don't even know what you are talking about. . . ."

The pot-bellied, twinkling-eyed inspector patted my shoulder confidently :

"You can trust me!" he said, in a very French voice, quivering with emotion.

I shrugged. This would mean no confession nor a denial. But the inquisitive little man kept on bothering me till in the end I had to give an answer.

"No, I didn't write the article," I said, virtuously. "But I supplied the material."

This was just what he wanted to hear. We became fast friends in half an hour. He introduced himself as Inspector "Delaporte," probably because he lived just outside the gates of the little town.

"For God's sake!" he implored with Gallic enthusiasm, "don't be your own enemy! If you have such material in the future, don't take it to a beggar of an editor! Bring it to me! I assure you, I'll pay you much, much better than even *les Americains*."

M. "Delaporte" was so full of hopes of a rosy future, his own advancement, and my financial success, that he forgot to ask me where I had got all this interesting material. And I was rather glad that he did not raise this unpleasant question.

My train to Metz had gone a long time ago without me. M. "Delaporte" was very much concerned about my well-being and took me to his little house, presented me to his plump, fair, and hospitable wife, and offered me a "modest" real French supper which I enjoyed greatly.

Later at night I returned to Forbach. I had become an agent of M. Inspecteur "Delaporte," a position which fulfilled exactly my requirements. Later, I often visited the kind inspector, stopping at his house whenever I passed to Thionville on my way to Luxembourg. Later, when I had joined the "firm" of the amiable gentleman in Forbach, we still remained good friends. That pleasant intelligence officer had soon turned up after my arrests in Strasbourg and Thionville. Of course, he had ordered these arrests, "just to make sure," before he employed me. I had been weighed and not found wanting—therefore, I was qualified to join the host of the agents of the "Deuxième Bureau."

In spite of the caution and suspicion which the masters of the French Secret Service showed in my case, I have not too high an opinion of them. Although the "Deuxième Bureau " had never permitted me to look into its cards, their tactics against Germany were all wrong, and even to-day they have not improved. They are too petty, too narrow-minded. This view I formed through my experiences as chief of the Security Service for Special Purposes of the S.S. Reich Fuehrer, and every small incident has supported it.

What did the French Secret Service expect of me ? Or what did I want to attain by joining it as a pseudo-agent ?

With Buerckel's and Heydrich's knowledge and full approval, I composed "reports" for the French. These reports were nothing more than a summary of all that could be read in refugee papers days or even weeks before. Some of them were rather daring political competitions wholly without foundation ; others well-known facts which could be found in any military paper of Germany without even reading a foreign daily or a refugee publication.

It was with rather a neat touch of irony that I wrote all these reports which I delivered to the " Commissariat Spécial " in Forbach—in Ludwigshafen, at the Police Headquarters. When, later on, I was unable to travel to Ludwigshafen or Neustadt for the composing of my reports, I typed them out in Forbach or Saarbruecken on my portable machine. But I always sent a copy to Buerckel, one to Heydrich, and kept one for my own files.

I had hoped that the French would be gullible enough to send me to Germany where I could find out in time the most important names and connections of their long-established agents ; perhaps I could uncover the whole net of their espionage against Germany. But this remained an idle hope, frustrated by the fact alone that the German military authorities were unable to supply me with the necessary material— " Material for disinformation," as the technical term goes—for offering to the French. Buerckel was justified in his doubts, although later I stumbled by accident on something rather important.

" Disinformation " is briefly to supply to a foreign power false military or political information, manufactured for this express purpose. Such material should not only mislead the foreign power, but move it to erroneous dispositions and calculations which might prove highly damaging in case of war. As long as there is war on earth disinformation is destined to play a decisive part in espionage. Many a battle has been won by skilfully suggested, forged news ; by a pseudo-betrayal of painstakingly prepared false plans, battle orders, etc.—provided that the enemy swallows the bait.

To-day, when the gathering and transmission of information has been made simple, swift and secure ; when every modern military formation is more or less generally known and internationally publicized in its technical details, many countries refuse to use disinformation, especially in times of peace. You cannot supply to a foreign power disinformation on a large scale without giving about 80 per cent correct data to make them believe you, the rest of false material. And even if the foreign power knows all about the 80 per cent, and is able to examine its correctness by its own intelligence service, no General Staff is willing to risk delivering proof for the truth of this 80 per cent. Such activity is left to-day mostly to political swindlers and adventurers who still believe that they can have any success with their forged documents. They always last only a short time and are engulfed by their own stupidity.

I tried to do my best with the French, yet I had little success. Dr. Best managed to get for me from the Reichswehr in Darmstadt two of the unimportant " orders of the day," issued to a regiment of artillery in Kassel. I took them to Forbach—but that was just chicken feed. My colleagues were naïve enough to offer me the plans of a marine torpedo— prepared in 1911—but I refused point-blank. I was sure that the French would have arrested me at once. Even so, they became more and more suspicious.

At least I tried to attain a complete freedom of movement on French soil. Even that was difficult. I was only helped by the circumstance that the " Deuxième Bureau " took such a long time in making up its mind about me. During this comparatively long period I could wander in my role as pedlar and refugee through Alsace-Lorraine, especially in the vicinity of the famous Maginot Line. I continued my trips even after my two arrests in Strasbourg and Thionville, although I felt rather uncomfortable all the time.

I took good care to brag more or less openly about my direct connections to the French Intelligence Service. These partly veiled allusions helped me to a great extent in my work in the Saar. It impressed a man like Max Walz that his one-time protégé had become an " important " agent in French service; it also helped me in making new contacts and tapping sources of information which had remained closed to me up to then.

I have already mentioned that when I started my work in the Saar the Gestapo was especially interested in the leakage of information which came from Hindenburg's closest circle ; someone was sending information (and highly correct information at that) not only to refugees, but directly to the French. This was a very serious matter, and both Buerckel and Heydrich were anxious to clear it up.

Heydrich suspected three prominent persons. One was a countess of old Prussian nobility, the second a high official in the German Foreign Office, and the third an important industrialist. I must state at once that these suspicions were unfounded. Only much later did I succeed in finding the real culprit—and even then only by an accident. The three people whom Heydrich suspected may have no idea even to the present day in what mortal danger they were as nothing happened to them.

I approached the French with the offer that I would like to carry on espionage for them in Germany. We had carefully discussed the plan in Ludwigshafen and Munich. I mentioned to the French intelligence officer in Forbach the names of the three suspects, and told him that they would supply me in the future with information about the events in the Reichswehr, the German Foreign Office, and the Nazi Party. The whole idea was that the Frenchman might betray through a chance remark or a single gesture that he knew all three or at least one of them—or at least had some knowledge of their connection with the " Deuxème Bureau." But the Frenchman was more cunning than we were; he did not betray himself; nor was there, in this instance, anything to betray. My task had failed before I had really begun my double role in the French Intelligence Service.

I was told by my amiable French chief to go through Germany and get in touch with these three people. In order to prove that they were willing to do espionage for France I was to bring some small piece of writing in their hand.

I could not do anything except to go on with my play-acting. I told the French intelligence officer that it would be impossible for me to use my genuine passport; as a Trotzkiist refugee I would be in instant danger. But it was no use; he would not give me another forged passport; I had to get some document of legitimation myself, " secretly," and, as I told them, through an illegal channel. For this purpose I used Oskar Pfarr's Saar passport, which bore his photograph—and committed thereby my first serious blunder. The French, of course, became interested in Pfarr, although for the time being without any serious consequences. I travelled a few times to Germany and back, although I did not go to Berlin, only to Neustadt, Ludwigshafen, and Munich, where the reports on my alleged contacts with the three " suspects " were manufactured. As proof of my activity I brought a few worthless, out-dated S.S. orders which Kemmet had given me; two regimental orders by Dr. Best, and the courier plan of the Foreign Office which any postman could have acquired.

There was always a considerable lapse of time between my trips so that I could carry on my work in the Saar and in the district of the French fortification. Buerckel and Heydrich were much amused by the scanty pay which I received from the French and which went to swell my funds, out of which Quindt—or " Hansi "—paid my agents in the Saar. Although the French were not very magnanimous, they had contributed a useful sum towards the costs of espionage in the Saar— against themselves and the Saar Government.

Narcissus Quindt had proved a genius in collecting monies for our purposes. The bigger our apparatus in the Saar became, the more expensive its organization—and yet the less it cost Germany. Quindt filled our coffers with contributions

G

from commercial and industrial firms ; both Buerckel and
Heydrich approved highly of this method. The nearer the day
of the plebiscite, the bigger the contributions turned out to be.
The merchants and industrialists wanted to ingratiate themselves with the masters of the Third Reich. These gentlemen
all trusted Quindt ; the monies went to a " special fund,"
and were acknowledged by receipts stating only the amount.
Whenever they asked Quindt what the money was for, he
made a most mysterious face and hushed the question. Our
patrons hoped to get later State orders ; the building firms
were the easiest to approach. Some of them really received
orders from the State later on—and went bankrupt in trying
to execute them on ruinous terms.

Heydrich was much interested in Quindt's method ; later,
when he transferred his seat to Berlin and became chief of the
Gestapo, he organized a system of " voluntary contributions "
which was on a gigantic scale. Often such sums were unofficial
" fines " for alleged political offences—but they all were
" voluntary." The great Siemens A.G., for instance, paid
several hundred thousand marks to Heydrich for the discovery
of industrial espionage in its plants. For " money talks," and
Heydrich likes its voice.

CHAPTER VIII

★

GOERING IN DANGER

WHILE I WAS IN Strasbourg someone called my attention to a former German officer, possessor of the highest war-decorations. He had fled from Germany and was now up to his neck in left-wing intrigues and plots. He conducted a small but efficiently functioning organization which mostly dealt with the smuggling of political pamphlets—violently anti-Nazi—into the Reich.

I became interested in the man and started special investigations. Soon I found out that there was something more dangerous in his activity than pamphlet-smuggling. This man—as he is still living abroad I prefer not to mention his name nor the names of his associates in Germany—tried to build up a daring group of fanatics modelled on the *Narodniki* in pre-war Russia. Their aim was to spread a mood of panic in the Third Reich by a series of terroristic actions.

It was just before the Reichstag Fire trial ; the would-be terrorists planned in the first place the assassination of Hermann Goering. The Prussian Prime Minister, as founder and organizer of the Gestapo, was especially hated in refugee circles.

All this may sound fantastic—but the leader of the terrorist group was such a matter-of-fact, clear-headed, and brilliant man that his plans constituted a real danger. At the end of 1933 the Nazi rulers did not feel themselves at all secure ; even the existence and possible activity of such a terrorist group meant a lot of worry for them. Especially as the real opponent, i.e. the chief of the group, was abroad and organized his underground units invisibly.

The members of this group, both leaders and " executives," were mostly middle-class people, intellectuals, and fanatical proletarians.   They were indignant about the passivity of the German Communist Party and the inefficiency of the Party leaders.   They could not imagine that any political unit could remain idle while the Nazis were ravaging Germany. Therefore they had formed a sort of Bolshevist unit, independent of the Communist Party, and decided to start on their own.   They had certain sympathies with the Trotzkiists.   As they felt their surplus energy wasting away in exile, they wanted to organize a series of assassinations, to make the German people restless and to intimidate the leaders of the Nazi Party.   As " revengers " they would prepare the way for a Proletarian Dictatorship in Germany.   There was a great deal of romantic nonsense in their ideology, but their organization was sound and might have proved highly dangerous.

I found it impossible to get acquainted with the chief of these terrorists.   He was much too wary and much too experienced.   But I pursued patiently my investigations and managed to find out the names of two of his fanatical followers living in Berlin.   I traced them through the pamphlets smuggled into the Reich.   At the same time I found out about the planned assassination of Hermann Goering.

When I reported to him, Buerckel did not demand that we should arrest the two men in Berlin.   He gave me full power to carry on, and told me to report the matter to Heydrich, which I would have done in any case.   He was " officially " concerned only with the smuggling of pamphlets into the Pfalz or the Saar.   But he remained interested in the whole matter and supported me in my attempts to discover the whole widespread plot.   This could be done only if the Berlin Gestapo refrained from taking precipitate steps.

In this respect Heydrick and Himmler supported me more than readily.   These two were still sitting in Munich while their beloved " Fuehrer " spent months in Berlin without seeing them.   They both had a devouring ambition and schemed incessantly to get their hands on the wheel of the Gestapo.   Himmler had become chief of all police forces outside Prussia—but Prussia, he felt, was more important

than the whole of the rest of Germany. Hermann Goering
sat enthroned in Berlin, apparently all-powerful and without
a vulnerable spot. Goering was clever enough to cling to his
self-appointed deputy, Dr. Diels. It was their joint success
that the Gestapo was well known in the Reich and abroad.
Neither Goering nor Diels cared a rap that the fame of their
secret police was a sad, often a tragic, one. Himmler and
Heydrich felt that they simply must get the control over this
powerful organization. But Goering would not budge—not
only because he was greedy for power and wanted to have as
much as possible ; he had more matter-of-fact considerations.
He knew Himmler as a weakling and sentimentalist ; but he
knew very little about Reinhard Heydrich, who was the
opposite of his direct chief. Therefore Goering would not
trust Himmler to direct the Gestapo ; if there was a job which
demanded a strong man, this was certainly one.

Heydrich received with enthusiasm my proposition that for
the time being we should keep all the plans of the terrorists a
strict secret, and that I should not use the Gestapo in my
further investigations in Berlin. He did not hide his main
reasons for his approval. If the Security Service of the S.S.
Reich Fuehrer succeeded in disclosing a widespread plot
against the person of Goering, while his own police organization had not the slightest idea about it, Dr. Diels would become
an impossible man ; he would probably lose his position at
once. After all, the Gestapo had such a huge organization of
spies and informers that it ought to know about an attempt to
assassinate its own overlord. If it did not—so much the worse
for the Gestapo and Dr. Diels. It was a very neat scheme
which Heydrich explained to me without the slightest shame
or shyness. And if Dr. Diels committed such a colossal
blunder, no one else could be his successor but the twin stars
Himmler-Heydrich.

There was another point. If the Special Service of the S.S.
saved Goering's life, Goering would certainly be grateful—or
at least acknowledge the use of the Special Service which, at
that time, had been the butt of many criticisms by prominent
leaders of the Nazi Party, government officials and eminent
business men. If Goering backed it, there could be no other

authority against it—no, not even the Fuehrer himself. And
Himmler, as head of the Special Service, would become chief
of the whole German police. Truly, I must have appeared
like a messenger of extremely good tidings to the ruthless
Heydrich.

The plan succeeded. The fact that Himmler and Heydrich
are to-day the chief police executives of the Third Reich proves
it to the fullest extent. They managed to break Dr. Diels and
get the control of the Gestapo. Their mainstay is not the
Gestapo—but the Special Service, which has a more elastic
organization, a more deadly power than the State Secret
Police. Perhaps I was a modest instrument of their success.
I cannot tell. I certainly had a considerable part in it, although
many events, currents, and influences co-operated here. Not
that Heydrich or Himmler acknowledged their debt. They
were not of that kind. They knew how to use people and how
to discard them if convenient.

Of course, it was a dangerous and devilish game which
Himmler and Heydrich intended to play. The stake was
Goering's life—but one life did not count much in their eyes
even if it was that of a Prussian Prime Minister and Hitler's
right hand. It could quite easily happen that while I was
following my investigations in Berlin, a bomb might explode
suddenly, killing Goering—or even Hitler. . . . At least I
could assure my chief that there was no acute danger, hardly a
possibility of an unexpected early action on the part of the
terrorists ; at least I would know about their plans in good
time. But, of course, I could not offer any absolute guarantee.
Those terrorists in Berlin might even act without waiting for
the command of their chief in Strasbourg. Heydrich accepted
all my propositions, but told me bluntly :

" You are responsible with your life that nothing untoward
happens to Goering through the terrorists."

But even if he got rid of the responsibility, the free hand
he gave me was a dangerous thing ; dangerous both for
Goering and Heydrich. I was, however, much too wise to
express my opinions in this matter.

Heydrich instructed Dr. Best, who at that time was chief
of the South-West Branch of the Special Service, to accompany

me to Berlin. There he introduced me to Dr. Behrends, who was chief of the Special Service in the East Branch. In Berlin we also met Kemmet, who took part in the first conferences as Buerckel's representative.

Dr. Behrends was responsible for Greater Berlin, the surrounding Mark Brandenburg, the German-Polish frontier, and the whole of East Prussia ; a highly interesting and important job. I was rather surprised to see that he was quite a young man, although he seemed to be efficient, even if not very intelligent. In 1934 he was about 27 or 28, and had not yet finished his law studies. But he had the highly important task of organizing and enlarging the essential information service within the frame of the East Branch of the Special Service.

Just like all Special Service branches—except the centre which at that period was in the Prinz Albrecht Palace, Wilhelmstrasse 112—Dr. Behrend's office was in a quiet, small sidestreet near the Reichskanzlerplatz. Later it was removed to Jagowstrasse 18, Berlin-Grunewald. Here, among well-built and unostentatious villas, stands the private house of Heinrich Himmler and the important training school of the Special Service which is more efficient and has a better teaching staff than any fancy espionage school in the world. These houses were all rented under the name of some innocent private person to whom all letters destined for the different offices were to be addressed ; all telephone numbers were strictly secret. Every main branch of the Special Service has its own short-wave transmitter and a direct telephone cable to the Gestapo and the Special Service Centre. These lines can only be used by the different branch leaders and their aides-de-camp.

Dr. Behrends was ill, and therefore we discussed the whole difficult problem at his bedside. He received me with extreme friendliness ; he felt that this was his big chance just like mine ; after all, it was his domain which was involved in the activity of the terrorists. Dr. Best was, on the other hand, rather shorttempered ; he did not relish the thought that Behrends would earn all the credit, apart from myself, if the plot were discovered. He sharply criticized the " primitive " housing of such an important branch of the Special Service.

"I couldn't work in such low rooms," he said importantly. "Even if they were large, they would depress me. For work like mine, I need huge rooms—almost halls. Otherwise I can't think . . . and you all know how important my thinking is."

Dr. Behrends murmured something; I suppressed a smile. Dr. Best was certainly a clever man, even if a very vain one. His office in the former Crown Prince Palace at Stuttgart was nothing if not luxurious. There he could "think." True, later, when he was transferred to Berlin with Heydrich, he had to be content with ordinary office rooms—and was happy to have them.

But for the time being we did not go into the question of the size of the rooms in which the Special Service could function well. I soon noticed that both Dr. Best and Dr. Behrends were anxious to take the whole investigation out of my hands as soon as I had made the necessary preliminary steps. Dr. Behrends, my new "comrade," hoped that he would gain all the kudos of the matter. He was visibly disappointed when I refused point-blank to conduct my operations from his headquarters. He was flabbergasted when I showed him my credentials and Heydrich's instructions. These instructions gave me a completely free hand to deal with the group of terrorists and also empowered me to use the services of any Special Service group leader in matters of espionage in whatever part of the Reich I was working. In fact, ambitious Dr. Behrends became, for the time being, my subordinate, and had to fulfil my orders.

Our relations—and those of Dr. Best to us—were rather characteristic of the spirit of the Gestapo and the Special Service. Dr. Best's words when he spoke to me privately about Dr. Behrends betrayed his hate and envy of the younger man. I had come to the Special Service with the honest conviction that I would find willing co-operation and a spirit of comradeship in the service of the common cause. I disliked Dr. Behrends from the beginning, but I trusted him; I believed his fine words and assurances of friendship. Weren't we working for the same great goal, for the final triumph of the National Socialist ideals? I was gullible and trusting enough to forget the principle which was, and is still, valid among the big and small potentates of the Third Reich—the principle of the " survival of the fittest," of the fang and claw in the jungle. Everybody was willing to sacrifice the little finger of his left hand when he could cut off the right hand of the other man, his alleged friend. Of course, all this was done in the glorious name of the Fuehrer, the demi-god.

Dr. Behrends was clever enough to treat me with flattering amiability ; he hastened to fulfil all my requests and apparently did not make any difficulties. I only found out much later how quickly he started his intrigues against me and how tenaciously he tried to oust me from Heydrich's doubtful favours.

Dr. Behrends was a typical example of the new Nazi leaders, and therefore it may be instructive to describe his career. He was a short, bow-legged North German, with sandy hair and a decorative scar on his cheek. He had watery blue eyes and had been born in Wilhelmshafen, the base of the German North Fleet. His parents kept a prosperous restaurant which had many naval officer guests ; one of them was the young naval ensign Reinhard Heydrich. Heydrich (whose father had been a prominent member of an old Prussian Free Mason Lodge) had given up his university career after the war and became a naval officer. He was already a Chief Lieutenant (corresponding to a Lieutenant-Commander in the British Navy) when he had to resign on account of a duel in which he became involved in connection with one of his lady loves. Just before he had to leave the Navy he was a frequent guest in Dr. Behrends' paternal establishment, where he ran up gambling debts. At last he was appointed a member of the S.S. Reich Command, after he had served it as an illegal informer and " general handyman " on the coast. Later he rose quickly to chief of the Security Service. In Dr. Behrends he found a pupil who was just as unscrupulous as blindly loyal. Dr. Behrends was his accomplice in his first daring escapades as S.S. Leader. No wonder that the son of the Wilhelmshafen restaurateur became a favourite of the later master of the German police and has kept his position till this very day.

Dr. Behrends had come to Berlin to get his doctor's degree ;

Heydrich appointed him at once to the important post of leader of the Special Service, Main Branch East. During this period when Goering and Diels ruled the Gestapo, and there were still some German Nationals in the new Nazi Cabinet, Heydrich needed a man in Berlin who was absolutely loyal to him; who organized a network of spies around the non-Nazi Ministers such as Hegenberg and Papen; and who could also supply his chief with full information about prominent Nazis like Goering and Goebbels. Dr. Behrends was probably also entrusted with the task of watching over my own humble person.

To-day, Dr. Behrends is one of the most influential men around Heydrich. He is the more dangerous because Heydrich kept him in the background though still in the Special Service, and did not give him an official post in the Ministry of Interior or the Gestapo. His only serious rival is still Dr. Best, who has climbed higher on the official ladder, but the latter is a great favourite of Heydrich.

Dr. Behrends does not like work, but knows well how to make others toil for him. He has a certain amount of primitive cunning, but, otherwise, his intellect is not especially brilliant. His speciality tends rather towards daring exploits; he dares everything, risks everything, takes the blame for any base act unhesitatingly. He is unscrupulous and ambitious and stops at nothing if he has hopes of personal gain. If things turn out well, it's his achievement; if they turn out badly, someone else is always the culprit and he knows nothing. Lack of responsibility is one of the main characteristics in the Third Reich.

Such is Dr. Behrends, one of Heydrich's chief assistants who decides the fate of thousands of people—according to his own interests.

I saw that my investigations would take several days, even several weeks. Therefore, I took rooms in the Hotel Steinplatz, near the Zoo Railway Station. I sent for Oskar Pfarr as I needed an assistant, and he arrived from Saarbruecken, highly excited at the prospect of "great doings." Dr. Behrends had given me one man whom he named as especially efficient and trustworthy, Josef Pospischil. Later he became my constant deputy; his "given name" was mostly Baron Wronski; this feudal title helped him considerably to gain access to different places.

About this time Heydrich had secured his first foothold in the Gestapo. An S.S. Special Command had been established which—without Goering's or Dr. Diel's knowledge—consisted wholly of members of the Special Service RFSS. They were all under Dr. Behrends' authority; their task was to undermine Dr. Diels' position from the inside. Officially, they were commanded by Obersturmfuehrer Sohst, who later became the head of Heydrich's private terrorist group. Pospischil was a sort of liaison officer between this Special Command and Dr. Behrends' Branch of the Special Service. He had an office in the Gestapo building and there he could use all the instruments of the Gestapo, among them the notorious files of political suspects.

At first I could do my work very well alone; I used Oskar Pfarr for local enquiries and confided in Pospischil only to the extent which explained why I needed his files. Our work was rather dull, but promised complete success; from the nucleus of the two names which I had found out, a list of forty people grew. They were not all terrorists, but a group of political fanatics who had no part in the plans of the former; they were, however, mixed up in the smuggling of Communist pamphlets.

Buerckel and his circle had grown so afraid of an unexpected coup by the terrorists and an attempt on Goering's life, that Captain Buchmann came to Berlin from Ludwigshafen and visited Dr. Diels. He told him all he knew. This, of course, was a bad setback for Heydrich's plans and my own. But Buerckel had nothing to do with this "double-crossing." I was still sending him a duplicate of my reports; yet Buchmann could have no idea of their contents; he simply made some vague allusions to a widespread plan, and Dr. Diels was unable to take up any action. This was rather lucky for us—both for Heydrich and myself.

Buchmann's vague information and Diels' inability to act had given Heydrich a great advantage; in the end this cost

Diels his position. Buchmann, however, lost Heydrich's sympathy and was dismissed some months later in spite of Buerckel's backing. I think he was even sent to a concentration camp for some time. He was accused of " freemasonry," whatever that meant, and vanished from the scene of the secret police.

The Special Service of the S.S. Reich Fuehrer had no executive troops in Berlin, and, therefore, we could not do anything against the terrorists without some outside help. If it had been five or six people, we could have put them into a private car and transported them to Munich where Heydrich held the post of Chief of the Bavarian Political Police. But as my suspects numbered over forty and were scattered all over Berlin, such an action would have at once directed the attention of the Gestapo to our beginning. The Gestapo was very jealous of the Special Service, and Goering was very quick to take revenge if anyone trespassed on the territory of his beloved political police.

Nor could Sohst and Pospischil make any arrests on their own authority without having the official permission of Dr. Diels. This meant a serious snag. None of us dreamt of giving up our precious secret to the Gestapo to let them earn all the credit. There was no time to lose—therefore, without consulting Heydrich at all, I turned to my old acquaintance and former superior Kurt Daluege, Chief of the Uniformed Police, who had just attained the rank of Police General.

The old rivalry between Daluege and Dr. Diels was still very bitter, therefore the Police General was only too glad to help Heydrich in discrediting Dr. Diels. I had a long discussion with him, and he promised me his help. We considered different possibilities ; in the end he advised me to call on the retired Admiral von Levetzow, President of the Berlin Police, who had good cause to hate the Gestapo, since it had become the " highest authority in Prussia." There was another, personal reason for his willing co-operation. About the end of 1933, Dr. Diels had a quarrel with Goering, whereupon he lost his job at the Gestapo for a short period. But he had sufficient influence to become the Vice-President of the Berlin police for a few weeks. During this short time he behaved outrageously towards Admiral von Levetzow, who was still thirsting for revenge. All this gave us the guarantee that von Levetzow would at least not betray our plans to Dr. Diels, and that we could be sure of his co-operation should a legal way be found.

I told Daluege that I had to keep my incognito in the whole matter and therefore could not see von Levetzow. I sent Dr. Behrends. Von Levetzow declared that he would be willing to lend us several detectives on the day for which we planned concerted action against the terrorists. He acceded to our request that these detectives of the political branch in the Berlin Police Headquarters had to keep strictly within the instructions given by the Special Service; they would only figure on the day of the arrest and everything else would be left to us. In the beginning, Heydrich objected to my pact with von Levetzow, but later agreed to all we had discussed.

During the last days, my rooms in the Hotel Steinplatz were like a beehive. Two other members of the Special Service had joined me, also from the Special Command in the Gestapo; they sat day and night in my hotel. Pospischil did not leave my side for a moment. We formed four groups to arrest the terrorists. Each group was headed by a Special Service man, supported by a Criminal Commissioner of von Levetzow's forces.

At my request, all Special Service men of the Greater Berlin branch had been mobilized and were constantly ready to support us. Two days before the arrests I inspected everything. Everybody was to wear civilian clothing; another step to prevent the Gestapo finding out about our plan too early. Daluege had put a company of uniformed police at my disposal, but I did not want to use them.

On the day of the arrests, I moved to Dr. Behrends' house where I could be in constant touch with Heydrich. We collected the necessary number of private cars. At the agreed hour, the Berlin Criminal Commissioners arrived first, then von Levetzow in person. He gave a few last-minute instructions to his own people and vanished. We had a little difficulty with the criminal officers who did not like to accept the authority of the young Special Service men, but, in the end, everything was settled.

During the night I was in constant touch with the different groups and was informed about the time and circumstances of every arrest. Throughout the night I was also reporting almost hourly to Heydrich, who kept impressing upon me the necessity for not letting a single terrorist escape. Just to be on the safe side, we collected not only those figuring on my list, but all the members of their families whom we found in their domicile. During the next eight days, plain-clothes policemen occupied the flats or rooms. The arrested persons were taken to the Berlin Police Headquarters; there were about eighty of them, and within the next eight days another twenty were added. One hundred and sixteen men and women were later sentenced by the court; about thirty were sent for a short term to a concentration camp and the rest released.

Our plan had succeeded fully. Dr. Diels' prestige received a mortal blow and the danger which threatened Goering was averted. In consequence I was transferred to Berlin, although I still directed the work in the Saar and visited the district from time to time. But the period of my espionage work had ended.

Before I return to the description of my work within the Gestapo, and my close association with Heydrich, I should like to add a few words about the methods of modern espionage.

My experiences have taught me that the best intelligence service of the world is that of the Third International, the so-called Party Communists. The G.P.U. has a sad notoriety, is hated and feared not only in Soviet Russia, but in all countries where there is an officially organized Communist Party, and, therefore, a legal Communist organization. It is not important what mask the G.P.U. wears in the individual countries or what it is called within the different sections of the Party. In Germany up to 1933 it was C.O. (Counter Organization) under the leadership of the Communist Reichstag Member Hans Kippenberger. Kippenberger was one of the cleverest and finest intellects among the German Communists—that is the reason perhaps why he has been imprisoned in Russia and by now probably shot. Willi Muenzenberg, the Red Press Chief and propagandist, has also been expelled from the Communist Party and lives in France. If the political leaders and party organization of the Communists had been working half as well in Germany as Hans Kippenberger's " Counter Organization," Hitler would have been fully justified in talking about the " Red danger," and the Reichstag Fire would not have been necessary at all.

I am convinced that the G.P.U., namely the Communist intelligence organization abroad, especially in all democratic countries, is fully equal to the famous " Intelligence Service " of Great Britain; in some respects, as for instance in industrial espionage, it is even superior.

The strength of the French is in the field of military espionage, but not in a large scale intelligence service covering all walks of civilian life. The French are sober, narrow-minded officials who never risk anything. Their intelligence service tries to economize where they ought to spend freely and pays huge sums to people who would be willing to work for less. The French prefer the " star-system " even in espionage. But the G.P.U. uses a mass of small fanatics who are severely disciplined and controlled by the party organiza-tions all over the world; as comrades of the Communist International often they supply precious material to their local centres without having an idea that they work for the G.P.U.) They are just as useful as they are cheap, mostly they are not paid at all for their services. But the G.P.U. commissars know very well how to spend large amounts if necessary.

As for Germany, German counter-espionage was never really bad and active espionage was never too good. A few occasional successes do not change these facts. To-day when their army is strengthened in all fields, active German espionage abroad is reorganized and enlarged.(Inside the totalitarian states like Germany and Italy a large-scale defensive organization against spies can be created much more easily than in a democratic country. On the other hand, there is the constant danger that often very influential persons suddenly become spies in their helpless rage against the dictator, while, under normal circumstances, they would never lower themselves to such a role. Of course, the foreign powers have to pay enormous sums to these people, as they are living in constant danger of the axe. They all try to earn as much as possible in a few months in the hope that they can start a new life somewhere abroad. This hope is usually vain ; but, even so, there are a great many such among the high officials and even the minor party leaders. . . .

Apart from plenty of money, great psychological talent and understanding is absolutely necessary for successful espionage. In the espionage against Germany, only the Russians possess these qualities. They are the most dangerous enemies in every field.

In Berlin a new life began for me ; a hectic and not always pleasant one. It was marked at the beginning by the terrible events of June 1934.

CHAPTER IX

★

ST. BARTHOLOMEW'S NIGHT—IN THE TWENTIETH CENTURY

I HAVE BEEN IN a great many scrapes and often found myself in a particularly tight spot. Excitement and adventure have entered my life without knocking—and even if they were unwelcome guests, I have tried to make the best of their visitations.

A great deal of optimism, a certain easy-going trust in the future, helped me through the most trying periods. I never made plans for more than a few weeks ; things and circumstances changed so quickly in my days, that it would have been silly to dream of a time when I would be able to smoke my pipe in peace in the front garden of a Thuringia cottage. To-day I seem to have lost even what little chance I had. Nothing haunts my dreams with such persistence as the memory of those days at the end of June 1934.

Immediately following the 25th June, I was in constant danger of a quick and painful death. I don't think that any of us felt safe or secure. At any moment men might enter my room and shoot me without bothering about preliminary small talk ; or they might take me to some barracks to face an execution squad.

And yet I was on the " right side." But in these days the biggest shots like Papen, Goering, Goebbels, Blomberg— even Hitler himself—were worried about their own safety.

Now, in the distance of the years, I clearly see how manifold were the dangers. The S.A. numbering three million men had to be decapitated at the request of the Reichswehr and heavy industry. But what if the S.A. should revolt ? Himmler

had three hundred thousand S.S. men who had been entrusted
with the grim " spring cleaning." But who could guarantee
that Himmler would stop at anything ? Perhaps when he had
settled the score of the Nazi left wing, the S.A., he would
also " eliminate " the right wing. The Reichswehr was
standing by in case the S.S. be " tempted." But would
Blomberg's army try to save Hitler, Goering, and Goebbels ?
Probably not. They would have waited calmly till everything
was " cleared off " and then swept away the S.S. to establish
a military dictatorship.

These were the dangers and it was only by a narrow margin
that they did not become realities. This time everything went
according to schedule. Roehm and his followers died, but
beyond that nobody dared to do anything. When everything
was finished, I began to breathe again ; and I think my
superiors felt exactly as I did.

This is no place to discuss the political background of the
bloody events ; I simply want to record the facts as I saw
them.

The Special Service of Himmler had its agents everywhere
—even in the S.A. In the spring of 1934 disquieting reports
began to reach us. The S.A. had become impatient and dissatisfied. Where were the promised jobs ? What had become
of all the rosy hopes held out by their leaders ? Hitler had
promised three days' free looting if he should come to
power—the Jews and the enemies of the Party would be
easy prey for the faithful S.A. Every group had already
chosen its victims—and yet it was all in vain. The beautiful
prospects faded, the great *Tag* did not arrive.

On the other hand Roehm had started a large-scale collection
for the benefit of the S.A. Hitler had approved it and it was
organized all over Germany. But strange rumours were
connected with this " collection." Not only the Jews, but
other wealthy men too were simply assessed for taxation at a
certain amount, and were forced to pay it. Our information
gave us immense figures, but Roehm and his staff only
accounted for a small part of it. Perhaps the collectors kept
most of the money, but Roehm became suspicious when
no action was taken against them. Had he been wiser in

this respect, he might have got away with a short term in a concentration camp. . . .

On the 24th June I was sent for in the early morning and detailed for permanent duty with several of my colleagues. There was high tension behind the scenes. Heydrich interviewed us singly. He seemed to be nervous and troubled. He looked at me with a searching glance, as if he were debating in his mind whether I was worthy of his trust. The result seemed to be satisfactory; he reached into a drawer of his desk and took out a file. There were several lists which he gave me to read. I noticed that they were all S.A. leaders with Roehm, Heines, and their friends at the head. Heydrich explained what he expected me to do. The names must be grouped according to cities and districts in which the people on the lists were to be found at the moment; any changes were to be marked when the III Department, which was watching them, turned in its reports. The lists could not be taken out of the building; so I started my work with two colleagues in the adjoining room. Through the open door we could see Heydrich at his desk, working, telephoning, seeing visitors. Sometimes when the phone rang, he motioned to me, whereupon we closed the door hurriedly; then, when he had finished, he opened it himself.

All the next day the conferences went on in Heydrich's room. Late in the evening he came into our room and brought new lists. When we glanced through them, he asked:

" Have you a friend or relation among them ? "

We all answered in the negative, although I saw several names whose bearers I knew well; among them the name of my friend, Heinz Guertler, with whom I have spent many a pleasant hour.

" These are all enemies of the Fuehrer," said Heydrich in a queer, strained voice. " File them like the others."

It was only now that we understood; something was being prepared against these men. But we had no idea what it was. Nor was it our business to worry about it. I was a little anxious about Heinz but it would have been more than risky to warn him. I hoped that he would somehow save his skin. Perhaps these people would only lose their jobs, or be taken to a concentration camp. . . .

It was late at night when we finished our lists. In the morning Heydrich gave me permission to go home for a few hours ; I felt that I wanted a bath badly. But I had hardly walked a few yards when I noticed that I was being followed. I hid a smile. Heydrich was much too cautious— he trusted me, but safety came first, and he would not let me walk about unattended in Berlin. I did not dare ring up anyone from home ; I knew that my wire was tapped. I had breakfast and changed, then I hurried back to the Prinz Albrechtstrasse.

During the forenoon I had plenty of opportunity to admire Heydrich's histrionic talent. Two men visited him. I knew well that their names were on our list. I watched them through the open door while they talked with Heydrich. He did not betray himself—with a single gesture or inflection. He discussed their errands amiably, and in the end even accompanied them to the door.

We knew now that this would be a large-scale " purge." In the background discussions went on as to the limits within which it should be organized. At the beginning it was only the S.A., but later the list was enlarged. A great many " old debts " were to be settled. Rudolf Hess, Hitler's deputy, arrived, and had a long talk with Heydrich behind closed doors. When he left, our young chief again brought some lists for us to work on. These had been prepared before the Nazis came to power. When they did, they had intended to " eliminate " these men, but the time did not seem to be suitable, so they postponed it. The people might have been resentful if Hitler's first action had been revenge. But now the time had come. We also realized that this would not be a bloodless purge, and this thought did not actually improve our mood. We worked silently and at great speed.

On the 28th June, Heydrich saw each of us alone and gave us detailed instructions. Fiedler and I were to go to Munich. We were to keep in constant touch with Berlin and to watch those S.S. leaders who were chosen for the " executive work." Fiedler would stay with Wagner, I with Major Buch ; officially we would be liaison officers. If the S.S. should for any reason fail or—although this seemed to be impossible—in the last moment join the side of the S.A., I was to deliver a sealed envelope to the local C.O. of the Reichswehr.

I knew that in such a case I would be the first victim of the S.S. and could never deliver my sealed orders ; but I hoped that everything would go smoothly. As far as it was possible to calculate anything, there was no reason for anxiety.

Fiedler and I took our leave without attracting any attention after we have fixed a rendezvous in Munich.

When I arrived in the Bavarian capital, I called on Major Buch whom I had never met before. After the first glance, I saw that he was the right man for the gruesome task. His thin lips showed energy and decision ; he certainly would not become " sentimental." Buch explained the situation, then the representative of Department III reported about the supervision of the suspects. Roehm's whole staff was watched day and night ; every movement was reported at once. We had to take care of about two hundred people in this way. I rang up Berlin asking for Dr. Best. According to my orders I only had to report if something was out of order, so I merely said :

" Marie is very well ; the doctor says that the confinement will take place without any complications and at the time expected."

" I hope they won't be twins," replied Dr. Best, but I did not see the point of the joke.

Our work started on the night of the 29th–30th June. The leaders of the whole S.S. main group gathered together and received their orders at two o'clock. Everybody had his strictly limited task. They left one by one ; first those whose troops were the farthest from Munich. At dawn the " operations " began.

The Reichswehr had been standing by in the barracks since the 24th June, all leave had to be cancelled, and the officers spent the nights with the men.

At dawn the S.S. groups started. First they placed the machine-guns according to the detailed plan at cross-roads, on rooftops, etc. In a few places they had to use the windows of private flats. The owners must have been rather unpleasantly surprised on being wakened in the middle of the night and having machine-guns installed among the aspidistras or the flower-pots.

At the same time the S.A. barracks were surrounded, and the men lined up. They asked the officers to accompany them for an urgent discussion; then, in the privacy of a room, they arrested them. The men were disarmed and their weapons taken to lorries and carted away. In the end they called up the forty-three men who were especially loyal followers of Roehm—or the loudest in their dissatisfaction—and led them away.

Everything went smoothly. I was rather surprised how meekly the S.A. submitted. Of course they had their own intelligence service—but in this case it had failed dismally.

The S.A. officers and men were taken to the Stadelheim prison. At eight o'clock everything was finished.

In the Bavarian Ministry of the Interior, where Wagner directed operations, there was a great bustle. Every minute new reports arrived. It was rather difficult to keep track of everything, as it all happened simultaneously. But among the tense, dramatic incidents, I still remember vividly the scene when Schneidehuber, the C.O. of the Munich S.A., and his deputy, Schmidt—both of them close friends and important allies of Roehm—were brought in.

Schneidehuber had no idea what was awaiting him, and he was surprised to see all his aides under the guard of armed S.S. men. He turned to Wagner and sharply demanded an explanation.

"You know the reason well enough. You planned a Putsch against the Fuehrer."

Schneidehuber looked flabbergasted and rather silly. I smiled. He still did not grasp the situation and asked Wagner that he should be allowed to use the telephone on the desk and speak to Roehm.

Wagner refused.

"You are arrested," he said. Schneidehuber became very pale and almost collapsed. Schmidt behaved much more courageously. He protested and threatened—all in vain.

There were a few questions. Schneidehuber would not believe that the end had come for him. He even started to make jokes—but they were very bad ones. He said that he did not know about any Putsch.

" If something was being prepared, Roehm left me out of it because he knew that I would give my last drop of blood for my Fuehrer," he said.

" Perhaps you'll be able to do that soon enough," callously replied Wagner, and gave orders that the whole company should be taken to the Brown House.

Civilian prisoners were brought to the prison in the Ettstrasse. There were several hundreds of them there ; the most important persons were under lock and key before they realized what had happened. And now the questioning and execution of sentence could begin.

Of course, there could be no question of regular proceedings. Everything would be summary ; the arrested people were mostly well-known enemies of the Nazi regime.

And yet the first victims were of " our " side. Three S.S. men who had fallen under suspicion were shot in Stadelheim. Their group was put on a train at once and taken away.

The drama commenced in the courtyard of Stadelheim. I was standing in a doorway ; above my head a dirty bulb was shedding a scanty light. I watched the victims surrounded by S.S. men and prison guards. The commander checked their names once more, then they were led to the wall in the back of the courtyard where a few people were holding torches or sticking them into the loose, reddish soil.

The first group—four men, among them a priest, the Munich vicar Muehler—realized only here in the courtyard what was to be their fate. A nauseating, ugly scene followed.

" They told us we would only be taken for questioning," screamed one of them.

Another embraced the legs of the priest, imploring him to save his life.

The guards swiftly and brutally ended the scene, dragging them to the wall where the execution squad was waiting. Three sharp commands, a short volley. The four men collapsed, but the priest lifted his arm in a last gesture of benediction. An S.S. man walked up to him and shot him through the head.

The bodies were dragged aside and another group followed. . . .

There was absolute silence around the Sanatorium Hanselbauer, but I knew that the S.S. were invisibly watching. Buch and his men entered the building first; after about ten minutes they reappeared with Roehm's men who had to dress in a hurry. They seemed to be very much surprised and frightened. They were hustled into cars and started towards Munich. Now the Fuehrer and his escort entered the sanatorium. Armed sentries were placed in the corridors. Hitler himself knocked on Roehm's door.

" Who is it ? " asked a sleepy voice.

" Adolf Hitler."

There was a shout of surprised joy and in the next moment Roehm's stocky figure appeared in the open door. He excused his pyjamas, but he had not known. . . . He glanced at us then, the Fuehrer and three of his entourage entered the room. The door closed behind them.

We waited about fifteen minutes, then the Fuehrer and his companions emerged with Roehm from the room. He seemed to be gay. At the stairs Heines joined us; he saluted Hitler, who nodded and lifted his hand. Then we all went down the stairs.

The drama began when we reached the cars. I was at some distance and could not hear the words spoken by the Fuehrer. Roehm seemed to be terribly staggered, but both he and Heines were surrounded by armed men, keeping their revolvers ready. Hitler entered his own car, which started at once. Roehm stared after him.

But Heines proved difficult. When Major Buch told him to get into the car, Heines rushed at the armed guards, although he must have known how futile it was.

" Dirty dogs . . . " he shouted furiously.

In two minutes he was securely tied. But he still shouted abuse at Buch and called out to Roehm :

" I told you not to trust this scum. . . ."

A few minutes later the column started back to Munich.

On our way we met the S.A. leaders who were innocently making their way to the supposed " conference " at Wiessee. They were halted ; the suspects separated from the " good little boys." And Hitler silently dragged his prisoners to the place of execution.

Roehm and Heines were taken to the Brown House. All Roehm's officers were collected here. It was a sad meeting for them.

Roehm was guarded alone in a room : Adolf Wagner tried to get him to make a confession.

" If I have anything to confess it will be only to the Fuehrer. I prepared no Putsch. I want to speak to Adolf. He has been misled by my enemies. I demand to be heard by him."

But Hitler would not face his trusted lieutenant.

" I want to see Goebbels," shouted Roehm. " Let me spit in his face . . . the dirty traitor ! "

In the other room where Heines—still handcuffed—Schneidehuber and Roehm's whole staff waited, there was utter dejection. Most of them knew that the end was near. Heines and a few others still protested hotly, but in vain. In vain they declared their loyalty to the Fuehrer and the Party, but their fate had been sealed.

During the forenoon a strong S.S. guard took them downstairs. Roehm, Heines, and four others were put into an armoured car and taken under the guard of two S.S. companies to Stadelheim.

Here, in the grim prison, I saw the last act of the drama. Roehm was alone in his cell, the others together in a larger room.

A young S.S. man approached the latter. The prisoners received him with loud shouts.

" We want to see Hitler. We want to be questioned." The officer demanded silence.

" In view of your past services," he said, " the Fuehrer gives you permission to choose a solitary cell and a loaded revolver."

After a moment of staggered silence shouts came again :

" No, no . . . let them shoot us. We prefer that. We're innocent. . . ."

Only a young man came forward.

"Don't do it, Willi," the others tried to restrain him. "Let us die together. . . ."

"It doesn't matter," he replied. "Everything's finished, anyhow. Why should these dirty swine enjoy themselves?"

The officer gave a signal, and Willi was led away. Then he told the rest of the prisoners that they had one hour to think it over, and left.

He went straight to Roehm's cell and offered him the same choice.

"I won't do it!" Roehm roared. "You dogs . . . kill me. . . ."

The officer put a loaded revolver on the small table in the cell and left, keeping his gun ready.

Minutes passed with excruciating slowness. After some time the officer returned and called through the grille of Roehm's cell.

"Wollen Sie nicht?" ("Don't you want to do it?")

"Send Adolf," shouted Roehm. "He shall shoot me with his own hands if he doesn't want to listen to me."

An hour later the guard appeared in the corridor, and the door of the large cell was opened. The prisoners were led out. Schneidehuber and another young prisoner cried like children. Weeping, they repeated their assurances of innocence and begged to be given a chance of clearing themselves.

A few minutes later a volley rang out from the courtyard . . . another . . . a third. Roehm must have suspected what was happening because he started to rave in his cell.

All the afternoon the volleys crashed outside. I saw the S.A. officers being led downstairs; most of them still did not understand what was happening. I saw hopeful and anxious faces, dejected and gloomy ones. A tall, fair young man asked of the S.S. men:

"Comrades, are they taking us to a concentration camp? We haven't done anything. . . ."

One of the S.S. men looked at his companions and replied:

"Don't worry, such men as you never get to concentration camps."

The tall, fair young man seemed to be reassured. A few minutes later there was a new volley. No . . . he didn't go to a concentration camp. . . .

Three of the Gestapo's agents became the victims of duty— or rather, they died because they were ill-informed.

They were arrested with a group of S.A. men. They did not know what was to be their lot, and so did not say anything. They thought they would have plenty of time to reveal their identity during the questioning ; at least, they could carry on their work of observation as long as possible.

But there was no questioning. Hubert, Krause, and Mueller only realized this when it was too late and no escape was possible. At the last moment Krause was able to tell the commanding officer who he was and the appointment he held.

" Get back to your place," the officer replied, " we haven't time to bother about things like that."

The stupid Krause returned to the line, rather dazed. He was still surprised when the bullets struck his body. He died— flabbergasted.

In the evening Major Buch appeared in the corridor. Up to that time an S.S. officer asked Roehm every hour whether he would execute the sentence of death on himself. But Roehm did not reply. He walked up and down in his narrow cell ; rage and despair alternated in his mood, sometimes he sobbed, at other times he shouted abuse. He knew that everything was futile, that his companions had died. A guard asked him whether he wanted anything.

" Bring some coffee," he said.

They brought him coffee in a tin cup. He tasted it and threw it to the floor.

" This is dishwater, you dogs ! " he roared.

" We can bring you another cup, but the coffee is just the same," the guard said.

" Drink it yourself ! " he shouted and continued to walk up and down.

Major Buch nodded ; four men led Roehm from his cell. When he passed me, I saw his fat chest heaving, his eyes were full of tears and perspiration ran down his face.

In the courtyard he saw the firing-squad. He called out and threw himself at Major Buch, roaring like a wounded animal. The guards took hold of him and fastened his hands behind his back. He kicked out and they tied his feet together, then dragged him to the wall.

" Dogs, swine, dirty swine . . ." he shouted, till the very last moment when the volley crashed out. . . .

The climax of the drama had passed, but the epilogue was still to be played. The S.S. men worked all night ; about one hundred and forty to one hundred and fifty people were executed in Stadelheim alone. The next two days, Sunday and Monday, a great many others were brought in who had escaped their fate in the first rush.

Stadelheim was not the only execution place. People were shot in the Munich police prison. The hearses were rolling all night, taking the bodies from private flats and offices. The S.S. men had strict orders to shoot at the slightest sign of resistance or attempt to escape. Sometimes a surprised gesture was misconstrued and the revolvers barked.

Near the railway station, those S.A. men who had been taken from the trains were collected in a cellar. Those who could be suspected of trying to escape or who could not give a good reason for travelling, were executed. Some of them might have been Roehm's couriers, wanting to take the news all over Germany.

The big " spring cleaning " went on in the whole country, and how big it was we found out only much later—and even then we only guessed. Victims included not only those who figured on Heydrich's lists. Some of the S.S. leaders and Party chiefs were empowered to order the execution of those whom they knew as the enemies of Nazis at their own discretion. A great many used this heaven—or rather, Hitler-sent opportunity—to rid themselves of their rivals or personal enemies.

I never tried to find out further details and I think I was wise. In those confused, grim days it was better not to attract attention.   When it was all over, I missed a great many people from Berlin and guessed what their fate had been.

This was the Nazi " Night of Long Knives," a St. Bartholomew's night of the twentieth century—and, incidentally, the final consolidation of Adolf Hitler's supreme power.

★

CHAPTER X

A HANDSOME POLE

I<small>T ALL BEGAN WITH</small> a small slip of paper on my desk. The Reichswehr had sent it, asking for information which seemed to be utterly unimportant and hardly interesting. And yet it started one of the largest and most important espionage affairs of the last ten years.

About this time hundreds of such requests reached the Gestapo. We were asking how a small clerk or typist, working in some State office, was spending his or her free time. If he or she appeared in a new suit or with a new piece of jewellery, the " Supervisor " working in his or her branch (who was also a delegate of the Gestapo) reported it to us. In ninety-nine per cent of the cases suspicion was unfounded ; we spent weeks in investigation only to find out that the man or woman suspected was honest and hard-working ; a girl had saved and scraped till she could buy the new bracelet ; a boy walked to the office for months to get a new suit. But the hundredth case brought consequences which reverberated across the whole of Europe.

This was the case when we had to find out how Miss Natzner spent her time after she put the cover on her typewriter. The strange thing was that her own mother had called our attention to her. The reports gave the story briefly. Mrs. Natzner, whose daughter was working as a typist in the Air Ministry, accidentally met her daughter's chief and reproached him mildly for keeping her little girl so late at the office ; hardly any day in the week but she stayed there until the small hours.

And the naïve mother added :

" Of course, you pay well for her overtime—but still I don't want the poor child to work herself to death. . . ."

Miss Natzner's boss did not bat an eyelid. He did not tell Mrs. Natzner that in his department there had been no late work done for several months. He kept this highly interesting information to himself; but when he returned to the office, he filled in a slip of paper which, in due course, found its way to my desk.

And so it began.

In forty-eight hours the result of our investigations had reached me. Not that there was anything you could call a " result." Miss Natzner—so it seemed—had lied to her mother, told her the fib about working overtime at the Air Ministry, because she had succeeded in getting into rather distinguished society. She did not want to introduce her mother into the same company; she was probably ashamed of her old-fashioned, middle-class parent who would have fitted ill into such a modern, very high-class and cultured circle.

Miss Natzner, as soon as the office hours were ended, hurried into the cloakroom reserved for female employees and changed into an evening gown. This was nothing out of the ordinary; most of the girls who lived in the suburbs, if they had tickets to a concert or play, changed at the office. Miss Natzner, however, did not go to the theatre or concert. She went to the villa of Baron von Berg.

Baron von Berg's spacious house was well known as the gathering place of Berlin's most distinguished society. The Baroness, a lovely woman, was a favourite of the highest circles. The former German Crown Prince, the members of the aristocracy and Nazi civil servants in high positions were frequent guests in the beautiful villa. The Baron himself was above all suspicion; he was one of the most talented German airplane designers, a director of the Siemens works. The Baroness had been born in the aristocratic family of Zollkofer-Altenklingen; her first husband was a Felkanhayn, a near relative of the famous general; after divorcing him she married Baron von Berg.

I made a marginal note in Miss Natzner's file :

" If little Miss Natzner had managed to get into such swell company, she ought to be forgiven for telling fibs to her Mamma."

And there the matter rested.

A week later Miss Natzner's name came to my attention again. We had introduced the system in the Air Ministry that every four weeks, after office hours, the Gestapo unexpectedly searched the desks, cloakrooms, and waste-paper baskets used by the employees. This system was later taken over in connection with all State offices. The clerk who pushed his things hurriedly into his drawers and was glad to get away after finishing his work, often left on, or in, his desk, or in the pocket of his working-coat, something which helped us to nip an espionage attempt in the bud.

I found Miss Natzner's name in the report about the search in the Air Ministry. It stated that they found three evening gowns in Miss Gerda Natzner's locker. According to the labels found in the dresses they were designed in the " Iris " dressmaking establishment of Fasanen Strasse.

" Strange," I told myself. " Why does the little Natzner girl need three evening gowns . . . and even more strange that she should have them made in the ' Iris ' . . . where she probably had to pay two or three hundred marks . . ."

I did not know this lucky little girl with her three evening dresses and her parties, I did not know what she looked like, but I tried to excuse her instinctively. Perhaps, I thought, she had found a rich protector and friend in that distinguished company who could well afford to pay several hundred marks for her dresses.

But there was something else in the report which caught my attention. During the search they found evening dresses in the lockers of two other girls—the Misses Engelhardt and Telge—and these, too, had been made by the distinguished dressmaker, " Iris."

An hour later, on my instruction, an income-tax inspector visited the " Iris " *salon*. The management of the dressmaking establishment found nothing strange in his call ; it was usual from time to time to go over the books. This he did now, going over the accounts, bills, correspondence : then he assured the managers that everything was in perfect order and left to prepare his report—which had nothing to do with income tax.

The cardinal fact of this report was that neither in the books nor among the bills did he find anything about the three evening gowns which " Iris " had supplied to Miss Gerda Natzner. Nor was there any mention of the two other gowns which the Gestapo had discovered during the search.

The last paragraph of the report was even more interesting.

According to the official incorporation of the firm, the " Iris " was owned by Princess Katia Berberian.

" Well, this begins to be interesting," I told myself. " This exotic princess, well known by the whole of Berlin from the time when she had been a dancer and called ' Black Angel ' by the habitués of night life . . . why is she giving away expensive frocks to young girls . . . working in the Air Ministry ? "

The last sentence of the confidential report said :

" We have also found out from the correspondence of the ' Iris ' that the firm has a ' sleeping partner,' a gentleman called Sosnovsky, who supplied capital to the extent of 25,000 marks."

Who was this Sosnovsky ? Did anyone know about him ? What was he doing in Berlin ?

Soon the reports gave ample information on these three points.

Sosnovsky was born in Galicia, on territory which now belongs to Poland, but which was once part of the Austro-Hungarian monarchy. He was the scion of an ancient Polish noble family. He received an excellent education and later became an officer in the Austro-Hungarian army. When modern Poland was born, he joined its forces, fought through the Russo-Polish war and gained great distinction. Polish newspapers called him the " Lion of Wilna."

Peace came for Poland ; but the young, adventurous, hot-blooded man was unable to find his place in everyday life.

I

He roamed over the world and one day appeared in Berlin. He was supplied with a stack of letters of introduction ; the most distinguished circles were opened to him ; he became a familiar figure of Berlin night life. He seemed to be rich and independent ; every night he was to be seen sitting in the night-club where the lovely exotic princess, Katia Berberian, presented her strange dances. A few days later everybody knew that a great, romantic love was blossoming into being between the rich Polish nobleman and the beautiful dancer. The princess was fully entitled to her rank ; she was a niece of the last king of the Caucasus.

A year ago, to the great regret of all her admirers, the exotic Katia retired from the night-clubs. She opened a dressmaking *salon* and now everybody knew that sooner or later Sosnovsky would marry her.

This was about all we could find out about Sosnovsky and the owner of the " Iris."

No need to say that from this moment both the princess and Sosnovsky were under constant observation. At the same time we controlled every step of the Misses Natzner, Engelhardt, and Telge, who still worked at the Air Ministry.

Twenty-four hours later I read the reports :

" Miss Natzner to-day visited Baron Berg's villa, where she spent half an hour. Then she left with Baroness Berg and drove to the flat of Princess Katia Berberian where she left only after midnight."

" Miss Engelhardt and Miss Telge left the Air Ministry together ; after having dinner at the Kurfuerstendamm "— here a well-known restaurant was named—" they walked to the Fasanen Strasse where Princess Berberian has her flat."

Now we felt that we had got hold of something really big. And now, instead of progressing slowly, patiently, piecing together the puzzle, we employed the typical Gestapo methods.

Which of the suspects seemed to be the weakest ? Which could be expected to make a confession after the first threat ? We selected Miss Telge. She was about twenty, slim and very pretty. Her parents lived in the provinces, she was alone in Berlin.

Next morning, Miss Theresa Telge was informed at the Air Ministry that she had been transferred temporarily to Kiel, where she would probably spend a week. Such transfers were fairly frequent; the fair young girl did not find anything surprising about it. She said good-bye to her friends, went back home to pack a suitcase, then hurried to the railway station to catch the Kiel express—and half an hour later she was in the Prinz Albrechtstrasse.

It was my official duty to be present at Miss Telge's questioning, but I managed to avoid it. It was always a deeply distressing sight to watch a young, terrified girl in the middle of a huge, glaringly lit room, facing five or six tough-looking men . . . with the dictaphone in the corner which recorded the smallest sigh. . . .

We had made an excellent choice from our point of view. After barely three hours (which was indeed very rare) she broke down and we had her whole appalling confession.

This was the gist of it:

When she was invited for the first time to the flat of the Oriental princess, she felt very flattered and happy, having no idea what serious consequences this invitation would have. There she found an exceedingly gay company; young men and pretty girls; they danced, drank champagne and enjoyed themselves. But about midnight, probably under the effect of all that champagne, morals began to become a little lax . . . and, as it sometimes happened in the most distinguished Berlin societies, the fine and enjoyable party degenerated into a nasty orgy. . . .

Next day Miss Telge reproached herself for taking part in such fantastic revels and decided never to go again. But she was greatly surprised when, after office hours, she met Baroness Berg who had also been at the party and who was apparently waiting for her. The Baroness said that she had something important to tell her and took little Miss Telge to her own house. And there the girl had to face a grave and unpleasant shock.

During last night's orgy—without the knowledge of the gay company—a skilful photographer had prepared a series of amazingly life-like and realistic photographs. And distressed

Miss Telge saw herself on these photographs in such a compromising situation, that she closed her eyes in shame.

At the same time the Baroness said softly :

" My dear child, if you want me to destroy these photographs, you have to obey me in the future. If you try to defy me in the slightest instance, I'll send some prints to your parents—and they'll be published in a magazine which enjoys having such material. . . ."

Now, the unfortunate girl was completely at Baroness Berg's mercy.

But what were the orders she had to fulfil ?

Miss Telge's reply was like a bombshell :

" Baroness Berg wanted me to prepare for her a copy of any document referring to the new aeroplanes driven by heavy oil. She knew that sometimes we had to copy such documents. . . ."

This confession deeply alarmed the whole Air Ministry.

Up to now they had thought that the new experiments had enjoyed full secrecy. Now they had to realize that this jealously guarded, highly important military secret had probably already been sold to a foreign power.

What was involved here ?

Henschel, proprietor of the Kassel Railway Engine Factory, had conceived the brilliant idea of trying to build steam-driven aeroplanes, the so-called " Dampfmotor Flugzeuge." If Germany succeeded in such an experiment, her air forces would be superior to that of every other power. It is well known that if the petrol tank of an aeroplane is hit in an aerial battle, an instant explosion follows, involving the loss of the machine and the probable death of the pilot. A steam-driven aeroplane would not be exposed to such a danger.

The first trials had taken place on the Johannestal air field. Every possible precaution was taken that no unauthorized person should be near the aerodrome during this time.

But the experiments did not bring the expected results, whereupon the Siemens factories took over the whole problem. It was Baron Berg, leader of the Aircraft Department of Siemens, who was in charge of the work. The original idea had been modified to some extent ; instead of steam-driven aeroplanes the object was to build crude-oil, i.e. Diesel, engines into the bombers, avoiding the use of easily inflammable, and therefore very dangerous and expensive, petrol.

Experiments were highly successful; it seemed as if the greatest problem of bombing planes had been solved. And now, like a bolt from the blue, came the news that foreign powers knew about the experiments and probably about the smallest details of the perfected planes.

And everybody was clear in his mind that a secretly prepared military weapon of which the enemy knew everything was just like scrap metal—worth almost nothing.

This was the situation when Heydrich felt that Adolf Hitler himself must be informed about our discoveries. We received a most satisfactory reply:

"Take the necessary steps . . . without considering anyone . . . if you suspect my own sister, you can arrest her."

The same night, about eleven o'clock when we knew that the last invited guest had arrived, the Gestapo surrounded the block of flats in the Fasanen Strasse and arrested everybody in Princess Berberian's flat.

Among those who were taken to the Gestapo was Baroness Kitty von Berg, who protested hysterically against her arrest. She maintained that as her husband was above all suspicion, we could not trifle with her personal liberty.

I reassured her myself.

"Baroness, your husband also has been arrested . . . in spite of being above all suspicion. . . ."

I told her the truth. On the Fuehrer's authority we thought that we had better arrest a thousand men than to let the real culprit slip through our fingers.

Arrests had taken place in the same night, not only in Berlin, but all over Germany. At least six hundred people were rounded up. We used the special powers vested in us by the Fuehrer in its widest sense; we arrested Mrs. Natzner, little Gerda's mother, although we were convinced of her innocence. But we wanted to see under lock and key all the characters in this mysterious drama.

Arrests were followed by a series of house searches. Next

morning we had all the data we needed; but it was an enormous task to sift it all and find the essentials.

Then the questioning began. I shall never forget the half an hour which I spent at Sosnovsky's examination.

He was suave and well-groomed, as always, although he had spent the day in prison. He was also rather superior and cynical. Before the Gestapo official conducting the questioning had said a single word, Sosnovsky drawled:

"Excuse me, gentlemen . . . may I tell you something? I hope you don't mind if it's rather personal. You see, during the Russo-Polish war I was captured by the Bolsheviks. They tortured me for two days and nights to make me betray a Polish military secret which I was not inclined to divulge. After two days they gave it up and sentenced me to death. . . ."

He glanced around with a supercilious smile and added with well-staged dramatic effect:

"But I managed to escape and this gave me the dubious honour of your company. . . ."

We all knew what this unusual introduction meant; he wanted to give us a hint that nothing could be forced out of him; he would accept no bluff, only absolute proof.

And we were right in our expectations. Sosnovsky evaded every question with a slight smile; he behaved like an innocent man who had happened to get in this curious place by pure accident. And then a whole, rapid machine-gun fire of questions was concentrated on him, he only said:

"But, gentlemen, have you any proof against me? Have you any support for your ridiculous accusations?"

The examination of the other suspects was wholly different. Unlucky Miss Natzner tried to deny everything at first, but soon she gave up her pitiful defiance and told us everything. She had been inveigled in the same way to the exotic *salon* of Princess Berberian and been caught in the same trap as her colleagues; but she was also able to tell us exactly which documents and files she had copied.

A strange, moving human document was Baroness Berg's confession. In the moment of her arrest she tried to jump out of the window. The Gestapo agents succeeded in saving her at the very last moment. She began her confession by saying that her husband was completely innocent and did not know anything about the things which were going on behind his back.

" When Sosnovsky made me the first offer to spy out my husband's work, I apparently agreed, but I decided at once to tell my husband and have Sosnovsky arrested. But then . . . some inexplicable curiosity took hold of me. . . . I had read so much about spies and their fantastic adventures. . . . Instead of betraying Sosnovsky . . . I fulfilled all his demands . . . I gave him all my husband's drawings and letters. . . . He visited me a great many times when my husband was away and spent hours in my husband's study. . . ."

And then she added :

" I never accepted a single *pfennig* from Sosnovsky, I didn't work for money. . . . I was only interested in the excitement, the adventure ! "

It took us two weeks to question and sift the evidence of all the arrested people. Sosnovsky was the last to be examined again. He did not change during his imprisonment. He was still superior and cynical.

When we read to him the strongly incriminating confessions, he replied with the same elegance and nonchalant manner :

" You are quite right, gentlemen, I approve of everything you say. . . ."

Thus it came to the trial. Baroness Berg and Miss Natzner, the unlucky girl who wanted to have three evening gowns, were sentenced to death.

Sosnovsky, being a foreign subject, got off with ten years' prison ; the others received various sentences.

Headed by the Crown Prince—who was a constant visitor to the Berg villa—the bearers of the greatest names of the German aristocracy tried to intervene with the Fuehrer to make him change the death sentences. But Hitler was adamant. Important interests of the Party demanded the execution of the two death warrants. About that time the monarchist movement was still strong in Germany ; the Nazis felt that by these two executions they would compromise this movement and German aristocracy for ever. . . .

I did not assist at the double execution, but a colleague of mine told me about it. And what he told me was terrible enough. Baroness Berg had behaved with remarkable fortitude, but when she faced Goelpl, the executioner of Magdeburg in the prison at Lake Poeltzl (Goelpl wore the usual prescribed tails and white gloves) she began to scream and had to be forced to put her head under the axe. Miss Natzner resembled a walking corpse by the time she walked to the block, and then her pretty head also fell in the sawdust. . . .

Of course, this affair had its painful reverberations. Germany had just made a pact of non-aggression with Poland ; the Foreign Office tried everything to prevent Poland's name being mentioned during the trial. They wanted to let Sosnovsky go ; nothing would be gained by keeping him a prisoner, as he had sent on the documents, plans, and reports he had procured almost immediately to his chiefs.

When the Polish ambassador in Berlin offered the exchange of a German spy arrested in Warsaw for Sosnovsky, there was no difficulty. After a few weeks in prison this strange adventurer returned unscathed to the Polish capital. . . .

We found out a little late that we had acted rather rashly when we released the greatest Polish spy. Sosnovsky had been in Poland for some time when we realized that the espionage organization we had managed to destroy in connection with the " Iris " dressmaking establishment was only one of his " sidelines."

Much later we discovered that he had organized four parallel groups in Germany. Three of them continued their work undisturbed during the whole investigation and subsequent trial . . . continued it for years.

We were rather naïve to think that Sosnovsky was only interested in the new aeroplanes. There was hardly any part of German defences which he had not succeeded in discovering and betraying to foreign powers.

After the Sosnovsky affair, the situation was almost catastrophic. All that had been invented or prepared in military matters had to be considered as well known to the master-spy. Everything had to be changed and re-built. A high officer of the Reichswehr told me that Sosnovsky had cost Germany several milliard marks.

. This strange man, with whom we had thought that we had finished, had a new victim, a new dupe and scapegoat, almost every month.

It was a world-wide sensation when—a year after Sosnovsky's trial—the Leipzig People's Court sentenced the Polish Countess Boregia Vielopolska to death *in camera*. When the sentence was made public very few people knew that this was only a new chapter in the tragic and adventurous story of Sosnovsky's life.

The Countess had been an important member of Warsaw society; she gave large parties and appeared at every social function although her husband, Count Vielopolsky, who was much older, had lost most of his fortune after the war. His estates were mostly situated on Russian soil and the Soviet Government had confiscated them without paying any compensation.

The beautiful young Countess was of middle-class origin; her mother lived in France. She often went to the French Riviera to visit her mother, Madame Kouzevemenska. In August, 1937, she wanted to go to Paris and see the exhibition, and intended to continue her trip to the Riviera, when the detectives of the Gestapo stopped her on German soil.

They forced her to leave the train where she shared a compartment with a Polish diplomat; they took her to the Moabit prison and told her that she was arrested on suspicion of espionage. She protested hotly against the accusation; she said that she had never stopped in Germany whenever she travelled to France; nor had she left Polish soil during the past two years.

But the German authorities declared that they had full proof and did not accept her defence. Count Vielopolsky did everything to free his wife. At his request, the Polish Legation in Berlin sent a diplomatic note, but its intervention failed. They were told that she had been watched for a long time and the preliminary investigation had produced highly incriminating material, they were forced to arrest her.

During the months of investigation nobody was allowed to

visit her, and she could not correspond with her family, not even with her husband.

And the new chapter of the horrible espionage story ended by the beautiful, twenty-nine-year-old woman being sentenced to death. She, too, was to face the executioner of Magdeburg in his tails and white gloves. . . .

But in the meantime, her husband, unhappy Count Vielopolsky, left no stone unturned to save his wife. He tried to get official support from Poland, he visited all the ambassadors accredited in Warsaw—but all his hope was lost when he was told that no intervention would help—his wife had been arrested and sentenced in connection with Sosnovsky. . . .

It is highly probable that the lovely Polish Countess did not even know for what purpose Sosnovsky was using her. Her task was only to travel through Germany and accept the letter offered her in Berlin by someone coming into her sleeping compartment. This letter—the contents of which she did not know at all—she was to take across the frontier.

This was all Sosnovsky asked of her—but it was enough to take her to the block.

Long months passed. The Count did everything to find some useful connection, to communicate with his wife—all in vain.

Months and months went by . . . at last the first news.

A Berlin diplomat managed to find out further details.

After the death sentence she waited for weeks for the execution. But a few days before her time was up the Fuehrer remitted the sentence . . . to life imprisonment.

It was said that in spite of the sentence the Germans would release Countess Vielopolska—just as they had let Sosnovsky go. The Poles were offering four German spies in exchange.

At home in Warsaw they were expecting her . . . but the whole matter was dropped . . . and the Countess was still left in the German prison.

Why ? What had happened ?

Sosnovsky again intervened. The Germans arrested a young man called Helmuth Kullmann—Sosnovsky's latest victim.

The unfortunate Kullmann became mixed up almost

innocently in the fatal affair. He spent his summer holidays in Warsaw and made the acquaintance of a very distinguished, very worldly Polish gentleman. He found out much later that this gentleman was—Sosnovsky.

It was easy for a man like the master-spy to convince the inexperienced young man that he could earn large sums by small, unimportant-looking services. A foreigner would be watched in Germany, but a Berlin youth could get about without attracting attention.

The young man fulfilled his duty loyally. He had to take the documents which Sosnovsky had put into a safe place before he was arrested, to a still safer place—abroad.

Young Kullmann worked without a hitch. He did not suspect that he was perhaps smuggling across the frontier those drawings which had cost two lovely heads. . . .

His next task was a little more difficult. In some way he had to get in touch with Countess Vielopolska, give her a little encouragement, and find out what had really happened to her. She had been in prison for over a year and Warsaw was still uninformed about her fate. Kullmann carried out the difficult task.

He succeeded in getting into Moabit prison. He even talked with the Countess—but he never left the prison . . . at least only when he was taken to the other building at Lake Ploetzen where the executioner of Magdeburg was waiting for him. Heydrich and his men had worked efficiently.

The official German News Service only reported :

" Helmuth Kullmann, who had been sentenced to death by the Reich Court of Justice, was executed to-day. Kullmann had made contact with the agent of an espionage organization when he visited his relatives in a neighbouring country. This agent enlisted him for his organization and employed him for over two years. . . ."

After the lovely Polish Countess, unfortunate Kullmann is the latest victim of cynical Sosnovsky.

Who will be the next ? Sosnovsky is not the man who can rest idly on his laurels. . . .

CHAPTER XI

★

THE FATAL FILE

WHEN I ENTERED HEYDRICH'S room, the chief of the Gestapo introduced me to the tall, fair gentleman sitting at his desk :

" This is the man whom you'll find very useful in Vienna, Herr von Papen. . . ."

It was the first time I had met Hitler's former Vice-Chancellor, although I had felt his influence (and his blunders) in my work in the Saar. I knew that the most contradictory rumours were connected with his person. Some said that he was one of the most bitter enemies of the present system and was doing his best to engineer Hitler's fall ; others maintained that he was in reality one of the mainstays of the Nazi regime, and attained his results because Hitler's enemies trusted him and thought that he belonged to them. We in the Gestapo were intrigued by him and felt a certain respect for his achievements. Everybody knew that it was he who, during the war, had organized the formidable German espionage system in the United States—and it was only a minor blemish on his efficiency that his brief-case had been stolen in the New York " L," and rather important documents discovered. The Americans called him Secret Agent No. 7000—and now when I was facing him I felt a pardonable curiosity what work I was expected to do under him.

At that time von Papen was Germany's ambassador in Austria.

Everybody thought that in such chaotic times Germany could not have chosen a better man for the position. They did not choose a diplomat of the old school ; for von Papen, even if he had been an attaché in Washington before and during the war, was nothing if not up-to-date. He had to be—the new Germany expected everyone to turn over a new leaf and begin on a virgin page.

His task was much more than a simple diplomatic representation of his country. The new ambassador to Vienna had to keep up good and amiable relations with the Chancellor of Austria, and at the same time conduct the underground movement which had almost died in consequence of Schuschnigg's energetic measures. He had to know what was going on in Schuschnigg's closest retinue and to follow all the plans of the Austrian Government.

No, an old-fashioned diplomat certainly wouldn't do in Vienna. This was no ordinary embassy. Only a man who knew what a secret agent had to do could cope with the situation ; a man who had done such work in the past. When Hitler appointed von Papen ambassador to Austria in 1934 he could not have chosen a better man.

Three years passed and von Papen had done excellent work. The brilliant methods which he employed were such outstanding movements of underground diplomacy that they were destined to become shining examples of double-crossing and intrigue, to be taught in the future schools of Macchiavellism.

His first action was to create a pleasant and almost friendly relationship, a neighbourly contact, with Schuschnigg. This went smoothly ; von Papen succeeded in a very short time in working out the first agreement between Austria and Germany. Now he no longer was the spy of an enemy state, but the likeable representative of a friendly country.

The second task was to remove from Schuschnigg's closest circle all those who might prove obstacles to his later plans. One of the first was Prince Stahremberg, Germany's stubborn and dangerous enemy. In every speech he held, in every article he wrote, he repeated :

" Austria will never become a German colony. . . ."

But Stahremberg failed just at the moment and had to be satisfied with a minor part in the future, when everybody had thought that he would succeed in ousting Schuschnigg and take the helm of Austria. Von Papen did brilliant work when he engineered Stahremberg's fall and reduced him to the status of a private individual.

Nor did he fail in his third task. By stubborn and tenacious work he slowly organized his agents at the police, the law courts, the different state institutions, and even in the Chancellery. He had someone everywhere on whom he could count, " just in case. . . ."

This was the moment when Germany changed her policy towards Austria. The ground was well enough prepared to start a decisive action on a large scale. And then—suddenly it seemed as if everything was lost. . . .

That was the reason why von Papen returned to Germany and had a long conference with Himmler and Heydrich.

It was almost a catastrophe.

What had happened ?

Heydrich only gave the answer to this question when I was left alone with him in the privacy of his office.

" This Jesuit Schuschnigg," he said, " wants to—blackmail the Fuehrer. I really wouldn't have thought that he had it in him. . . . He has a file containing data against Adolf Hitler and now he threatens to publish it in a ' White Book.' "

" Well, what are the contents of this file ? "

Heydrich shrugged.

" This impudent Schuschnigg is so sure of his position, so sure of the data contained in the file that he sent a copy through Mussolini to Hitler himself. Your task will be—and that's why I sent for you—to get the original documents of the file . . . at any cost."

" But . . ."

" There is no but. This file has cost three lives up to now. It doesn't matter if it costs a dozen more . . . we have to get it."

He took a blue file from his desk and gave me the copy of the tragic Schuschnigg documents.

" Sit down here in my room and go through it," he told me. " These copies are all typewritten, which seems to prove that they have not been photographed. This is our only hope, because otherwise not only the originals but the negatives would have to be destroyed."

I sat down and began to read. I want to emphasize here and now that I have never seen the originals of these documents. They may have been forgeries. I have no proof that they were genuine. But they certainly caused such a havoc as no file in the world has ever caused before.

Heydrich had prepared three groups. The first was headed:

Documents collected by General Schleicher

General Schleicher, who was the last Chancellor of pre-Nazi Germany, and who had so tenaciously withstood Hitler's demands, wanted to prevent the Fuehrer's coming to power. At the last moment when the Nazis had become the strongest political party in Germany, he tried to make Gregor Strasser Chancellor in Hitler's place. During his own chancellorship he began to collect the documents against Hitler.

His file dealt mostly with Hitler's war service.

Adolf Hitler was an Austrian subject. On the 3rd August, 1914, he sent a petition to Louis III, King of Bavaria, asking permission to serve in the Munich 16th Regiment, as he was living at Munich and did not want to go to Linz for mobilization.

The different propaganda books of Nazism have always maintained that Hitler had spent the four years of the war in the front-line trenches, and fought in such a heroic way that he had earned the First Class Iron Cross.

But the investigations conducted by Schleicher purported to have ascertained the following facts:

Hitler never served in a trench or in the front line.

After he had been attached to the 16th Munich Regiment (called the Lister Regiment after its commanding officer) he was trained and sent with his troop to the Western Front. There he was attached to the Regimental Staff, where he served as a runner.

Naturally the Regimental Staff was never in the front line; according to the lie of the land it took up a position at a distance of 4–5 or 10–15 kilometres from the trenches. Here they constantly needed a few efficient and trusted men. These runners had two kinds of service. First they had to care for the comfort of the officers and to do all the dull office work ; second—and this was the most dangerous, but also the most coveted work—they had to remit orders to the different company commanders. The runners liked this work best, because such errands sometimes took them to the *hinterland* or the neighbouring regiments. Of course, sometimes such work could become very dangerous if the runners had to pass through ground shelled by the enemy taking the orders to the front lines.

" There is no doubt," the report continued, " that such service can well be construed as front line service. But contrary to the romantic legends that Hitler had fought in the trenches, it has been ascertained that he never spent a day there."

The Schleicher documents also dealt with Hitler's rank of corporal. Whoever knew what a terrible scarcity of N.C. officers there was in the German Army about the end of the war, must find it highly mysterious that Hitler, being a good and efficient soldier, was still a corporal after four years.

There was only one answer. If he had been promoted to a sergeant he could not have remained a runner. The Regiment Staff had a strictly limited strength ; all supernumerary men, especially N.C.O.'s and officers, had to be sent at once to the front line.

Now either his superiors liked Hitler so much that they did not want to promote and thereby lose him ; or it was Hitler himself who avoided promotion to keep his comparatively safe berth.

The file included the results of the investigation which Schleicher had ordered to ascertain how Hitler received the Iron Cross, first class. About the end of the war it was comparatively easy to get the second class Iron Cross if a soldier served at the front and was honest. If Hitler had got that, nobody would have been surprised. But he owns the first class Iron Cross. . . .

This could be given only by the Kaiser, or the High Command of the Army, to whom the Kaiser relegated his prerogative during the war. Even officers received it only for outstanding achievements, great personal bravery, and if a corporal became the proud owner of it he must have done something quite extraordinary and be a hero of the first rank.

Immediately after the war the history of the Lister Regiment was published. It enumerated all the outstanding deeds of privates and non-commissioned officers and recounted the heroic deeds of all the officers. But there was no mention of Hitler's name in this imposing book.

Now all the Nazi propaganda pamphlets and books told the story in great detail of how Hitler was awarded the Iron Cross, first class, because single-handed, with only a revolver in his hand, he captured twelve French soldiers with their machine-gun. But why this reticence of the official history of the Lister Regiment about such a wonderful exploit when much less worthy deeds were described at considerable length ?

Careful investigation—during which all the comrades of Hitler were questioned—elucidated the fact that Hitler had received this high German decoration not during, but after the war. It was Field-Marshal Ludendorff, whose connections with the Fuehrer were well known, who awarded the Iron Cross, first class, to the Fuehrer, some time after the war.

These were the contents of the Schleicher file. Hitler and his staff knew very well that the General was collecting these documents against him. A great many attempts were made to rob Schleicher of them. When, a year after his coming to power, on the 30th June, 1934, the time came to " eliminate " the enemies of the Nazi regime, Schleicher and his wife were among the victims. This file was not the least reason for Schleicher's death—but afterwards when the Gestapo went carefully through his papers, they discovered to their dismay that the original documents were no longer in his possession. He had sent them to Dolfuss, Chancellor of Austria. . . .

Documents collected by Dolfuss

The second bundle in the blue file contained the documents collected by Dolfuss. The small-statured but big-hearted Austrian Chancellor must have known that by such a personal file he might be able to check Hitler. The great number of

K

the documents showed what care and energy he spent on gathering them together.

When Dolfuss became Chancellor of Austria, Hitler had been the cynosure of the world's interest for a considerable time, yet strangely enough little was known about him. Nobody could explain how he came to bear the name Hitler, as his father had been called Schueckelgruber. Nobody knew how many brothers or sisters he had . . . the greatest mystery enveloped the Fuehrer's private life, family relations, origin.

Chancellor Dolfuss, after receiving the documents collected by Schleicher, started to investigate Hitler's secret. His task was not very difficult; as ruler of Austria he could easily find out about the personal data and family of Adolf Hitler, who had been born on Austrian soil.

Through the original birth-certificates, police registration cards, protocols, etc., all contained in the original file, the Austrian Chancellor succeeded in piecing together the disjointed parts of the puzzle, creating a more or less logical entity.

And there was one thing—whether true or not—which might have been a dangerous weapon in Dolfuss' hands.

This was what he had ascertained :

A little servant maid from Upper Austria called Matild Schueckelgruber came to Vienna and became a domestic servant, mostly working for rather rich families. But she was unlucky ; having been seduced, she was about to bear a child. She went home to her village for her confinement. Her little son, being illegitimate, received his mother's name and was called Alois Schueckelgruber. (In some documents, Schickelgruber).

In spite of his origin he grew up to be an honest, kindly man entering the civil service and becoming a minor clerk in a tax office. He married very early ; his first wife was Anna Glaser-Hoyer. Their only child, Ida Schueckelgruber, died in infancy ; Alois Schueckelgruber buried her at the side of his first wife in the graveyard of Braunau.

His second wife was Franciska Malzsalberger. Their union was blessed with one son who bore his father's name. He became a waiter, emigrated to England and there married Brigid Dowling, daughter of an Irish cobbler. Later he divorced her and returned to Berlin, where he opened a restaurant. He also adopted the Hitler name when his father changed his own name. The second child, born of Alois Schueckelgruber senior's second marriage was called Angela ; she married a Viennese named Raupal.

Alois Schueckelgruber was rather unlucky with his wives. Franciska also died ; the honest clerk was not very young when he met his third wife, Clara Poltzl.

Clara's father was a well-to-do farmer. He did not want his only daughter who was quite a heiress to marry a middle-aged man, but Clara insisted stubbornly. Alois was still a handsome man, and he had such a nice uniform. At last rich Poltzl relented ; but when his future son-in-law showed him his birth certificate, he was rather horrified to see that Alois was illegitimate. The certificate said that the father's name was unknown, his mother was Matild Schueckelgruber. After that Poltzl demanded that Alois should give up his " shameful name " and take a new one.

And Alois Schueckelgruber wrote a petition himself (this was also contained in Dolfuss' file) asking the " hochwohl-georen " Ministry to permit him to change his name. Instead of " Schueckelgruber " he would like to become " Hitler."

But why Hitler ?

This was a totally unusual name among Upper Austrian peasants. It was no more familiar in Galicia where several Jewish families called Hitler were living. How did the honest Alois hit on this rather Jewish name ?

Schueckelgruber himself gave the answer in his petition when he mentioned that the maiden name of his mother-in-law was Johanna Hitler, and he chose it at the request of his father-in-law.

The Ministry granted the petition of the well-deserving minor clerk in the tax office. His original name was a rather funny one in Austria, hardly fitting a " civil servant."

After the legal formalities had been complied with, Alois Hitler married Clara Poltzl. She bore him three children : Gustav, Adolf, and Paula. All three of them bore the name Hitler.

Gustav died young and was buried in the Linz public

cemetery. The second boy became the " Fuehrer," while Paula had been living in Vienna for a long time before she joined her brother in Berchtesgaden.

Now followed the most important and perhaps most compromising piece of the Dolfuss " collection." I must repeat that I have no proof of its genuineness. It may have been manufactured as a fitting weapon against the Nazi chief, who was not squeamish about his own weapons. Certainly it was rather shattering in all its consequences.

This document aimed at clearing up the great life tragedy of a small Upper Austrian maid—after more than sixty years. Matild Schueckelgruber, grandmother of Adolf Hitler, had come to Vienna to get a job. And there something happened to her which was a common thing in the great capital, and yet a private catastrophe ; she was bearing a child under her heart ; she had to go home to her village and face the disgrace.

Where was the little maid serving in Vienna ? This was not a very difficult problem. Very early Vienna had instituted the system of compulsory police registration. Both the servants and the employers were exposed to heavy fines if they neglected this duty. Chancellor Dolfuss managed to discover the registration card. The little, innocent maid had been a servant at the . . . Rothschild Mansion . . . and Hitler's unknown grandfather must be probably looked for in this magnificent house.

The Dolfuss file stopped at this statement. But in the margin of the protocol there was a note in the Chancellor's characteristic handwriting :

" These data ought to cheer the writers of history who may want to publish some time in the future the true life story of Hitler. Here is the psychological explanation of Hitler's fanatical hate of the Jews. Hitler, born in peaceful Upper Austria where there was hardly any anti-semitism, was filled already in his childhood with a burning hatred of the Jews. Why ? This may be the answer. . . ."

And now I was reading the third bunch of documents in the file, the data collected by Schuschnigg.

He had continued the work started by Schleicher and Dolfuss. He knew very well that this file had an immense importance for Hitler. Hadn't it already cost the life of two eminent politicians ? And Schuschnigg wanted to continue his investigations in the most dangerous directions.

His collection was in two parts.

The first consisted of documents trying to elucidate the origin of Johanna Hitler, the Fuehrer's grandmother, and the facts of when and how the Hitlers came to Upper Austria.

The second part contained documents referring to the mysterious suicide of Hitler's niece, Greta Raupal. Schuschnigg had succeeded in finding out more about this tragic affair than anyone else, although even he could not discover all the motives and details.

These were the main contents of the blue file which I read in Heydrich's room. I must confess that I was rather shocked when I closed it. This file had killed men and now I had read it. What would be my fate—after being initiated into all these uncomfortable secrets ?

Only four living persons knew its contents—Schuschnigg, Mussolini, Heydrich, and myself.

Who would be the first to suffer for this dangerous knowledge ?

For the time being I " only " had the seemingly impossible task of robbing Schuschnigg of the original documents.

Twenty-four hours later a Berlin stamp merchant, Karl Krause, took a room in the Viennese Hotel Metropole. It was a very modest room. Karl Krause—your humble servant —had arrived with a regular passport in the Austrian capital ; he had a bona fide Austrian visa ; he was an honest stamp merchant standing above all suspicion. Should they search his hotel room during his absence they would find nothing incriminating ; just a man interested in stamps who intended to spend a few weeks on business in Vienna.

I met von Papen at the German embassy. He explained the situation frankly.

Up to the time he had succeeded in getting two members of Schuschnigg's closest entourage into his services. One of them was the Baron Froehlichstal of whom it was common knowledge that he was not only Schuschnigg's friend, but his intimate, personal secretary and *alter ego*.

The Chancellor did not make a single step without him; he could not bear the absence of the well-dressed, suave, gay young man for a single day. They had become friends during their student days. Schuschnigg had been educated at the famous Stella Matutina College of Feldkirch; when he became Chancellor he recruited his closest collaborators from the former pupils of this ancient institution. Baron Froehlichstal was known everywhere as the most devoted soldier of the Austrian ideology who proudly wore the red-white-red emblem of the Vaterlaendische Front; he was known as a man ready to die for the ideals of Dolfuss, the great thought of an independent Austria and who enjoyed the fullest confidence of the Chancellor. When von Papen told me that he had " won over " this man to our side, I could hardly restrain my admiration for his diplomatic talents.

The other man was none other than Guido Schmidt, the young diplomat, also a former pupil of the Stella Matutina. He was the son of a very rich family. While in the case of Baron Froehlichstal I could not imagine what had made him change his loyalty, I realized what good reasons Guido Schmidt had for such a step. The family estates and factories of the Schmidts were all situated in the Sudeten German territories of Czechoslovakia. Germany was already preparing her drive and Guido Schmidt wanted to be sure that his patrimony would be safe in case of a German annexation.

The situation was rather difficult at the moment. Both Guido Schmidt and Baron Froehlichstal informed von Papen that Schuschnigg kept the fatal file in his own flat. My task was to find out the best way to open the small safe in the Chancellor's study and to steal the famous documents. All this had to happen without attracting attention.

But for the time being our plans were foiled before we began. It was Mrs. Schuschnigg who proved the obstacle with an almost miraculous intuition. Once one of my men succeeded in getting into the Chancellor's study disguised as a telephone mechanic, but Mrs. Schuschnigg would not leave the room for a moment till he had finished his " work."

At the same time Froehlichstal and Schmidt brought disquieting news to von Papen.

" Something's wrong," both of them said. " Schuschnigg trusts us, but he's sensing some danger. Up to now he has written even his most confidential letters in the Chancellery and conducted his most secret discussions there ; but of late he has taken his important papers home and either he writes his letters himself or dictates them to his wife. His private conferences are at his flat, the only witness his wife. The same applies to the confidential telephone conversations he has with Paris, London, Rome . . ."

The counter-measures we took against Schuschnigg's new tactics proved only partially successful. I succeeded in organizing a " watcher's group " in the Viennese telephone exchange, but its efficiency was not continuous. Only when our people were on duty could we control the telephone talks ; the same applied in the General Post Office. Sometimes we managed to get one of Schuschnigg's personal letters for an hour, to copy it before sending it on—but this was not enough. Nor did we succeed in placing a microphone into Schuschnigg's study or in tapping his telephone line.

Our progress was extremely slow and I was afraid of losing Heydrich's confidence and favour. I returned to Berlin to report to him and he gave me advice—almost classic in its simplicity.

" If a man doesn't succeed, use a woman. Why didn't you try it ? You must find someone who can win Schuschnigg's confidence—or his wife's."

The idea was brilliant. It conformed to the best standard of spy stories. The beautiful blonde spy who spins her silken net around her victim, ferreting out all his secrets. . . . Yes, the idea was brilliant, but there was no way to realize it. We could have easily found a lady—but Schuschnigg was the type of man who was completely unassailable even by the charms of the loveliest woman on earth. A strong believer, a deeply religious Catholic, an intimate friend of Prelate Seipel, he lived almost a monkish life ; he was a recluse who seldom went to parties, did not drink . . . he was almost a priest himself.

And greatest of all our trouble ; he was in love with his wife . . . deeply in love. She was the only being with whom he discussed everything, to whom he dictated his confidential letters. Sometimes when he talked to Rome or Paris, his wife went along to the telephone exchange and watched the operator to ensure absolute secrecy.

As for Mrs. Schuschnigg—she lived almost exactly like her husband. She was suspicious, reserved; it would be very difficult for the most cunning woman to gain her confidence.

And yet I had already found the woman who was destined to seal Schuschnigg's fate.

She was the ideal choice for the difficult part.

Countess Vera von Fugger. . . .

This lovely woman in the early thirties had almost been born into high politics. Her uncle was the famous Count Czernin, the last Foreign Secretary of the Emperor Francis Joseph. Before the war he was considered as one of the chief actors in European politics. Countess Vera was educated in the atmosphere of high diplomacy—but after the war the famous family became very poor indeed. Only the illustrious name and the high rank were left. The Czernins had trusted the Monarchy too much—they forgot to send their money to neutral states. Czechoslovakia confiscated all their estates. It was the duty of the lovely Vera to re-gild the somewhat faded glory of the Czernins. And so she married Count Leopold Fugger von Babenhausen.

The Count was also the scion of an ancient family. His people were very rich, but Vera's husband would only become so after his mother's death, and the old lady kept a tight hold on the purse-strings. Nora von Fugger, the mother, gave him an allowance on which he could barely subsist—if he wanted to live according to his rank. His mother did not like Vera very much; she would have preferred a better match and rather despised the poverty-stricken Czernins.

So after all this marriage was not a success. Vera did not attain the goal she had set herself. She was thirty-two . . . and old Countess Nora clung so tenaciously to life that she seemed likely to hold on for another thirty years. Would she have to live in poverty for all that time? Countess Vera had other plans—one day she simply left Countess Fugger. When a woman is thirty-two she cannot afford to wait if she wants to realize her dreams. . . .

But what could a divorced lady do if she had no money? The war had ended; standards had changed and work was no disgrace for ladies of the aristocracy. The name of Czernin sounded well enough to get a job for Countess Vera with the Phœnix Insurance Company where she became a department leader. No work was expected of her; she simply " loaned out " the Czernin name so that the salesmen could do better business in the circles of landowners and monarchists.

I could pride myself on my choice.

Vera Fugger-Czernin was ideal from every point of view. Excellent family, wonderful manners, great beauty, widespread connections. She had a cunning, refined brain—and, as for the most important part, the whole family was very poor and so she would be willing to play the part which we set her.

Still Schuschnigg was unapproachable. Von Papen gave a big party at the embassy and presented the two to each other. But they exchanged only a few, commonplace words. Nothing more. . . .

" A very difficult task . . ." said Vera. " This man's defences are too strong."

" Yes, even she may fail," said von Papen.

But fate came to our aid.

Next day startled Vera read the tragic news of Schuschnigg's motor accident. Mrs. Schuschnigg, his devoted wife and faithful helpmate, was killed. . . .

I know perfectly well that to this very day many people attribute this stupid and inexplicable accident to the Gestapo. But although I know that apart from Himmler and Heydrich nobody could tell what the Gestapo had done, I must maintain that in this case it was pure accident which cost Mrs. Schuschnigg's life. The Gestapo had nothing to do with it.

On July 13th Schuschnigg lost his wife. While the whole of Austria sympathized with him in his bereavement; while von Papen visited him officially to offer the condolences of the Third Reich—we knew that we had made a great step forward. . . .

That hidden safe and the fatal file would be ours as soon as the Chancellor, suffering from a heavy spiritual depression, left his flat for the first time. His study would remain unguarded—and we could get the documents at last.

For long days Schuschnigg did not leave his rooms. When, at last, he returned to the Chancellery, we were startled to find out that he had cautiously removed the file himself and taken it along—not to the Chancellery, but to the Vienna branch of an important American bank.

Short of burgling the vaults of the bank and killing a great many people we could not get hold of the coveted documents.

Twenty-four hours later I left Vienna, disappointed in my hopes. There was nothing I could do and Heydrich had new work awaiting me.

It looked as if all our work had failed.

But three months later I was again in Vienna. And now I could see with satisfaction that we were again making progress.

Von Papen had again worked brilliantly.

After Mrs. Schuschnigg's death the road was more or less open for Countess Vera; now she had been able to get into Schuschnigg's confidence.

During my second visit I met von Papen only for a short time. I gave him Heydrich's message; Countess Vera was not to forget for a moment the fatal file; she had to find some pretext and persuade Schuschnigg to remove it from the safe of the American bank.

Her relation to the Chancellor was close enough by this time to make such a request possible . . . she could even find some plausible reason for it.

Her task had been not so difficult after all. Even a woman of less brains and beauty could have tackled it.

The Chancellor was a lonely man, almost broken by the blows of fate; he was living helplessly, unhappily in a large town; he still guarded the memory of his wife and took care of his ailing little son. . . .

It was child's play for a skilful woman to spin a net for him. And Vera solved her problem in less than four weeks.

She visited the Chancellor ostensibly on behalf of the

League of Austrian Catholic Women and expressed the deep sympathy of her whole sex. Next day she had a discussion with Schuschnigg representing a committee of distinguished ladies who wanted to take care of the orphaned little boy. . . . A new orphanage had been built by the League of Austrian Catholic Women—they wanted to call it after Mrs. Schuschnigg who had died so tragically and, of course, needed the consent of the Chancellor. . . . The home for crippled children wanted to invite the little Schuschnigg boy to a party. The Chancellor was very busy—and Countess Vera, who had brought the invitation, took the small boy in her own car. . .

She was inexhaustible in producing new and new ideas. Old General Schuschnigg felt very flattered when the beautiful Countess Vera Czernin visited him in his villa at the shores of Lake Garda and asked him to accept the presidency of a new patriotic association. The retired father of the Chancellor was happy that he had not been wholly forgotten ; a warm and pleasant friendship was born between him and the young Countess. After a few weeks she was a familiar guest at the villa . . . and when the Chancellor visited his father, he found Countess Vera there in the company of his brother, Walter Schuschnigg, manager of the Radio Ravag. The lovely young woman almost belonged to the family ; the old general addressed her as his daughter, little Kurt had come to love her dearly. . . .

It was fine and highly skilful work. . . . Countess Vera had reason to be proud. She had certainly earned her reward. Her " act " would become a classic example.

Vienna began to take notice. There was no doubt about it ; a fine and gentle romance was being born at the Belvedere. The jovial Viennese were not at all shocked by the behaviour of their popular Chancellor. They had shared his misery and now when he seemed to find new interest in life, they did not grudge him his happiness. They thought that with the lovely, gay Countess Vera at his side he would be better able to carry on the fight for an independent Austria.

And the later news coming from the Belvedere seemed to

confirm the idea . . . this lonely man, who had nobody to support and befriend him, had found the great romance of his life. He hardly made a secret of his feelings.

The Chancellor and Countess Vera spent three weeks together in St. Gilgen. . . . It was only for appearance' sake that she kept her flat on the Graben ; she spent most of her time in the Belvedere. Schuschnigg bought her a beautiful villa near Vienna where they stayed over the week-ends.

And Vienna slowly got used to the idea ; after the year of mourning Schuschnigg would marry the beautiful Countess. After all there could be no difficulty. Schuschnigg was a widower, the Countess legally divorced. Of course, the Church did not acknowledge such a divorce—but the Pope was free to give his consent in exceptional cases.

Would Schuschnigg, the Roman Catholic Chancellor, create such an example ? Yes, he would. He started the necessary proceedings. The Archbishop of Vienna was the first forum ; he sent it on to the Primate of Salzburg and then the petition went on to Rome. No doubt, the Holy See will understand. . . .

An idyllic time followed—the finest months in Schuschnigg's tragic life. There was no cloud on Austria's sky. Quiet and order within the frontiers. Since von Papen had become ambassador, Germany had behaved herself. He reassured Austria again and again that Germany did not want the *Anschluss ;* she only wanted to live in peace with her Austrian kinfolk.

Guido Schmidt, the Foreign Secretary, gave optimistic interviews to the Press. There was no danger ; Austria's independence had been guaranteed—not by the Western Powers, but by Mussolini. Mussolini had already shown Hitler that ten millions of Italian soldiers would occupy the Brenner if the German Fuehrer dared to attack Austria.

Schuschnigg seemed to have changed. Those who met him during these months noticed the change. His face became brighter, he could laugh again, he had new plans and ideas . . . the horizon seemed to have opened to him, showing far and fine vistas.

He was only in his late thirties and on the pinnacle of his career. Did the thin, bespectacled law-student who was taken a prisoner by the Italians during the War ever dream that twenty years later he would become the dictator of Austria ?

Austrian school-children were already learning his life-story. It was a brilliant career. When he returned from the Italian prison-camp, most of his fellow-students were idling helplessly, trying to find some place in the new life. He had already finished his studies in law ; a few years later he became an M.P.—and the favourite of Prelate Seipel. It was Seipel who raised him from the rank and file ; and when he lay dying he nominated Schuschnigg as his successor.

He was hardly thirty when he became Minister of Justice in the Buresch cabinet. When Dolfuss was killed, he was a member of the triumvirate guiding Austria's destiny. He seemed to be the weakest, the softest of the three—everybody thought so and the newspapers voiced the same opinion. But a short time afterwards this weak man was holding the helm of the ship of state alone. Who could doubt that Schuschnigg was Austria's real ruler ?

During these happy months he went about his work with an easy heart. Everything seemed to be quiet and settled.

A happy and contented man is always less suspicious—less cautious—than one oppressed by grief. That was the only explanation why the Chancellor did not notice the things going on around him.

Von Papen had continued his tremendous work. A few months passed and there was hardly a man in Schuschnigg's closest circle who was not in Papen's pay. There was no magic about it ; such things could be organized quite simply with some money and more tact. Schuschnigg had no conference, did not write a letter about which Germany would not have known. Appointments of civil servants were subject to von Papen's secret approval. If Schuschnigg chose someone, either his secretary, Baron Froehlichstal, or Countess Vera or Guido Schmidt notified von Papen ; and the German ambassador always found ways and means to win the candidate for his purposes. If he did not knuckle under, the Countess could easily prevent his appointment.

" This man visited von Papen yesterday," she would say.

" He is an agent of the Nazis . . . you cannot give him the position."

This was all. Schuschnigg smiled gratefully ; he thought he had found a wonderful collaborator in the lovely Countess.

Now the problem of the fatal file became important again.

" The documents have been taken back to Schuschnigg's flat . . . I hope your trip will have better results now," Heydrich told me when he again gave me the task of procuring the compromising documents.

The next day Karl Krause, a Berlin stamp merchant, arrived again at the Hotel Metropole and started to live the quiet, busy life of an honest business-man.

Twenty-four hours later the microphone was rigged up in Schuschnigg's study which we could never install in there during the life of his wife. We had tapped his telephone-wire ; it was only the question of days or even hours before the plot which we had prepared so carefully and systematically would finally succeed.

But even now something went wrong.

The first sign of trouble was when the microphone in Schuschnigg's room became suddenly silent. Someone had taken it away and we knew very well that it was not Schuschnigg himself.

This had happened at the moment when the Chancellor announced that he was going to marry the Countess Vera Fugger.

We knew perfectly well that this must not happen. If Countess Vera and the Chancellor became man and wife we would not only lose our best agent but no doubt she would unmask the whole plot. We had to prevent that—at all costs.

Von Papen had enough dummies in high positions to make the necessary moves. Schuschnigg suddenly noticed that everybody was against his marriage. Mayor Schmeitz—a loyal follower of the Chancellor—voiced it first.

" This marriage cannot take place. There are a million unhappy matches in Vienna and husbands and wives all bear their crosses. All these people will say ; if Schuschnigg can do it, why can't we do it, too ? Schuschnigg must not marry a divorced woman . . . at least not so long as he is Chancellor . . ."

The intelligent Vera soon discovered that this counter-campaign had been started at the German embassy.

I was in Papen's room when Countess Fugger was announced. So I became the witness of the most dramatic encounter I ever saw during my rather chequered career.

Vera Fugger had to experience the same thing as was experienced by a thousand different secret agents if they revolted against their employers.

I had to formulate her death warrant.

" Countess, I am deeply sorry, but if you refuse to co-operate, I shall be forced to present the Chancellor with the proof of your past activity. . . ."

It was a painful scene ; the most distressing I ever lived through.

But von Papen the diplomat spoke a different language. He offered a seat to the Countess and tried to reassure her.

" You must understand, Countess," he said. " Don't you love the Chancellor ? You do, don't you ? Well, then you must know that you can't become his wife as long as he holds this office. Our aims are identical. Go on helping us and you'll see ; in a few weeks Schuschnigg will become a private individual and there won't be any obstacle to your marrying him. . . . Or do you want him to share the fate of Dolfuss ? " he added significantly.

The unhappy woman raised her eyes, deeply startled. But the ambassador continued mercilessly :

" You're a clever woman and know as much about the situation as we do. Schuschnigg may still resist—signing his own death-warrant by his obstinacy. You love him—I understand your feelings, but you must make sacrifices for this love . . . all of us have the same goal. Schuschnigg must leave his place and in that moment both of us have attained our aims."

Three days later the famous meeting at Berchtesgaden took place.

Historians and publicists describing the tragedy of Austria mostly maintained that the catastrophe was caused by

Schuschnigg's acceptance of Hitler's invitation. The Fuehrer received him, their version ran, as a real dictator, he showed him brutally the mobilization plan of the German troops and then presented him with his ultimatum.

The truth—at least according to my knowledge—was quite different.

The fate of ancient Austria was in a woman's hand.

After many delays Schuschnigg decided to go to the fatal meeting, accompanied by Guido Schmidt and von Papen.

He went calmly and composedly because he knew that he could balance Hitler's exaggerated demands.

Schuschnigg knew that Hitler had realized what a fatal weapon that file could be. Should Schuschnigg publish the documents in a " White Book " he would deal Hitler a mortal blow. Even if he did not succeed in bringing him to fall (it was hardly probable that such a book could be smuggled in a large number of copies into Germany) any Nazi movement abroad would be discredited in the moment when the Fuehrer was shown in the merciless limelight of cold facts . . . not at all complimentary to him.

Schuschnigg had no other aims beyond that. After the White Book had been published there would hardly be a substantial group of Austrians belonging to the underground Nazi movement.

This file, this thick bundle of documents, all original, was in Schuschnigg's study between the steel walls of his safe.

And it was guarded by Countess Vera Fugger.

Himmler and Heydrich were both at Berchtesgaden and in constant touch with the Viennese events. Heydrich's instructions were outspoken, decisive, and strict.

I myself had to open the safe, take the file and prevent even Countess Vera from looking into it.

Early in the morning of the momentous day a member of the Special Service had arrived from Berlin who was an artist in burglary and could open almost any safe within a few minutes—and without leaving any traces.

I confess that I felt a strange excitement when I arrived with this man at Schuschnigg's flat.

His valet led us into the drawing-room. A little later the Countess Vera appeared, behaving as if she already were the mistress of the house. She greeted us pleasantly; but there was some strange expression on her lovely face which I could not at first fathom.

I was burning with impatience to fulfil my duty and said rather rudely when she sent the servant for some refreshments:

"For God's sake, Countess, we haven't got any time for polite small talk. Everything has been prepared for the transfer of the documents."

She seemed to be surprised.

"The file? Don't you know that von Papen has made other arrangements?"

I felt my hands growing cold; there was a clammy feeling around my heart. For heaven's sake, what had happened— just now when I believed that everything would be all right?

Countess Vera seemed to be rather startled at my lack of information.

"Baron von Kettler, von Papen's secretary, was here some time ago. I gave him the file and as far as I know he has left Vienna already. Von Papen thought that the documents would be in a much safer place in his secretary's courier's bag which won't be opened at the frontier, than in your hands. Even if you had perfectly organized the smuggling of the file into Germany, you might be exposed to the danger of an over-zealous customs officer."

I thought she had some particularly deep game of her own.

"I . . . I don't believe you," I stammered. "How could you open the safe?"

She smiled and showed me a key.

"Here it is . . . the Chancellor gave me the key. The poor man told me that if there should be any danger I should take them away to a safe hiding-place."

In order to convince us she led the way to Schuschnigg's study, opened the safe and showed us the empty inner drawer.

What could we do?

I had to get in touch with Heydrich . . . at once. The whole story was extremely suspicious . . . von Papen must have prepared some devilish intrigue. Perhaps his secretary had already left the country and now, instead of Schuschnigg, Papen would be able to threaten and blackmail Hitler. . . .

I rushed to the German embassy to ring up Heydrich. He was furious and almost roared in his despair. But he still had enough presence of mind to give me the instructions : I had to find out which route von Kettler had taken.

We knew that he was travelling by car and I knew its number. But I did not want to alarm the Austrian authorities. What if von Kettler was really going to Berchtesgaden? Our organization was not strong enough to have an agent in every town on the Vienna-Berchtesgaden route, whom I could have instructed to watch out for von Kettler's car. We were more or less helpless.

Hours went on in nerve-racking waiting.

The same tension reigned during the famous meeting at Berchtesgaden, described so often by different minor actors in the drama. Heydrich told me himself it was not true that Hitler treated Schuschnigg rudely and brusquely. But the Fuehrer seemed to be very nervous. He asked Himmler every thirty minutes whether there was any news about the file.

Schuschnigg, of course, had no idea what was going on behind his back. He behaved in a rather superior manner. He knew that he had a weapon in his hand which he could use to the fullest advantage if Hitler should prove difficult.

The forenoon passed and lunch was served.

In the afternoon Hitler broke off the conference ; he refused to continue the discussion till the fatal file should have arrived.

We had figured out in the meantime that von Kettler—in case he was trying to reach Berchtesgaden at all—had to pass the frontier about half-past eight in the evening.

But it was nine o'clock and he had still not crossed the border.

There was deep consternation both at the Viennese embassy and in the mountain chalet of the Fuehrer.

Another hour passed.

Still no news of von Kettler.

Another difficult, tense, painful thirty minutes went by.

And at last, after thirty more minutes the news came: Kettler's car had reached the frontier and . . .

The fate of Austria was sealed.

About 11 p.m., when Hitler knew that we were in the possession of the accursed documents, the discussions could begin again. But they soon took a tragic turn.

". . . and if you do not fulfil my conditions, German troops will occupy Austria," Hitler ended.

And now tragi-comedy followed.

Schuschnigg replied . . . alluded cautiously to the publication of a " White Book," which would . . .

" Consist of empty pages," the Fuehrer interrupted him ruthlessly. He walked to a cupboard in the wall, opened it . . . and Schuschnigg paled. He recognized the file which he thought safely in his own study. . . .

" What happened ? " he asked himself, losing all his poise and assurance.

At the moment when Hitler received the file, my mission had ended. I had succeeded and Karl Krause, the Berlin stamp merchant, could return to his home—or rather to the desk in the Gestapo building.

In Austria, history marched on with gigantic strides. On a memorable day Heydrich gave the command with a beaming face :

" Start for Vienna . . ."

And he added, laughing :

" But this time you can leave Karl Krause at home."

No, there was no need of any camouflage now.

The *Anschluss* had taken place.

It was rather a strange coincidence that I stayed again in the Hotel Metropole. This during these first, feverish days became the headquarters of the Gestapo.

One of the first victims of the *Anschluss* was—Baron von Kettler, Papen's secretary. As I found out later, Heydrich had given instructions from Berchtesgaden. A few trusted men were detailed to find out why the secretary had been late —by almost two and a half hours.

The unlucky man tried to explain it by a motor accident. But Heydrich's investigation soon found out that there had been no accident at all. Von Papen had again organized a brilliant *coup*.

It was at the German ambassador's orders that the secretary received the file in my place. Von Kettler drove to Salzburg where he took a suite in an hotel (the Gestapo found out all about it) and there, in a hundred and fifty minutes, he photographed all the secret documents of the file with the intention of creating a formidable weapon for von Papen's hand. . . .

A few days after the *Anschluss* von Kettler's bruised body was discovered in the Danube.

The Gestapo knew how to punish.

As for von Papen, everybody knows about his fate. Just before the *Anschluss* all the German papers announced that he would be appointed Germany's envoy to Turkey. But since the *Anschluss* no German paper ever mentions his name. According to my information—which may or may not be reliable—von Papen succeeded in sending the photo-copies to London where they are safely guarded. Probably this fact explains why von Papen is still alive. But he had to leave politics and was more or less exiled.

The file had cost the life of another man . . . unhappy von Kettler. A strange and fatal bunch of documents ; there is hardly anything in world-history to which it can be compared.

During my Vienna days I renewed my contacts with Buerckel and talked over our past co-operation in the Saar. He offered me a job in Austria, but I refused ; I felt that my place was in Berlin, in the Prinz Albrechtstrasse. Of course I did not speak to him about the file—it would have been sheer suicide. But anyhow, Buerckel was a much-occupied man in these days and beyond exchanging a few memories and giving me some encouraging words we did not speak much.

My story would not be complete unless I tried to finish it with the little I know about the beautiful Countess Vera's fate.

Her really great task began when Schuschnigg returned to the Austrian capital after the tragic meeting at Berchtesgaden.

Soon after his car drove up to the Belvedere, Schuschnigg and his fair traitress faced each other. It must have been a scene worthy of any romantic novelist's pen. She stood there, without tears in her eyes, and looked at the man who had trusted her so much.

And she bowed her head.

" Yes, it was I . . . I who deceived you . . . a thousand times in every hour of every day . . ."

Schuschnigg looked at her and felt : it must have been the strange will of Fate that ancient Austria should fall because he trusted this lovely woman.

But why wasn't she fleeing ? Now that she had done her task so well, fulfilled the command—why didn't she go to Germany and claim her reward ?

The tragedy had taken a curious turn.

Only the real expert in feminine psychology could fathom Vera Fugger's heart.

" Everybody is a traitor around you . . . all whom you trust. . . . Guido Schmidt . . . your secretary and intimate friend . . . the Cardinal with whom you talk every day . . . I . . . and all the others."

Schuschnigg listened almost dazed to this terrible confession.

" But why . . . why did you do it, Vera ? "

And now there were tears in her eyes.

" This was the only way to save you . . . for myself. I didn't want you to share the fate of Dolfuss . . . I didn't want you to remain Chancellor . . . and never to be able to marry me . . ."

Schuschnigg may have bent his head too and murmured :

" A woman who sacrifices a country for her love . . ."

Was everything lost or could the country be saved ?

" A limit must be set," Schuschnigg gave the new parole.

And he wanted to save in the last moment whatever there was to be saved. . . .

His whole day was a terrible chase for help ; he telephoned to London and Paris ; conferred with the Socialists whom he had once sent to prison ; he tried to get Stahremberg who had been such an enemy of Hitler ; he tried to fight. . . . A plebiscite. . . . But it was too late, the last hour of Austria's thousand-year-old history had arrived. And all through the tense hours Vera, repentant Vera was at his side. . . .

Yes, Countess Fugger was there, trying to do her utmost

for Schuschnigg who had forgiven her. She encouraged him
to make his last stand, and when the Nazi troops surrounded
the Belvedere, these two were alone . . . the Chancellor and
Vera. . . .

The *Anschluss* had taken place ; parades, festivals, and long
speeches . . . Guido Schmidt, who was now bragging openly
that he had been the secret agent of Germany, went off blithely
to Berlin to accept the decorative position which the Fuehrer
gave him. The others, Schuschnigg's former associates, all
unmasked themselves . . . for months they had been obeying
the Fuehrer and dancing to the tune of von Papen's pipe. . . .

And Schuschnigg ?

Schuschnigg, the prisoner, received the Papal dispensation
and married Countess Vera. As he could not leave the prison
of the Hotel Metropole, his father, the old general, led the
bride to the altar.

Is Schuschnigg still in the prison established on the third
floor of the Hotel Metropole ? Or has he been taken to the
Dachau concentration camp ? Will he face a charge of high
treason or—just as von Papen has been interned on his estates
—will he have to live in a certain, prescribed circle ?

I am afraid I cannot supply the answer to any of these
questions.

CHAPTER XII

★

A THOUSAND EYES, A THOUSAND EARS

My NEW JOB WAS rather dull—or at least so I thought. From the Special Service I was transferred to a sub-department of Department III in the Gestapo—the branch under the leadership of Dr. Hans Schmidt, with whom I co-operated on an equal footing. Our task was economic and industrial espionage and counter-espionage.

At first this sub-department worked only with about twenty men and in three rooms ; but in the ratio in which Germany continued her rearming, this branch of the Gestapo was increased and enlarged.

In the beginning our work was simply to try and trap the foreign agents lurking around the armament factories and putting them " out of circulation "—but slowly we noticed with increasing anxiety that the Reichswehr and Air Ministry declared daily new industries as coming under their authority ; in the end we were forced—figuratively speaking—to surround the whole German industry with barbed wire.

In modern war fighting is not solely the business of the army. Every industry, every producer, every commercial occupation has its part in it. The different branches of armament industries are hardly different in importance. Munitions plants, aeroplane factories certainly belong to the most essential ones. But the rubber factory supplying the pneumatic tyres for lorries or gas-masks is just as important. And the otherwise innocent oil distillery whose by-product is glycerine is just as vital ; glycerine is needed for nitro-glycerine and dynamite. And what about the tar factory with its by-product, benzol, which is a fundamental element of ecrasite and

167

lyddite, the deathly contents of grenades and shrapnel? Lead can be turned into tin. . . . And what would an army do without tinned food nowadays? Almost all raw materials have a similar role; whatever may be of a third or fourth-rate interest during peace time may prove highly precious during war. . . .

Soon after I started my work with Dr. Hans Schmidt, the first foreign agent was arrested. He was interested in the plant of a Dusseldorf silk factory. He protested furiously and maintained that he was only interested in artificial silk and our military secrets left him quite cold.

But we had learned our business.

Any artificial silk factory turning out silk stockings for girls with little money, but a longing to look smart, can be transformed without great difficulty into a plant producing smokeless gunpowder. Its output of stockings gives an almost precise calculation basis for its possible output of gunpowder; the difference may be that the plant will work twenty-four hours a day instead of eight. A toy factory could become a manufacturing place for detonators because that would best suit its machinery and fulfil the greatest need. All an agent had to find out was its number of machines and the rest would be easy.

In the third week of my work at the sub-department, a Reich law was issued. In the future people caught engaged in industrial espionage would have to suffer the supreme penalty—even in peace time.

The first death sentence was executed on the industrial spy Ludwig Maringer and his helpmate, Katherine Kneup. Their story is not only interesting because it presents an unusual case, but also because it offers insight into the fantastic world of commercial and industrial secret agents.

When Ludwig Maringer returned from Paris to Berlin, nobody found anything out of the ordinary in his arrival at the German capital. After all, he had been living in France for some years and he might have been homesick. He was fed up with roaming abroad and wanted to settle down in his home country. He took an office opposite the Anhalter Bahnhof, in the busiest business district of Berlin, and put out his sign :

REPRESENTATIVE OF FACTORY EQUIPMENT

L. MARINGER

If an expert strayed into the office, the young proprietor of the firm explained at length that he was representing several foreign enterprises ; he had a substantial backing and the great companies which he was introducing in Germany were able to deliver in the shortest time any factory equipment, even the most complicated machinery.

Soon his undertaking began to prosper. Maringer was no longer alone. The administration of his office was done by a strikingly beautiful woman in her early thirties—Katherine Kneup. The young man did not find it difficult to achieve considerable business results ; this was the time when Germany was starting to rearm with a vengeance. All the factories were working at full capacity, day and night ; new plants and companies were formed almost every week and Maringer knew how to profit by the " boom."

Whenever a new factory was inaugurated, the clever young man appeared first at the scene, presented his credentials and had such an attractive offer for equipping the plant that his German rivals were more or less helpless. Maringer was personally present when the machines shipped from abroad were established and installed . . . even later when the factory was working regularly he visited it from time to time. It was perfectly natural that he should be interested whether the machinery he supplied was giving satisfactory service.

After a few months there was hardly an important plant where Maringer had not become a familiar figure. Even if he had no business connection with a factory, he visited most of them to make a tempting offer for the replacement of outmoded equipment.

He was just as much at home in the numberless shops of the metal factories of the Ruhr as in the district of Dusseldorf, where plants were guarded by regular troops and their buildings surrounded by barbed wire.

Nobody dreamed, nobody had any reason to think that this

young man with the rather melancholy smile could have other motives than his business interests—namely, prying into the secrets of factories.

I shall never forget the day when the scandal started.

Not only our sub-department, the whole Gestapo resembled a feverish, disturbed ant-heap.

All this excitement was caused by the report of a Moscow agent of ours. We were notified that Moscow had succeeded in acquiring a model of the new heavy submarine which had been launched only a fortnight before at Kiel.

Everybody was flabbergasted.

We had thought that we had taken all necessary precautions at Kiel to avoid the leaking of information. And now we had to face the fact that in spite of all the caution foreign powers were fully informed about the plans and achievements of German armament factories. In vain we posted guards in front of the plants, in vain we carefully selected the workers, it was no use. We even controlled every step of the workers, engineers and clerks . . . in some mysterious way we had failed to safeguard the most important secrets.

But now we felt that the mysterious spy who had betrayed the latest achievement in naval armaments could not escape our clutches. We had taken a step which seemed rather super-fluous at that moment, but which now proved vitally impor-tant. We had taken everybody's name who was present at Kiel during the period of the experiments—for whatever reason he or she stayed in the port. We only had to sift these few hundred names, to select those who must be innocent—in the end the culprit must be shown up by a process of elimination.

Ludwig Maringer also figured on this list.

One day two gentlemen visited the office at the Anhalter Bahnhof and enquired for the chief of the firm. But Maringer was away on a business trip ; only lovely Katherine Kneup received them.

The Gestapo used the brutal, well-tried method which seldom failed.

" Frau Kneup," one of the Gestapo men said, " any denial

would be waste of time and only an aggravation of your plight. Maringer was arrested yesterday; he has confessed everything. It's all the same whether you deny it or not; Maringer has given everything to us, we have signed protocol, all the details of your work . . . we have been watching you for months, and you must realize that unless you make a clean breast of it . . ."

Of course nothing of this was true. At the moment Maringer was just as much a suspect as several hundred others figuring on our list. If the poor, misguided woman had protested with a smile, the Gestapo men would have probably apologized for the rather bad joke and gone on to the next name on the list. But Katherine Kneup fell into the trap.

At the first words of the Gestapo agent, she paled; wringing her hands, she stammered, almost helplessly:

" I knew it . . . I knew it would come . . . that scoundrel, Maringer . . . he wanted to die and confessed everything . . . he did not mind that he was dragging me with him. . . ."

This was full admission of her guilt . . . we had caught our fish.

Katherine Kneup was examined in detail and gave us all the data about Maringer's past.

It was quite a fantastic story, deeply moving in its parts.

" Maringer was in love with my younger sister," began Katherine Kneup. " It was a great, romantic love affair. Last year in Paris they had a motoring accident. My poor sister was killed. Maringer, who drove the car, was only injured. After he was discharged from hospital, he wanted to commit suicide. He said that he was the cause of my sister's death and did not want to live with the stigma of this guilt. . . ."

A curious episode followed in Maringer's life.

He was living in a small Paris hotel, preparing for death. His neighbour opened the door of his room at the moment when he was putting the revolver to his head.

This unknown man took the gun from the German boy's hand, he patted his shoulder saying:

" It's silly to kill yourself. If you want to die, there are easier and better methods. . . . A man who isn't afraid of death is a very rare thing. But you belong to this kind. . . ."

And he persuaded Maringer to stay alive—to take the risk of death in . . . espionage. He gave him a letter of introduction. He was sent to the country where even peace-time industrial espionage is punished by death. Germany was the first country which introduced capital punishment—beheading by the axe—even for peace-time espionage.

So Maringer went to Germany, and began his dangerous work. He was quite indifferent to danger . . . after all, even if he were caught, the death sentence would mean that someone else was doing, in his place, what he wanted to do himself in the little Paris hotel.

Desperate Katherine Kneup told the Gestapo that Maringer visited her when he arrived at Berlin. He persuaded her to help him in his work. He sent his information openly, almost defiantly, to his employers. And the Gestapo did not suspect that the blue prints of machinery, the technical descriptions which the Maringer office mailed almost every day, enclosed with its orders, were German military and industrial secrets.

People who were present at the trial told me that Maringer behaved with incredible calmness and superiority. His melancholy smile was still on his lips. On the other hand, Frau Kneup fought desperately for her life—but her life was lost in the moment when she made her first confession.

Then came the last act of the tragedy. The black flag was hoisted on the prison near Lake Ploetzen . . . signalling that the executioner of Magdeburg had again a job to do.

Who could tell whether this strange man, Ludwig Maringer, who had chosen this curious form of suicide, was happy or not when he saw the glint of the axe ?

The work of our sub-department naturally did not consist only in guarding German factories against inquisitive strangers. We followed the industrial development of the whole world with keen and constant interest.

To-day, the industrial and economic sub-department of the Gestapo works with almost eight hundred clerks. But it has a world-wide organization which can be safely called unparalleled.

I am fully aware of my responsibility when I say that *all*

German subjects travelling abroad are forced and obliged to carry on industrial espionage on Germany's behalf. If they did the same on German soil for a foreign power, they too would have to face, sooner or later, the executioner of Magdeburg.

German firms, factories, branches, agencies, travel bureaux, banks, shipping offices abroad must consider themselves as supports of Germany's economic war; they are bound to furnish every scrap of industrial, commercial and economic information they can procure and send it to a Berlin address—which is identical with this particular sub-department of the Gestapo.

The material supplied by these Germans abroad is immensely helpful and of the widest scope. These patriotic amateur spies have done great service to the Fatherland. But naturally, our sub-department had its professional spies in industry almost everywhere.

In most places it is camouflaged by the " Deutscher Hafendienst " (German Harbour Service). These offices are in truth, under their peaceful exterior, the " embassies " of the Gestapo. They are independent of any other German organization abroad, and are instructed directly by the Berlin Secret State Police.

Naturally, this name applies only in those countries which have seaports. In other states the Gestapo chooses different names. It can be some charity association, or a German reading circle—the main thing is the effective camouflage, a loose " cover " hiding real activities.

All over the world in the Harbour Service Offices the economic sub-department of the Gestapo carried on industrial espionage.

It would be rather difficult to give a systematic account of this work. It changes according to countries and industries. But some examples will show the amazing versatility and gigantic scope of this underground activity.

In Amsterdam, a little commercial agency was opened. Its most important equipment consisted of address books published by French and English chambers of commerce, industrial syndicates, and similar organizations. The agency sent a circular to the factories informing them that it was looking for export articles and asking for offers. Of course, they received an enormous amount of letters.

In the hands of expert technicians, these offers represented extremely interesting material.

Next the agency proceeded to correspond with these factories, discussing the supply of certain articles. They also asked for further information ; offers for certain variations in price and quality. The replies gave almost everything which the agency wanted. It was also easy to find out what quantity the factory in question could " guarantee." The prospect of such large-scale business forced even the most cautious enterprise to give full and frank answers.

Sometimes the " engineering experts " of the Amsterdam agency even visited the factory. They were received with the respect due to such important prospective clients and shown everything that was worth seeing. These Gestapo agents— for, of course, they were Gestapo agents—looked at everything with expert eyes. Even that could not cause any suspicion, if, in spite of the visits, no business was transacted. There was no law in the world prohibiting a commercial agency from trying to do business and procure information for its purposes. In such a way the Amsterdam office was able to prepare extensive files within six months of a great many factories of Western countries. With the help of the col- lected data, it could notify the Berlin centre that it had a more or less complete picture of the industrial capacity of three important countries in times of war.

Another cunning method opened the gates of many jealously guarded plants—opened them so wide that not a single secret was left unprobed by our sub-department.

It was my humble idea to send skilful Gestapo agents all over the great plants of foreign countries offering the most up-to-date " sprinkler " equipment.

This was nothing else than a system of water-pipes reaching all rooms and halls of the factory. If for any reason fire would break out somewhere, the metal cap at the end of the pipes would melt very soon and a regular downpour flood the room. The added advantage of this system was that insurance companies were willing to grant lower tariffs to enterprises which had adopted it; therefore the money paid for such a " sprinkler " system would be soon regained.

Our agents made extremely cheap offers. In some places it was almost at cost price; they could easily prove that by saving on insurance the factories got it for next to nothing. After an agreement was reached, the mechanics of the " company " appeared; for weeks every part of the factory was open to them. Of course, among these mechanics we had our expert specialists who photographed everything which they found interesting enough.

Sometimes we used astonishingly simple methods. For a glass of wine highly important secrets of manufacture could be acquired. All our agents had to do was to make friends with a foreman of the factory, take him to a pub and stand a few drinks; a little well-staged interest and the honest man was only too proud to tell everything he knew—bragging of the efficiency and importance of his work.

In more difficult cases there was always some story which made our agents' interest explicable. For a small bribe we could get expert information which not even the chief engineer of the plant could have supplemented.

Very few companies worried about the blue prints of the factories. When the plant was built, they often paid enormous sums for them—but as soon as it was finished, they did not trouble about them. They were put away somewhere as unnecessary rubbish, being kept just for some sentimental reason. But these blue prints meant a great deal to us. Our agents always found ways and means to get them and they deduced a mass of valuable data from these forgotten and neglected plans. . . .

Quite recently another branch was added to the economic sub-department of the Gestapo. Its organization has not yet been completed. Its task is rather special; *preparation for sabotage in case of war.*

Of course, this sabotage was most important in the armament factories.

The specialists of this branch have considered almost every important foreign plant, choosing with expert eye the points which were most vulnerable and could be used for putting the factory out of working order. On their carefully drawn plans these vulnerable points are carefully marked. The intention and purpose of such preparations must be evident. A handful of sand suffices to make a sensitive dynamo or turbine useless for a long time. In other places a small detonator is enough to start a terrible fire. Or a time bomb placed in a particularly vulnerable spot can put hundreds of workers out of a job and cancel production schedules for a long time.

The activity of this branch both in peace and war-time can be fatal for a country.

This branch—with real German thoroughness—has a huge filing system of most of the factories of the world; this system can be called unique. Tabulated graphs and specifications constitute a full directory of Europe's industry and all its vulnerable points.

The compilation of this file cost comparatively little money, but enormous work. It cost little because the procuration of necessary information was rather simple and almost always free from danger.

Even experts often confuse *industrial* espionage with *economic* espionage. The two often interlock and are pursued in parallel.

The birth and foundations of German economic espionage are easy to summarize.

The armament programme of the Third Reich demands the import of great quantities of raw material; most of them can only be bought for foreign currencies. To procure this foreign currency, German exports have to be pushed to the utmost. In order to combat rivals, exact economic information has to be collected—by every means, both legal and illegal.

Let's take an example. Egypt needs twenty locomotives. This means a very substantial amount—in English pounds. British, American, French, Polish, Czech, Italian companies are fighting to get the order. Naturally it will be given to the firm which can make the cheapest offer for the best quality.

Our department is notified. The best German engineers are

sent to Cairo. The most efficient agents start away towards all points of the compass to find out the prices and qualities of all the different firms—by any means. If necessary, they bribe confidential clerks or commit burglaries.

If they succeed in finding out all the necessary data, a German firm sends an offer to Cairo at the last moment, which is better than any of the others. It is easily possible that the German factory makes no profit on such an offer; it may even suffer a considerable loss—but the Third Reich covers the loss, or pays the profit. For Nazi Germany needs the English pounds to buy rubber, petrol, nickel or other raw materials for the manufacture of arms. . . .

To attain similar results sometimes quite different means have to be used. One of the smaller countries wants to buy aeroplanes. Of course, German firms also send in their offers. The planes have to be presented in actual flight to the committee which is going to decide about the placing of the order. Not only prices and qualities are important—the impression of security and stability must be proved on an airfield.

Now let's suppose that in the critical fifteen minutes some accident happens, some defect is noticed in the rival make of planes. It won't figure as a rival any longer. Or at least a respite has been won and the German firm has the opportunity to prepare fully for the next trial.

To make such an accident " happen " just at the right time, German agents have a great many different methods.

In the fight for foreign currency, any weapon is permissible —at least, so Nazi Germany thinks. And foreign currency is vital for German armaments. It is almost the only goal of German economic life—to get sterling and dollars, even if they have to sell below production costs.

There is no profit? It doesn't matter. The German Foreign Trade Office has its budget for such emergencies and willingly pays export premiums. The main thing is to get the foreign currency.

In the office of a foreign commercial enterprise there sits a badly paid clerk or a young lady typist, who prepares invoices relating to the goods supplied. The underpaid clerk or the little typist holds in his or her hands the most important

M

business secrets of the firm.   And he or she does not even know the importance and value of these secrets.

It is not difficult to bribe such an employee.   Very few refuse to eke out the meagre salary with a little extra.   He or she does not dream that next time a German clerk or lady typist writes the same invoices—only at lower figures.

Even the man or woman who knows little about shares, debentures and the flutter of the Stock Exchange, has sometimes dreamed of winning a tidy little sum by an " inside tip." If the news of some world shattering event arrives—events like the *Anschluss* or the annexation of Sudeten German territories—a great many people think in the safe secret of their hearts : " My God, if I had known this a week ago, how much I could have made in the City ! "

Everybody must envy those who could earn millions on the Stock Exchange just by being sure about the happening of some great historic event—*in advance*.

For a number of years Germany has been more or less directing or staging world events.   But very few people know that every time something happens the Third Reich earns huge sums on the London, New York, and Paris Stock Exchanges.   Skilful German agents take good care to profit by their more or less perfect knowledge of coming events.

It is quite natural that such highly confidential affairs can only be entrusted to the most trusted men.   Such an agent often handles almost astronomical amounts, and if " something " happens to the money, the individual can be hardly caught as he is abroad.*

* The Publishers apologise to readers for the hiatuses on pages 178, 179, 180, and 181, but the deletion of material from these pages has been necessitated by the law of libel as it exists in this country.

I should like to say a word as to what this excellently functioning and widespread espionage system of Germany really means to the world.

It represents a huge advantage for the Third Reich. Official German circles are fully informed about the commercial, financial, economic industrial conditions of other countries, about the possibilities of supplies and hidden sources of raw material. Germany knows exactly where and how these supplies can be cut off or diminished ; thousands of agents serve her with information ; but at the same time, her opponents hardly know what to believe of the conflicting news connected with the Nazi state. There is a moral effect of this situation which is greatly disturbing for Germany's opponents. In case of war this would mean almost fatal handicap for the enemy.

To-day, all the well-informed people know that during the critical September days of 1938 Germany was far from being ready to fight Great Britain, France, and Russia. But she showed a fighting spirit and bluffed as hard as she could. Thus she gained her victory. Yet she could only bluff because thousands of her spies assured her that the three great powers would not make war. Russia had a formidable air force. But the German spies reported that Russia would not march.

British and French armaments had not reached the point yet at which the two allies could have started a war with the hope of quick and certain success. Germany knew that she could bluff as hard as she wanted; her opponents would withdraw. The Third Reich won a war without a rifle-shot, only with the help of her agents.

And the gigantic organization of these agents is supervised and directed by the Gestapo for which I was then still working.

CHAPTER XIII

★

KING CAROL'S TROUBLES

" Mme Tabouis reports that Count Ciano is to visit Belgrade
as soon as Mr. Chamberlain has left Rome. In view of his
recent journey to Budapest, it is evident that Italy is developing
Central European ambitions. It is believed, however, that
this is with German approval.

Italy is to be allowed to establish politico-economic domina-
tion in the south of the Danube, Jugoslavia, Albania, Greece
and Bulgaria, sharing a sort of condominium with Germany
over Hungary.

Count Ciano is busy arranging for the common
action of these States against Rumania.

Rome has been deeply stirred by the execution of the
Fascist leader Codreanu, and is anxious to get rid of
King Carol unless he is prepared to abandon all
alliance with the Western Powers and with the
Soviet Union."

From the *Evening Standard*, London.

7th January 1939.

THE ABOVE SHORT PARAGRAPHS of a London daily hide
one of the most exciting stories of international rivalry.
Germany's drive to the East—Italy's ambitious aspirations in
the Balkans—will they be ever co-ordinated? Sometimes even
the astute Madame Tabouis can be wrong. But perhaps the
following pages will give an answer to the Rumanian
riddle and show clearly the troubles of handsome King
Carol.

When I met Zelea Codreanu for the first time, it was already
settled that out of the three candidates for the part of a
Rumanian " Fuehrer " Codreanu, or as he was known in his

own country, " the Captain," would get Germany's full moral and financial support.

There were three aspirants in Rumania ; all three maintained that they had the masses behind them ; the people were willing to follow them through thick and thin. If only Germany would guarantee the necessary financial support, success would be assured.

The first applicant was the seventy-six years old university professor of Jasy, Cuza. Professor Cuza was an almost legendary figure in Rumania ; everybody knew that he never shook hands with a Jew and had propagated both in Parliament and in his newspaper for more than thirty years the ideas which the Third Reich had adopted with Hitler. Under Professor Cuza's leadership whole generations grew up in anti-semitism, the hatred of the Jews. And yet he was not chosen. Professor Cuza was not the right man for us. Although he hated and abused the Jews, he emphasized in every speech and article of his that he wanted to attain his aims through the parliamentary methods.

The second man who asked Germany's support to realize his plans was the poet, Octavian Goga.

He was a small, stocky man with big, burning eyes and soft, almost feminine gestures. His life had been almost like a novel.

During the war he was sentenced to death in Hungary for high treason. . . . He escaped to Rumania. With his fine poems and inflaming orations he had a great part in bringing Rumania into the camp of the Allies. After the war he became a politician ; he had gained his majority by the votes of the minorities, Hungarians, Germans, and—Jews. He became Prime Minister, but could hold his position only for a short time. He was suspected and accused by the other political parties of wanting to become a dictator . . . and was nicknamed a " pocket Hitler."

Goga would have been a suitable man. A wonderful orator who could almost hypnotize the masses ; one of the greatest Rumanian writers, a poet—but at the same time a bit of a weathercock, a turncoat. Then the political situation took him into Hitler's arms—but if it changed again he might very well desert Germany again. And Goga died soon after he had to resign. . . .

And so Germany chose the third candidate, Zelea Codreanu.

When I met him for the first time I was the bearer of pleasant news for " the Captain."

Not that the time would have been particularly suitable for a long, quiet discussion. In those days " the Captain " was a hunted man, a quarry of the Rumanian police.

The Siguranca, the Rumanian Scotland Yard, was hot on his heels; the provincial gendarmes were chasing him all over the country.

What had happened ?

A thin, anæmic student, barely twenty-two, went to the Ministry of the Interior at Bucharest and there waited patiently till he could get into the room of Under-Secretary Anghelescu. His name was George Beza. When he walked into the room, he took a gun from his pocket and fired four bullets at the unsuspecting politician. It was a wild and fantastic scene; the athletic Under-Secretary began to fight with the thin student although he was bleeding from four wounds. At last others hurried into the room, disarmed Beza and took the dying Under-Secretary to a hospital. . . .

The assassin was a member of the Iron Guard; everybody knew that it was the Iron Guard which had sent him to murder Anghelescu.

The whole country was scandalized, the Press protested, questions were asked in Parliament. Would Rumania endure that the men of the Iron Guard, Codreanu's gangsters, should kill freely ?

In the evening Codreanu's Iron Guardists put posters all over the capital. " The Captain " was daring enough openly to take the part of the assassin. He called his deed an action " worthy of a true Rumanian " and praised the courage of student Beza.

Twenty-four hours later the Rumanian Government issued the instructions: " the Captain " must be captured and brought to trial for condoning a capital crime.

But where was " the Captain " ?

The police, the gendarmes, the special branch of the Siguranca, searched for him in the whole country.   Where was he hidden ?

At the same time when he was hunted by ten thousand men, I had an appointment to meet him in a well-known and rather expensive restaurant.

I stopped my taxi and continued my way on foot.   And there, in the Café Floreazka, screened only by a few drooping plants set in pots, " the Captain " was smoking calmly.

He was a tall, very handsome man; his nose a little daring, his eyes steel-blue.   Every gesture was a little studied. His clothes were not the usual Western male garb ; a sort of transition between a civilian suit and Rumanian peasant dress.

We were sitting on the narrow terrace of the café . . . music floated over the dusty pavement . . . and the policemen of Bucharest were looking for " the Captain " . . .

He was talking slowly, searching for words ; after every question he stared for some seconds into the dusk, formulated the replies haltingly.   He had clasped his knees with his hands ; they were strong and shapely with a pale scar on the back of his right hand.

We were speaking of his past life, about his terrible start in politics.   Few men had started their public careers with— three murders, but Zelea Codreanu did this very thing.

And his quiet, even words painted a lurid picture.

A young student was waiting in the ante-room of the Prefect of Jasy.   The ante-room was full of people who had come on different errands.   The student was sitting peacefully, never protesting against the long wait.

It was long past noon when the door opened.   The Prefect stood on the doorstep, then walked forward and stopped in the middle of the waiting hall.

" I must ask you to come to-morrow, I have no more time to-day to see anyone."

But the student who had waited three hours to see the Prefect, rose and faced the head of the Jasy police.

" You have thrown into prison and flogged the heroes of

Rumanian liberty . . . my fellow-students. Do you know what you are to expect ? You're getting it now ! ''

He did not wait for any reply. In the hands of the young student—Corneliu Codreanu—the gun began to bark. The Police Prefect, George Manciu, collapsed—dead. Two police officers were standing near, they wanted to rush at the assassin ; but before they could take a step, the gun spoke twice more. Three dead . . . and as the autopsy ascertained later, all three bullets had gone through the heart.

This triple murder took place in 1925, at the time when the Rumanian movement of anti-semitism was at its height. Under the leadership of the seventy-year-old university professor of Jasy, Ion Cuza, the young students arranged a demonstration every day—in Bucharest, Jasy, Galatz, the Jews lived in constant terror. The police would or could not defend them against the pogromists.

1925 was the black year for the Rumanian Jews.

The Liberal Government of the country found that the time had come to suppress the extreme anti-semitic agitation. It was only after long discussions that they had arrived at such a decision. Up to then the slogan had been : " Don't touch the students ! " The students were the future leaders of Rumania and the future ministers, members of parliament, could not be sent to prison for their " political convictions." But the foreign countries had started to take notice, the American Press wrote about repeated massacres of Jews ; at last the Government issued the proclamation : anarchy must end.

Student demonstrations and revolts were naturally the sharpest and most violent in Jasy, old Professor Cuza's hometown. Manciu, the Police Prefect of Jasy, wanted to carry out the orders of Bucharest in every particular; he started to " smoke out " the anti-semitic wasps of his city. He used the same methods against the arrested demonstrators which he had used in the case of the Communist agitators. The cells of the police were full of arrested students. . . . It was for the first time in Rumanian history that anti-semitic students had really to . . . stay in jail.

And Corneliu Zelea Codreanu fired three shots. . . .

The murders had been committed at Jasy and the trial would

have to take place there. But the Liberal Government of Rumania thought it better to transfer the case to the farthest part of the country, the peaceful and idyllic Turnu Severin, where no reverberations of Jew-baiting had found their way. But the Government was mistaken. The small provincial town, which was almost like a village, was invaded by three thousand students. For three months while Codreanu's case came up for trial, they camped there and turned the peaceful little town upside down. Nobody knew which of the honest citizens of Turnu Severin would be the jurors, and so the students had to win every adult person in the town—and win through them the acquittal of their hero.

And Zelea Codreanu was acquitted.

His fellow-students organized for him a triumphal procession. All through Rumania they marched to the distant Focsani, and fêted the man who had committed three murders. It was like a triumphal entry in ancient Rome—only the gladiators and the slaves behind the chariots were lacking to make it truly Roman. Not for nothing do the Rumanians claim that they are descended from Cæsar's legions. . . .

Codreanu's followers marched from town to town.

The triumphal procession arrived at Focsani.

A chain of gendarmes closed the road and tried to keep them back. But nothing could keep back these enthusiastic warriors. They broke through the cordon . . . there was a tumultuous scene. . . .

The students won the battle, they marched into the main street of the city. But here a young captain of the gendarmes blocked their way.

A shot rang out and the captain fell to the ground, fatally wounded.

A new murder.

There was no proof that Codreanu had fired the shot ; but his friends advised him to vanish for a little time from the public scene. It would be better if he were out of sight of the authorities.

Codreanu left Rumania for France. He arrived at Grenoble and enrolled there at the law faculty to continue his studies.

He spent two years in the French university town, living the life of poverty-ridden, struggling students.

Every week the post brought him a letter from Rumania. His friends still wrote that he must stay away, they were still looking for him.

The Rumanian police had no idea that the man wanted for murder was in Grenoble. They looked for him somewhere in Moldavia; they thought he was living there, hiding at some mountain farm.

1927.

Codreanu felt that he was unable to stand exile any longer. Every drop of his blood longed for his beloved country. He had finished his studies at Grenoble and had graduated. He was entitled to call himself a doctor of law.

Without waiting for the advice of his friends, he left France and returned to Rumania.

It was with some trepidation that he crossed the frontier, but there were no gendarmes waiting for him, no armed police force to take him into custody. Two years are a long time. The authorities had simply forgotten about him. And even if they had not . . . there was no actual proof that he had killed the captain of gendarmes . . . and without proof they could not prosecute.

He arrived in Rumania and got in touch with his old friends. He was glad to find that his popularity had not waned. On the contrary. There were even more fanatics willing to follow him. . . . And a short time after he had set his foot on Rumanian soil, a gun barked again in the hand of a student . . . and a high civil servant collapsed with blood spurting from a deep wound. . . .

And now I was facing " the Captain," this young man who had four lives to answer for . . . if he would ever be called to answer. It was almost childish, the question which I put to him.

" What are your plans now, Captain? Wouldn't it be better if you came with me to Germany? I'm sure I could smuggle you through the frontier. . . . I have a few passports in my bag, one of them would suit you. . . . You ought to wait in Berlin till things quieten down here. You are due to be arrested almost any moment. . . ."

He laughed.

"That's just what I want . . . listen . . . you'd better wait a little . . . in an hour you'll see what's happening. Can you stay for a few days? Yes? That's splendid. Well, we'll continue our talk shortly."

I said good-bye to him and left the café.

An hour later the newsboys were running with the extras through the streets of Bucharest. I bought one and asked a friendly Rumanian to translate the screaming headlines. It must be a great sensation, I thought—and so it was.

After "the Captain" had said good-bye to me and I left, he walked out of the café, took a taxi and drove smiling, as if he were going to some lover's tryst, to the headquarters of the Siguranca, the Rumanian Secret Police.

He walked into the room of the Siguranca chief and said calmly :

"Here I am . . . you can arrest me."

He was taken under strong guard to the prison of Vacaresti. Ten days later he came up for trial in Bucharest.

And the events of this trial finally settled the fate of "the Captain" and his Iron Guard.

The jurors of Bucharest acquitted Codreanu. According to their sentence, his poster praising Beza's deed was not a crime. Their reasoning was rather difficult to follow ; but Codreanu was a free man again.

After this second acquittal Codreanu redoubled his efforts. He took charge again of the Iron Guard. The Rumanian newspapers were horrified. Up to now the Iron Guard had not amounted to much. Sometimes—and fairly often it happened in the last months—they organized noisy and unruly demonstrations. Once or twice they fired a gun and killed someone. But now, almost overnight, they had become a serious and important organization—a private army—a menace to the State.

Whence came the money with which "Captain" Zelea Codreanu used to plaster the whole city of Bucharest with his posters ?

Everybody talked of this mystery in the capital; newspapers wrote articles about it; questions were asked in parliament.

There was some innocent soul among the members of the latter institution who took paper and pencil and figured out that the Iron Guard must have spent millions to extend its organization. During the last weeks a branch had been opened in the smallest, most secluded village. All the pamphlets, posters, emblems, uniforms—they cost money. Where did Codreanu find this huge amount?

And where did he find the money to buy several hundred acres in the suburbs of Bucharest on which he could build the huge, new central building of the Iron Guard?

What was the source of all this money, the Democratic newspapers asked.

Who supplied the millions, the Democratic members of parliament enquired.

During these days it was proved that we had chosen well when we selected Zelea Codreanu as the man to back. In spite of the visits of police in the centre of the Iron Guard, in spite of postal censorship and constant watch over their telephone lines—no proof could be produced against them; no incriminating circumstance found. There was no trace of any connection of the Third Reich with "the Captain."

Suspicion was strong and everything pointed to its justification. The Rumanian authorities needed only a scrap of paper, a single receipt or some allusion to prove that Codreanu received his millions from abroad . . . from Germany.

But "the Captain" proved to be an excellent pupil in diplomacy. From the first moment he was on his guard. He took great care, with stubborn tenacity, that he should not betray the connection between Nazi Germany and the Iron Guard. He knew well that if he should "slip up," Germany would have to withdraw her support and the Rumanian authorities would try him for high treason. And this time there would be no acquittal. . . .

Yes, Zelea Codreanu was an excellent pupil.

He was efficient enough to adopt the methods through

which the Nazis had attained power in Germany ; but he was intelligent enough not to follow them slavishly. He counted on the rather mystic element in the soul of the Rumanian peasant ; he enlivened his parades and meetings with strange interludes which almost looked ridiculous to us, rather sober and stolid Germans.

Anyone who wanted to join the Iron Guard had to submit to a strange, almost archaic ceremony recalling the Middle Ages. He had to keep a fast, go to confession ; a Greek Catholic priest took his oath.

The text of this oath was horrible enough to have a deep impression on the new member.

He had to swear that he would fulfil the commands of " the Captain " under all circumstances, whatever these commands were. He was told that the Iron Guard would kill him mercilessly if he broke his oath or refused obedience. . . .

When I visited " the Captain " for the second time, the centre of the Iron Guard had already been finished at the so-called *Carmen Sylva Estate*. It was a huge building, furnished like an hotel. Here the different offices were situated and also some guest-rooms for the members. It was called the " Green House "—modelled after the " Brown House " of the Nazis.

" The Captain " himself lived in more romantic surroundings.

His tent-like little house stood in the middle of the large grounds, half-sunk into the earth. Around it regular trenches with sand-bags and loop-holes. The house was guarded day and night. Inside the tent was an iron camp-cot with an army blanket. Above the bed a collection of weapons, almost an arsenal. In the middle of the room a simple plywood table with a telephone—but on the wide empty wall opposite a startling picture.

There was a text running above it :

WHEN THESE GRAVES ARE ALL FILLED, THE CAPTAIN WILL
RULE THE COUNTRY

And the painting depicted a thousand graves . . . ten rows of a hundred each . . . drawn close to each other.

On the gravestones of the first there was a name : Police Prefect Manciu. The second and the third bore the names of the two police inspectors killed at the same time. The fourth showed the name of a member of the Iron Guard who was killed during a demonstration in the Bukovina. The fifth the captain of gendarmes whom Codreanu was suspected of having killed, and so on. . . .

When I visited the *Carmen Sylva Estate*, twenty-one crosses already bore names. . . .

So " the Captain " needed " only " nine hundred and seventy-nine corpses to attain his final triumph.

During my second visit there were important discussions between " the Captain " and the representatives of the German Foreign Office. Codreanu pledged himself in writing that should he come to power he would create the warmest and closest co-operation between Rumania and Germany.

As for my task—I had arrived with a party of three—it was nothing more than to explain to " the Captain's " staff the organization methods which had proved so successful in the Third Reich.

This was highly necessary. Codreanu did not trouble about any personal danger which might threaten him. There was a fanatic spirit of dare-devilment in him ; he travelled all over Rumania without an escort ; he did not seem to be afraid of his many enemies.

A few days later fifty rather " tough " men surrounded him. These fifty men who were destined to become the nucleus of a troop similar to Himmler's S.S. became Codreanu's body-guard. They took the oath for their new duties in a romantic and picturesque ceremony designed apparently by " the Captain " himself.

Church flags, Greek Catholic priests in ornate dress . . .

" You fifty men," Codreanu said, " are going to carry a loaded gun in your pockets. You are responsible singly and collectively for my life. . . ."

The fifty armed students, carrying the guns in their right hands, stepped in front of the altar and the priest " consecrated " their weapons.

" We swear," said these fanatic young men, " that our

N

lives shall last only so long as the Captain is alive. Wherever or whenever any harm may be done to him, we will die gladly."

I shall never forget the scene. "The Captain," at that time, was not yet thirty. There was a wild and cruel expression on his face as he stared at the fifty youths. He looked at them for a long time and said slowly, lost in his thoughts :

"Well . . . I don't think I need more than fifty loyal men . . . Believe me, they are enough to conquer a country. . . ."

This was the time when we were almost sure in Germany that it would take only days for Codreanu to grab the supreme power in Rumania.

The whole country was in a state of almost hypnotic terror ; the careful and cautious people wanted to find a place in time among the members of the Iron Guard. The German example was rather convincing and—threatening. The " wise people " thought that they ought to get the membership card of the Iron Guard as soon as possible ; otherwise they would fare as did many in Germany, where the ranks of the Nazi Party were closed and all those left outside had a rather bad time after Hitler's accession to power.

The Rumanian political parties also showed a warm interest in Codreanu's organization. For the time being only the less popular fractions, i.e. those with the fewest electors, tried to find some connection with " the Captain." They had, after all, very little to lose. Their leaders scarcely veiled their conviction that there was only one reason for making a pact with the Iron Guard. Should Codreanu gain the power, he would probably introduce the system of concentration camps. Such a pact, made before his coming to rule, would ensure a certain immunity. It was better to be armed for any emergency than to be caught unawares. . . .

It was like a bombshell when it became known that Maniu himself, who had been President of the National Peasants' Party for decades and had headed several cabinets as an " apostle " of Transylvania, had also started negotiations with the " Fuehrer " of the Iron Guard.

The big democratic newspapers began to handle them more gently. For months no article was published in the Bucharest

Press which would have been unpleasant for the Iron Guard. Mockery and satire ceased—they did not even dare to criticize. It seemed as if the Press could take no notice of the increasing terror ; the public of the capital could find out nothing about Codreanu's activities. They did not know—or at least only a few of them did—about the central building which was quickly growing on the outskirts of the town ; they did not know that the members of the Iron Guard wore green shirts instead of the brown of their Nazi brothers ; they were uninformed about the consignments of arms which arrived in large quantities at " the Captain's " headquarters. The man in the streets of Paris or London was following much more closely the dark danger threatening Rumania, than was John Smith of Bucharest who lived a few hundred yards from the " Green House." This was a dangerous conspiracy—a conspiracy of silence.

Something else happened which also seemed to be interesting. All political parties, seeing the great popularity of young Codreanu, began hastily to change their party programmes—in the Nazi way. The Bucharest Press noted rather naïvely that all the political organizations—and not only the small, but the large and well-established ones—found it necessary to " refresh their platforms." At such meetings, held behind locked doors, nothing happened, except the decisive movement to bring the old party programme into accord with the Nazi ideology of the Iron Guard.

During this period four agents of the Gestapo were constantly present in Zelea Codreanu's " general staff." Their duty was to transplant the well-tried German institutions and methods into the organization of the Iron Guard.

About this time " the Captain's " book of law was published ; fundamentally a copy of a similar book published by the Nazis in Germany.

It caused a nation-wide sensation when a Democratic member read out in parliament the laws of the Iron Guard which he had obtained by some means or other.

" The Rumanian who sells himself to the Jews is to be punished by death."

"The Rumanian who has anything to do with another Rumanian, already in the clutches of Jews, is also to be punished by death."

Death . . . death . . . death . . . Codreanu seemed to want to fill up those graves as quickly as possible. Nor would he stop at the first thousand. A great many other victims had been selected. . . .

In his book of laws there was no other punishment but death.

The Democratic M.P. did not dream that by raising the matter he would only serve Codreanu. By his interpellation the merciless sentences of the Iron Guard became widely known ; instead of harming them, it helped to win to them all those who were afraid of their power.

Following the German method, the Iron Guard had its branches and members in all State institutions and organizations ; its representatives were sitting safely in all ministries, civil service offices, even in the different units of the Rumanian army.

Nobody could tell whether in some highly important State bureau the chief or his deputy was a member of the Iron Guard.

No doubt all this could not have happened had not the Prime Minister, M. Vaida, silently approved of the Iron Guard's activities and thereby helped it in its almost fantastic development.

A politician of the old school visited the Premier and anxiously reproached him. This was a danger which would be extremely serious almost overnight. Vaida shrugged.

"I'm only following His Majesty's wishes. . . . It's his command that we should give a free hand to the Iron Guard."

Marinescu, the Police Prefect of Bucharest, received the same reply to his enquiries. He was so startled that he drove straight away to the Royal Palace and asked for an audience with King Carol. Marinescu had belonged to the old, intimate circle of the King ; he felt that he had to give an account urgently about his discussion with Prime Minister Vaida.

King Carol was horrified at Marinescu's report. Half an

hour later he sent for the Prime Minister. Some well-informed people maintained that it was a highly dramatic encounter. King Carol reproached Vaida ; told him that he had misused the name of his King ; it was probably his, Carol's, prestige which had made the Iron Guard so powerful—without his knowledge and approval. But the Iron Guard, even if it was protesting its loyalty to the Crown, steadily was undermining the authority of the King. He, Carol, would be only a shadow, a puppet, at the side of Codreanu, the dictator. Other examples had proved this fully.

And so the Iron Guard became the cause of Prime Minister Vaida's fall. He had to resign immediately. The evening papers published the sensational news. It was a political debacle and King Carol took a strong stand. He would brook no interference from any political organization.

And now Zelea Codreanu committed his blunder which finally led to his tragic death.

I shall never forget the night we spent at the telephone in the Gestapo building. I was working again for Sub-Department EAST in Main Department III of the Secret State Police, supporting Criminal Commissioner Dr. Riedel, that tall young man whose organization covered Poland, Czecho-slovakia, Hungary and the Balkans. As I had been to Rumania several times, I was consulted as an expert.

We were waiting for the news from Bucharest.

Prime Minister Vaida had resigned. Only one man could follow him, we thought—Zelea Codreanu, " the Captain."

Everything was prepared for his coming. Both the masses and the Government circles would accept him. The Iron Guard had its men in the ranks of the army and the police.

A single gesture, a strong stand—and " the Captain " would hold the highest power in Rumania.

But now, for the first time in his life, Codreanu flinched. He did not dare to give the command. He did not dare to take the decisive steps, although everything was prepared, the posters and handbills printed. . . .

We received a copy of the green-bordered poster for the files of the Gestapo. I still remember every word of it :

" To the battle, Iron Guards ! The last hour has arrived !

Take to your arms, whether they be sickles, spades, axes or rifles ; march for the last fight. To-day we proclaim the Iron Guardist Rumania. In face of death we cry out with a smile :
Long live death !
LONG LIVE THE IRON GUARD !
LONG LIVE THE CAPTAIN ! "

But even if the proclamation was rather bloodthirsty, Codreanu boggled at the responsibility at the very last moment. King Carol appointed Duca in Premier Vaida's place. Sub-Department EAST of the Gestapo soon received the news of the first declaration which the new Prime Minister made. It began :

" I assure the country : the first task of my Government will be to rid Rumania of the terror of the Iron Guard. . . ."

Then the first confidential report arrived ; our agent in " the Captain's " general staff had a long talk with Codreanu in the critical hour of Vaida's resignation, before Duca was appointed.

" I'm not a coward," Codreanu said, " but I know the spirit of Rumania better than you do. And I know better when I have to give the command to go. Every day makes the situation riper ; if I were to try to take over the power too early it would only mean a final failure."

When the Gestapo agent reproached " the Captain " sharply, telling him that every day of waiting cost millions, the Iron Guard's leader smiled.

" Believe me, this will prove the best investment for you. But I wouldn't be embarrassed even if you withdrew your support ; I would simply have to find other sources. . . ."

And Codreanu was right. In this period every money-bag, every bank safe, was open to the Iron Guard. As for foreign help, Rome was almost jealous that Codreanu had not yet applied for the secret funds of the Fascist Propaganda Ministry.

The Duca cabinet was duly sworn and began its administration. A few weeks later " the Captain's " fatal blunder became evident.

All the outward signs seemed to point to the fact that Codreanu's chances had only improved by Duca's appointment. Duca was a Democrat of the old school. According to his opinion a Democratic government must loyally guard the constitution and could not deviate from the path of law and order. Therefore, in the first place, it needed a strong parliament to pass all the Bills which would give it the necessary executive power for dealing with a so-called political party—in this case the Iron Guard.

The date of the elections was already settled. And Duca was startled to find out that the Iron Guard would probably carry a majority of the votes, indeed, most of the parliamentary seats.

Codreanu had contested elections in fifty counties ; the Iron Guard had fifty " legions," fifty well-organized centres. It seemed almost certain that his loyal followers would assure victory for Rumanian Nazidom. . . .

The disturbing news became more and more startling. A hundred thousand Iron Guards were roaming the country, armed with guns, bombs, hand-grenades. Duca had read a " daily command " of the organization which in essence said :

" An Iron Guardist never argues. He has his revolver in his pocket, the best answer to any question. . . ."

The horrified Bucharest papers reported that in the streets of Jasy barricades had been erected, a regular pitched battle was fought ; more than fifty shops were destroyed . . . there were three dead. . . .

In four villages of Dobrudja the village sheriff was killed because he objected to the Iron Guard propaganda. In Bucharest and in Transylvania one murder followed another.

The capital was already prepared for the victory of the Iron Guard. Even the most pessimistic calculations awarded 250 out of the 350 seats in the Rumanian parliament to them.

The Government was completely helpless in the face of the unscrupulous and relentless propaganda which Codreanu and his organization pursued. " Pay no taxes ! " " All debts will be cancelled ! " " The shops and factories of the Jews will be confiscated ! " " Big estates will be distributed to small farmers ! " These were the main slogans of the Iron Guardists. What could the Liberal Party, the middle-class organization built on old Conservative traditions, offer against such catchwords ?

We in the Gestapo began to have our doubts. Had we been mistaken ? Perhaps we did not know Rumanian local circumstances as well as Codreanu. Perhaps he had been right. Everybody had counted for sure on the Iron Guard's victory. The news from Bucharest was reassuring—for us. The Jews of the capital were so certain of the coming catastrophe that they fled in a panic. Whole districts became depopulated ; there was a wholesale migration.

Yes, it seemed as if for once the canny Gestapo had erred gravely. The young " Captain " seemed to have followed the right methods.

A little later the startling news arrived. Premier Duca had dissolved the Iron Guard, annulled all their constituencies, and—in a single night—had had three thousand followers of Codreanu arrested.

This was a terrible blow. What had happened ?

The Iron Guards had been so sure of their victory that they had overlooked even the most elementary precautions. They were too cocksure and invited ruin. Their car stopped openly in front of the German embassy ; without any attempt at secrecy, their envoys visited the Bucharest branch of a big German chemical factory which supplied them with their funds.

Prime Minister Duca was only waiting for such a slip. He had two or three Iron Guards arrested. In their pockets he found ample proof of Codreanu's foreign connections. According to Rumanian law he was fully entitled to dissolve a political party which was supported by a foreign power and financed by another country.

And then the fight against the Iron Guard began. No government had dared to touch them up to then ; but there were searches, arrests, almost every day. It seemed as if final and fatal blows would be struck. So the Gestapo had been right—and not the young " Captain."

Zelea Codreanu realized it—but much too late.

He felt that everything was lost if he did not check the strong-armed Duca in his persecution of the Iron Guard.

Something drastic had to be done—and done quickly.

" The Captain's " answer to Duca's crusade was a terrible one.

The Secret Council of the Iron Guard sentenced the Prime Minister to—death. Three Iron Guards : Belimac, Constantinescu and Garanica, were chosen to kill him.

Another trio was detailed to execute the first three men if they should fail. (This was a close copying of the Gestapo methods.) And a third group was chosen to supervise the first two in their grim duty.

In the end ten groups of three men were chosen in such a way. For days they followed Duca like his shadow. The " dead-line " was January the first—the assassins had to take a solemn oath to kill the Prime Minister before that date, and they also swore that they would commit suicide should they fail.

On the railway station of Sinaia the tragic shot was fired . . . the shot which ended Duca's life.

But this brutal and cowardly assassination did not help Codreanu to become Rumania's dictator.

It caused grave resentment even within the Iron Guard. Every sign pointed to a fatal split. The situation was almost identical with that which Hitler had to face in June, 1934— the situation which led to Roehm's execution and the terrible purge.

The Rumanian authorities did not dare to arrest Codreanu even after Duca's murder, although every trail led to the Iron Guard and suspicion was more than well founded. As the Iron Guard had been dissolved, he had to form a new party, to create a new organization. He called it, somewhat grandiloquently : " EVERYTHING FOR OUR COUNTRY."

But two of his most loyal men, Misu and Stelesku, did not enter the new party.

The two groups separated completely. Stelesku suddenly became a dangerous opponent. He published a pamphlet in which he unmasked Codreanu ; he had a file of documents which were highly incriminating. Among other things he proved that " the Captain " was not even a Rumanian subject ; his mother had been German, his father a Pole. And he told the compromising story of German funds supporting the Iron Guard.

Codreanu had no choice; he had to sentence Stelesku to death. This sentence was also executed—with almost bestial ferocity.

Stelesku was lying in the Brancoveanu hospital. Twenty Iron Guardists entered the hospital, held up the nurses and doctors; they penetrated to Stelesku's room and hacked him almost to pieces . . . with nauseating brutality.

Soon posters appeared in the streets :

" Stelesku the traitor has received his reward."

" All traitors will meet the same fate."

But Codreanu knew already that he had committed a serious tactical blunder when he had not listened to the advice of the Gestapo and failed to seize the power after the resignation of the Vaida cabinet. This served as a good lesson; he was only waiting for the opportunity to make his bid for dictatorship.

In the meantime he decided to restore the unity of his Party and then to begin the last battle.

Up to then he had always left the person of the King out of his political calculations. Yet everybody knew that he was a republican at heart. In case he should succeed he would reduce Carol to a figurehead—perhaps even force him to abdicate—and relegate him to the role the King of Italy was playing by the side of Mussolini.

But after Duca's murder, the Iron Guard gave up its past policy and started its campaign openly against King Carol.

" The Captain " knew quite well that the Rumanian people were loyal to their king. Ninety per cent of the inhabitants were more or less illiterate peasants to whom the person of the supreme ruler was—sacrosanct. Therefore the Iron Guard could not attack Carol directly; it had to be done by an intrigue which was hidden from the public. For this purpose Prince Nicholas of Rumania seemed to be an excellent implement.

Prince Nicholas had fallen in love, after his rather adventurous and stormy youth, with the married daughter of

Saveano, a well-known Rumanian politician. She divorced her husband and in spite of Carol's opposition, Nicholas married her. Through his morganatic marriage Nicholas lost his rank and rights.

Codreanu's emissaries sought and found easy contact with the dissatisfied royal prince. They hinted that if he would join the Iron Guard he would not only regain his lost position, but rise to be a highly important figure after Codreanu's victory.

Nicholas accepted the offer, and became a member of the Iron Guard. From this time on his name was the bait which Codreanu's men used in monarchist circles. . . .

King Carol anxiously watched " the Captain's " increasing activity, but he thought that the time had not yet arrived when he must interfere with full energy. And suddenly, through a pamphlet smuggled into the palace, he discovered that the Iron Guard was using his brother's name for purposes of agitation.

He had always possessed strong family feelings. He sent for his brother, laughingly showed him the pamphlet and asked him to find some tactful means of ending this idle gossip. Rumania must find out that Prince Nicholas has nothing to do with the assassins of the Iron Guard.

But Nicholas—refused. King Carol, who had never seriously doubted his brother, was startled to see the connection between Nicholas and Codreanu. He threatened to stop his brother's allowance and to confiscate his personal property. There was a stormy scene in the royal palace and not even the pleading of their mother, Queen Marie, could bridge the deep rift between them. Nicholas defied his brother and king—and Carol proceeded to fulfil his threat in earnest.

He realized that if he remained lenient for a single day, Codreanu soon would be installed in the Royal Palace at the Calea Victoria of Bucharest.

The same night Goga was appointed Prime Minister.

King Carol thought that Goga would simply steal Codreanu's thunder, adopt his programme and render the Iron Guard harmless.

And now the Gestapo was proved right again. We had refused to support Goga because we did not think him to be the right man—in the first place we did not think he would remain loyal to Germany. And Goga was only too glad to play the turncoat and form a cabinet—against the Iron Guard.

Luckily for Codreanu and for the Third Reich his attempt failed. It seemed that " the Captain " was right when he attacked the King and wanted to become a dictator in spite of Carol.

Another chapter followed in the struggle ; a chapter which is still wreathed in mystery. In the following pages I will try to give the gist of surmises, rumours and some inexplicable events. It is extremely difficult to get at the truth ; even the Gestapo is not omniscient, nor are those who work in its different departments fully informed about everything. But even so, it seems more or less certain that the following information is accurate and close to the truth, although its details may be different from actual happenings and actual words spoken.

King Carol was fonder of his son than of any other being on earth. Crown Prince Michael had experienced the strange fate of being King first and Crown Prince afterwards. He found in his father a perfect companion, a mentor, and a friend.

Following the advice of the British, King Carol solved the problem of educating his son in a thoroughly modern manner. He had a class organized for him which had only nine pupils. Nine districts of Rumania each sent a boy of simple family. In this way Michael had not only opportunity to learn the different idioms of his future subjects ; he also got acquainted with the different races and people living in Rumania. Carol's other aim was to create a compact, absolutely loyal circle of friends for his son—a fine bodyguard for a future king.

The whole country was startled and mystified when the King—apparently without any reason—disbanded this class and sent home the nine boys to their parents.

What had happened?

Codreanu and his Iron Guard had stretched out their tentacles after Crown Prince Michael. They had won over with skilful propaganda eight of the nine boys (the ninth was a Jew) to the youth brigade of the Iron Guard. It was all done very efficiently. Codreanu organized the League of Archangel Michael (which was a flattering allusion to the Crown Prince's own name)—the eight boys joined this decorative League . . . and unnoticeably Crown Prince Michael had been seduced to Iron Guard ideas.

The widespread intrigue of Codreanu was discovered through a tragic incident—at least, according to the information of the Gestapo, which may or may not be correct.

Crown Prince Michael, returning from some military manœuvres which he had attended, hurried excitedly to his father's study.

All the decent-feeling members of the court had taken good care not to speak a single word to the young Prince about Madame Lupescu, his father's friend. It was on her account that Michael's mother had had to leave the country. Perhaps —it was almost sure—Michael had never suspected that his mother had had to go out of his life . . . to give up her place to another woman.

During the military expedition one of the officers—naturally a member of the Iron Guard—had disclosed in front of the young boy the private affairs of the King; of course, on Codreanu's instructions. He also pointed out that Madame Lupescu, the evil influence in King Carol's life . . . was a Jewess.

It was said that the Crown Prince hurried to his father and reproached him with trembling lips—because he had sent his mother away and was now living with a Jewess. . . .

He implored Carol—this was the version of the scene— with tears in his eyes to give the power to Codreanu, the great patriot who would rid the country not only of Madame Lupescu, but of all the Jews. . . .

The king must have been horrified to notice that Codreanu had poisoned the soul of the being who was nearest to his heart . . . that he had won over his son.

Next morning, Crown Prince Michael was sent on a prolonged visit to Queen Elena in Italy. The same night in three hundred different towns and villages a sudden attack was launched on the Iron Guard.

The King had decided to break their power—once and for all.

It was early in the morning when the police report arrived stating that Codreanu had been arrested. . . .

This was the point to which I could follow the events as a personal observer, visiting Rumania several times, having many discussions with " the Captain " and perusing the reports of my colleagues at the Gestapo.

The rest I only knew from intermittent news, mostly received at second-hand.

Codreanu and his staff were sent to prison. The Rumanian newspapers and their foreign colleagues announced that King Carol would take the government into his own hands. Among his first decrees was one introducing the supreme penalty for organized revolt and seditious activities. Up to that time Rumania had had no capital punishment. . . .

It seemed that King Carol had decided to have " the Captain " sent to his death with full legal formalities, not creating a martyr, but executing a criminal.

This fact was supported by the newspaper reports. During the searches in the homes of Iron Guards, documents had been found which proved without doubt that Codreanu's men pursued regular espionage activities in all State departments, and communicated their discoveries to a foreign power. We at the Gestapo knew very well the identity of this foreign power.

It was also proved beyond doubt (at least so the Rumanian papers wrote) that Codreanu had planned a regular attack against Bucharest, on the model of the Marcia su Roma with the object of taking over the government as a dictator.

If all these proofs would be used against him, it would be easy to convict him of espionage and rebellion.

And yet he was not sentenced to death.

He was saved by Germany. Saved by the Third Reich

whose name had not been mentioned once—either during the preliminary investigation, or in the course of the sensational trial.

Whenever the questions took a trend which might have incriminated Nazi Germany or the Gestapo, the president of the court (no doubt acting on higher instructions) took good care to silence the witness or even the prosecutor.

Codreanu and most of his fifteen comrades were sentenced to ten years' hard labour in the salt-mines of Ramnicu Sarat. This was no formal death-sentence—but it almost amounted to that. Very, very few people survived ten years in those horrible wastes. . . .

It seemed as if order had been restored in Rumania.

The Iron Guard movement had apparently collapsed with the capture and imprisonment of " the Captain " and his general staff.

But although I had been transferred to another department meantime, I knew very well that a movement which had cost so many millions of marks, so many lives and so much energy, would not simply peter out because its leader and his henchmen were working in a salt-mine.

Where was the second " general staff " ?

During the period when I was in constant touch with Codreanu and had many discussions with him, I found out that there was a second " general staff " organized within the Iron Guard. Just as in Germany, " the Captain " thought of every emergency which might arise. He chose a second set of men who would automatically take his and his associates' place if anything should happen to them.

The following events were fully discussed in the world Press.

When King Carol arrived in London on a State visit with his son and heir, the Iron Guard which had been considered dead, grasped the opportunity and planned a large-scale rising, a dangerous Putsch. It was only at the last moment that their plans were frustrated and most of them killed.

The King returned hurriedly to his capital and could see with his own eyes what Codreanu's second " general staff " had inaugurated. A series of attempted assassinations, bomb outrages, armed revolts were prepared to seize the power for the Iron Guard.

And it seemed that King Carol wanted to settle the dangerous problem once and for all. All the newspapers published different versions of the following report about the execution of " the Captain," and his staff :

" According to the official report of the Second Division, the transfer of prisoners from the Ramnicu Sarat prison to Jilava had been started on the night of the 29th–30th November. At first o'clock in the morning when the prisoners and their escort were passing a forest, the cars containing the men were attacked by gun-shots fired by unknown people. After firing these shots, these attackers fled at once. At the same time, the prisoners taking advantage of the darkness, jumped from the cars and ran towards the forest with the evident intention of escape. After the gendarmes had called upon them to stop, they used their rifles. The bullets killed Zelea Codreanu, the leader of the Iron Guard who was sentenced to ten years in prison and six years' internment; the three murderers of Prime Minister Duca and the ten assassins of Stelesku, member of parliament who were all university students and all sentenced to twenty years' hard labour, were also killed.

" The military attorney of the Second Division and the civil authorities visited the scene. They confirmed the death of the fourteen prisoners and took a medical report. They gave permission for the burial of the bodies. Investigation is still going on. At the proposal of the State attorney and in the interest of public order, the burials will take place in the military graveyard of Jilava. The burial was effected during the forenoon by the prison guards of Jilava."

This was all—a few, bare sentences, covering the death of Rumania's " Fuehrer " and frustrating a great many hopes of Nazi Germany.

Most Rumanians think that with the execution of the Iron Guard's leaders this movement has ended. But in my opinion, the situation is somewhat different. They have killed Codreanu and most of his associates. The second " general staff " is in prison. But what about the third ? It had probably taken charge of the Iron Guard—and the future will show whether these men will fulfil their oath . . . sworn in front of their dead " Captain." It will also show whether Germany will be able to continue its penetration of the Balkans and whether the Gestapo will be able to go on with the work it started so " auspiciously."

★

CHAPTER XIV

THE GENTLE ART OF MURDER

" . . . And if these base attacks are continued against Germany, we shall take good care to silence our vilifiers. . . . We have the men who can put an end to the bleating of Germany's enemies. . . ."

These sentences were published in the *Essener National Zeitung* which must be considered as Field-Marshal Hermann Goering's official mouthpiece. They let loose such a howl of indignation, such a storm of outraged protest as have very few sentences ever before. Even the " Mother of Parliaments " under Big Ben's shadow heard their echo.

A member raised the question as to whether Herr Goering was threatening—among others—a well-known and highly respected English politician . . . with assassination ?

This was the first time that the " Death Brigade," or as we called them in the Gestapo : " Heydrich's Killers," were mentioned in public . . . either inside or outside Germany. The " death brigade " which punishes Germany's enemies —by killing them swiftly and ruthlessly.

When writing about the organization of the Gestapo, I mentioned the notorious " SD.RFSS. Alarm Command "— that special troop which is connected with the Special Service of the S.S. Reich Fuehrer and constitutes Heydrich's most private bodyguard. I have spoken about S.S. Flag Leader (Standartenfuehrer) Sohst, that tall, slim desperado who has killed and tortured more people than anyone in the Gestapo or the Special Service. But I did not give further details about him or his killers. . . .

Was there really a "death brigade" in Nazi Germany? they asked in Great Britain, in the United States, everywhere in the world.

I am, of course, fully aware what is entailed by betraying the secrets of this brigade of assassins.

In one or other form these men have been working for decades in Germany. Their story has never been told before. I know very well that they would make short work of anyone who attempted to tell this story. Probably—as I said before— I am signing my own death-warrant. But I also know that I have merited this death by most of the chapters in this book. You cannot kill a man twice—this trite truth gives me some support in my cynicism.

Sohst is not only the chief of the SD.RFSS. Alarm Command. With another man, Theodore Schultz, he presides over the secret tribunal of the S.S.

This tribunal has no permanent seat in Germany. It meets when and where it is needed. No accused is ever present at the trials. The president listens to the prosecutors and when he is satisfied as to the guilt of the accused, he proclaims his sentence which can only be . . . death.

And a few days later the "criminal" is found dead on some river-side. The police turn out with full apparatus; but there are no clues, no finger-prints . . . and so the case is closed. . . .

Both Theodore Schultz and Sohst first became notorious soon after the war.

Times were strange and passions ran high in post-war Germany.

The defeat of the German army and the shameful armistice was followed by a dark period. The German Reich had lost its historical rules. Hundreds of thousands of young men could not find a decent means of existence. Four years had robbed most of them of the taste and habit for regular work. Millions of people who had found employment in armament factories were now out of a job, in the street . . . and with no hope of a peaceful and prosperous future.

The officers of the army who had been assured of a safe and honourable career also faced bleak prospects. They had never learned anything but the gentle art of killing, the art of war. Tens of thousands of young men who had worn the Kaiser's uniform—preferably with a monocle—members of distinguished families whose birth-right was a high standard of living and a safe income—had lost their connections, their foundations, almost their right to live. Middle-class or even proletarian elements were sitting in the key positions for whom a well-sounding name was hardly sufficient recommendation for employment. The sons of " Junker " families, the scions of Prussian gentry had very little prospect of getting a job in Socialist Germany.

Naturally these people turned with fierce hatred against the ruling power, the left-wing men. They considered themselves to be the real Germany, robbed of their rights and privileges. It was easy to call them to the fray ; easy to make them believe that the present rulers of the Reich had betrayed Germany when they gave the order to cease fire, when they disbanded the army.

" Death to the traitors ! " became their slogan. The commissions of the Allied Powers had disarmed Germany. They collected the rifles, razed the fortresses, dragged away the cannon. And the former officers called everyone a traitor who was of any help to these commissions, who led them on the track of hidden arsenals.

All over the country secret societies were formed. A dismissed officer collected his comrades and organized a free guerrilla troop, a " league of revenge " under various names. One was called : " O.C." (Organization Consul), to which I had belonged for some time ; the other the Potsdam Free Corps, the third, Brigade of Order, and so on. Very often they bore the name of their commander ; there was a Reinhard Brigade, an Epp Brigade, etc. All these organizations were ready to participate in any Putsch against the Central Government.

But there wasn't a Putsch every week. The Free Corps had to be kept busy " between times." And in these free periods their main occupation was to " punish the traitors." If someone directed the attention of an Allied commission to a hidden arsenal, he was soon attacked and kidnapped by mysterious strangers, taken to some secluded place and killed. But the leaders of the ruling class, from ministers to the past petty secretary of a Trade Union, were also "traitors."

These underground organizations started a long series of political murders by killing Rosa Luxemburg and Karl Liebknecht in 1919. Their outrageous activities lasted for almost ten years; thousands of Germans died at their hands.

Ezzberger had to be killed because he had signed the armistice. Rathenau died for even less. Hundreds of unknown, simple citizens died for—nothing.

On the 11th January, 1919, Captain Franz von Stephani surrounded with his Free Corps the building of the Berlin Socialist paper *Vorwaerts*. His orders were simple; whoever left the building must be shot. Seven workers were killed before the police intervened. Stephani was acquitted by the court of justice. To-day he fills an important role in Nazi Germany as member of the SD.RFSS.

In March, 1919, the Berlin "Volksmarine Division" (Division of People's Navy), which consisted mostly of workers, lined up to receive its pay. About three hundred of them were gathered together.

An unknown clerk selected thirty at random and took them to another courtyard. Later it turned out that this unknown civilian was Lieutenant Marloh, a member of Reinhard's Brigade. In the courtyard Reinhard's machine-guns waited. They began to fire, without warning, on the thirty men. Twenty-nine died. The thirtieth escaped by a miracle. His companions fell on him, shielding him from the fatal bullets and the daggers of the assassins who after the machine-gunning examined the bodies, and completed the work they had started.

The court sentenced Lieutenant Marloh to a thirty-mark fine and two months in a fortress—for using forged legitimations. The commander of the Free Corps was not even summoned for examination.

. . . On the 2nd May, 1919, fifty-two Russian prisoners were walking on the high road towards Graefelfing. They would like to get home after their long, enforced absence. A " Free Corps " met them. Half an hour later the fifty-two prisoners were dead. . . .

. . . Members of the Luetzow Free Corps took twelve men into the cellars of the famous (or rather notorious) Munich Hofbraeuhaus. They were not even Socialists. All of them were executed. . . .

. . . On the 6th of May, 1919, twenty-six members of the Roman Catholic Young Men's Association named after St. Joseph met to discuss the details of a charity performance. Suddenly Captain Alt-Stutterheim entered with his men. The unsuspecting youths were led to the courtyard of the Prince George Palace and a volley fired. Seven lay dead on the flag-stones. The others were herded into the cellar and executed with knives, revolvers, truncheons. . . .

Captain Alt-Stutterheim defended himself in a strange way when he was brought to trial. He maintained that unknown men had fired at his troops which had enraged his soldiers ; he had been unable to restrain them.

And the court showed leniency and understanding. The Captain was acquitted.

During these chaotic times these fanatics were able to roam freely with their Free Corps all over Germany.

The newspapers never mentioned them ; there was never a brave man who dared to unmask their activities. Everybody knew well that he would sign his own death-warrant by doing so.

Strange and mysterious legends were spreading in the country.

The Holy Fehme. . . .

Some people recalled the mystical organization of the Middle Ages which had been kept alive for centuries in the Reich. But nobody knew what it was really doing. What was the Holy Fehme ? Who were its members and where did the secret court of justice meet whose only sentence was death ?

Most of these problems have not been cleared up even to the present day, although a great many historians were at work in pre-war Germany. All they knew was that it was the end of the man who called the attention of the Fehme to himself. It was invisible and present everywhere ; its members were in every walk of life and its sentences were mercilessly executed.

And in the years just after the war Germany realized with horror ; the Fehme of the Middle Ages had been resurrected. Its members were walking the streets of Berlin, Munich and other towns ; their ruthless sentences followed fast and sure.

Now that the Fehme murders increased week by week the Liberal and Democratic papers began to write articles about them. At first they handled the staff rather timidly, but slowly their courage became stronger.

All these articles mentioned two names. One of them was Sohst who later became the commander of " Heydrich's Killers "—the other was the former Lieutenant Theodore Schultze.

At last official republican Germany was moved to take action.

Investigation started. It was discovered that Lieutenant Schultze and Sergeant Klapproth had executed Fehme and similar sentences—at least eight times. Eight murders could be proved, although countless others were suspected.

Both Schultze and Klapproth were arrested. Their trial was a great political event.

The prosecutor disclosed every detail of the eight executions. The first victim was a worker called Brauer. His body was found sewn into a sack, his hands were bound with wire. The autopsy showed that he had been killed by stabs of a dagger. The police found out that he had last been seen in the company of a Lieutenant Kovalevski. This Kovalevski was supposed to be also one of the assassins.

The second indictment accused Lieutenant Schultze of the murder of a Lieutenant Land. Land's body had been found near the village of Dalgotz. He had been shot twice through the neck. What was his crime ? He had been spending money freely—much too freely. Lieutenant Schultze was sure that Land had betrayed the secrets of the Fehme courts to strangers and had received ample reward for his treachery. He was " executed as a traitor."

The corpse of a young baker was found mutilated by the strokes of an axe. He, too, was suspected of being a traitor. This time Lieutenant Schultze took almost fantastic measures to hide all traces of his foul deed. He buried his victim —standing . . . so that the body would be more difficult to find.

Another man killed. His name was Legner, and his only crime was that he had the legitimation of the Socialist Party in his pocket. Lieutenant Schultze and his companions made him drunk, took him to the forest of Busching and opened the arteries of the senseless young man. He was so drunk that he could not defend himself and quietly bled to death. . . .

After a trial lasting seven days, sentence was passed. Lieutenant Schultze was found guilty on all eight counts and sentenced to death. The same sentence was passed on Sergeant Klapproth who took part in all the eight murders.

But the sentences of death were never executed. Field-Marshal Paul von Hindenburg, President of the German Republic, pardoned the two men.

" Lieutenant Schultze and Sergeant Klapproth were both good and honest soldiers during the war. When they committed the eight murders, they did so in their misguided patriotic zeal. They cannot be considered common murderers." This was the explanation of the pardon.

The death sentence was changed to seven and a half years in prison and a few months later Hindenburg released the two men.

Lieutenant Schultze was free again. He was seventeen when he enlisted, he fought through the war and now, nearly thirty, he understood one thing only : how to kill.

What could such a young man do ?

There was only one possibility for him : Adolf Hitler and his Nazi movement.

By that time the brownshirts had turned the whole of Germany upside down. All over the country S.A. groups were formed. Their task was to keep order during the Nazi meetings and to break up the meetings of other parties, to terrorize the workers and act as Hitler's and his henchmen's bodyguards. For several years the S.A. and S.S.—this black-shirted organization was the Nazi police—worked hand in hand with the Free Corps. The S.A. even competed with them; they killed men of left-wing politics whenever they could. Their " territory " was identical.

In this rivalry Hitler's troops triumphed; slowly they incorporated the members of the Free Corps. Both sides gained by this process. Hitler found the men who were well versed in the art of killing very useful. On the other hand these gentlemen had no longer to worry about their pay-rolls. Hitler always found money to pay his S.A. and S.S. men. Gradually they merged completely with the Nazi organizations and continued their " patriotic " activity, persecuting, beating up, torturing and killing workers, Communists, Socialists and other enemies of National Socialism.

The authorities had a difficult task to check or imprison them. Crimes committed out of " patriotic indignation " were hard to classify as common murders. The members of the Free Corps, just as those of the S.A., always found pro-tectors in the police in the prosecutor's office or even in the law courts, who " sympathized " with them and helped them to escape just retribution.

Lieutenant Schultze—just like Sohst—became one of Hitler's most loyal followers.

He continued his work exactly at the point where he was forced to stop when he had been " unfortunately " arrested.

He was quite sure that the Nazis needed him more than he needed the Nazis—at least during these early years. Hitler needed a strong-handed man who knew how to punish mercilessly and who, at the same time, preferred to stay out of the limelight.

And Schultze began his work. . . .

Near the harbour of Kiel a small barge drifted on shore. There was a dead man in it; his hands were fastened together with wire. The autopsy stated that he had been killed by twelve stabs of a dagger.

They did not find a scrap of paper on the body; no clue pointed to his name. But when his photo was published in the newspapers, several people identified him.

It was Sergeant Klapproth, the man who had so loyally helped Lieutenant Schultze in all his murders. . . . And now the executioner had, himself, been executed. Why did he die ?

Sergeant Klapproth had lost his nerve. In the solitude of prison, while waiting for Hindenburg's pardon, of which, after all, he could not be sure, the killer began to feel remorse. He did not want to follow his career as an assassin. . . . He wanted to vanish quietly and lead a peaceful life. . . .

And Schultze mercilessly executed him—for hadn't he become a traitor ?

Nobody could say how many deaths were connected with Schultze, during the time he worked for the growing Nazi Party. So much is sure, however, he had his hands " full " in the years which preceded Hitler's coming to power.

At least he was relieved from the sometimes uncomfortable task of executing the sentences in person. He had his men, the members of the Special Service of the S.S. Reich Fuehrer, who fulfilled his commands precisely and swiftly.

One of his most lurid exploits was the murder of S.A. Troop Leader Schuenzel.

Schuenzel was a loyal and staunch member of the Party. As a primitive, simple soul he fulfilled every command without thinking about it. He showed great ingenuity in " punishing traitors " to the full satisfaction of his superiors. One day Schultze was informed that a case was being prepared against Schuenzel. He knew very well that if he were examined, this rather simple-minded man would probably betray himself ; one slip of the tongue and he would incriminate those on whose orders he had acted.

The same night Schuenzel's troop was called out on an alarm. Late at night he walked along the street at the head of his column. Suddenly there was some disturbance and noise ; the troop started to run, revolvers in hand. It was just a little " demonstration " to frighten the sleeping " Reds." Suddenly Schuenzel collapsed. His troop ran on. Passers-by found him on the pavement with a bullet in his back, dying.

He was buried as a martyr of the Party, a victim of the Communists. . . .

In September, 1931, there was another, similar tragedy in

Duesseldorf. Karl Vobis was an S.S. man, a model member of the Nazi Party; but he had one grave fault. After a few beers he became loquacious—and so there was some danger that he would talk in his cups and betray the Party.

On the 3rd September, late at night, the S.A. of the Klostestrasse received an alarm. They took up their position in the neighbouring street. After waiting a little, they saw a man passing them with rather uncertain steps. Wilhelm Scholl, an S.A. man, received a curt command from his leader. He hurried after the man and stabbed him in the back. The victim collapsed, dead; the S.A. vanished. Next day the police searched in vain for the murderer.

But on the same day Scholl was startled on discovering that the man whom he had stabbed to death was the brother of his best friend. He was a little drunk when he visited one of his superiors and reproached him; even uttered some threats. The S.A. leader thereon went to S.S. Leader Wetzel and reported the matter to him.

Twenty-four hours later Scholl was arrested for the murder. He had been denounced by the Party. According to their version Scholl was a Communist spy and agent provocateur. But the brother of Vobis had found out the real situation, and resigned from the Party. He might be rash enough to testify on behalf of his arrested friend. Not that such a thing could happen with the careful Schultze and his " death brigade "— some time before the trial the younger Vobis was found dead on the Rhine bridge near Neisse. His body bore the wounds of nine bullets. . . .

Another tragic affair happened in Upper Silesia. Bruno Novak, an S.S. leader who had executed several " sentences," began to get difficult. He, too, seemed to have lost his nerve and become an " uncertain element." One evening he was sent to a village to prepare a propaganda meeting. S.A. man Stephan Lemmer followed him, shot him in the back and then fled with his companions.

Unluckily there were some witnesses present. Lemmer was arrested the same night. It was too late to engineer his escape.

Next day Lemmer's chief visited him in prison and asked

him to save the honour of the Party.   He was to confess that
he was a Communist, that he did not really belong to the Nazis.
But Lemmer refused to make the sacrifice.

A few hours later two of his friends called on him and
agreed on a secret plan to free him the same night from his
police cell.   Everything was well prepared.   Late at night an
unknown uniformed policeman opened the door of his cell.
Outside, his friends were waiting in a car ; they started at
once, but did not travel far.   Next day he was found on the
outskirts of the town with two bullets in his head.

Lemmer had to be killed.   Whether he would have been
executed or not was a secondary question.   The main thing
was to ensure his silence.

After Hitler came to power the roles of Sohst and Schultze
became even more important.   This was the time when, under
Heydrich's guidance, they formed the Special Service Alarm
Command.   Its members were all trusted and well-tried men
who had no other task but to execute the death-sentences in a
way which would not leave any trace of the victim.   And
now their work began to spread abroad. . . .

Nazi Germany started its campaign against the refugees,
and this war, which has been going on for more than five
years, is still unfinished.

The " death brigade " took a great part in the silencing of
Germans who fled abroad.   The first case which caused world-
wide sensation was the so-called Formis affair.

A year after Hitler became Chancellor there was great
excitement in the circles of the Gestapo caused by a short-wave
radio sender.   This sender was making ruthless, well-docu-
mented propaganda all over the world—against the Third
Reich.   It worked undisturbed all through 1934 without
anyone suspecting where it was situated.   Goebbels was in a
constant rage, and the Gestapo was severely reproached
because its searches and investigations were all in vain.

The wireless experts who had been set on the trail of the
secret transmitter maintained that it must be somewhere in
Czechoslovakia.   But our local agents did not find any clue.
In response to the energetic protests and demands of the
German legation the Czech police also began to make inquiries.

But they did not show any special zeal, rather they felt malicious glee about the mysterious sender which was causing the Germans so much annoyance.

At last the Fuehrer himself became furious and during September Himmler and Heydrich lived in a constant panic.

Experts were sent in motor-cars to Poland, Austria, and Hungary, also to Slovakia. They took the finest instruments, the best equipment, and their work fixed the seat of the station somewhere in the centre of Czechoslovakia. New, strict orders were sent to the local agents, and a number of excellent spies were sent from Berlin to pursue the investigation.

At last, in November, 1934, a brilliant woman agent of the Gestapo, Louis Konrad, reported that the secret sender was installed in the Hotel Zahori near Prague, and was managed by the engineer, Rudolf Formis.

It was rather strange that we had found this out only with such great difficulty. We ought to have considered the possibility much earlier. Formis's name was not unknown to the Gestapo; we had had some trouble with him before.

Once a speech of Hitler was transmitted by the Stuttgart radio. Formis was one of its chief engineers. During the speech someone cut the cable so that the Fuehrer was speaking —into empty air. As a responsible man, Formis was placed under observation and soon sent to a concentration camp. He managed to escape and cross the frontier. He became acquainted with the former Nazi leader Otto Strasser who was himself an exile after his brother had been murdered. Formis offered him his brilliant technical knowledge and established his short-wave sender which transmitted the news of Strasser's anti-Nazi Party, the so-called Black Front—to Goebbels' intense annoyance.

Sohst and Schultze began their work at once to prevent Formis from pursuing his activities. A hand-picked group of agents was detailed. According to the plan, Formis was to be taken in a car to Germany; or if this should prove impossible, he must be killed on the spot.

At the beginning of January, a German Mercedes car stopped in front of the Prague Hotel Wilson and three people got out, two men and a woman. They registered as Mr. and Mrs. Hans Mueller (maiden name : Edith Kersbach), and Gert Schubert. After spending a few days in the Czech capital they left by car for the village of Stehvice and again took rooms at an hotel. It was only a few miles to the Hotel Zahori which was situated in a small, hidden valley of the River Moldva ; a one-storied secluded building in which Formis and his sender were installed.

The daring engineer knew very well that the Gestapo was out for his blood ; that was the reason why he chose this hidden little hotel for his *pied-à-terre*. He worked so well that not even the staff of the hotel knew anything about the sender installed in room number six.

Next day the little party took a walk to the valley of the Moldva till they reached the Hotel Zahori. Here they stayed overnight. In the evening they scraped acquaintance with Formis in the small dining-room of the hotel. The unlucky man must have been off his guard ; anyhow he became friends with his future murderers.

Next day Mueller returned to Prague and flew to Berlin, where he reported that contact had been established with Formis. Then he flew back to Prague and began the preparations with his associates. A host of other agents helped them.

The last development of the drama followed quickly. On the 23rd January, 1935, Hans Mueller and his wife again arrived at the Hotel Zahori and took room number four. Schubert stayed outside on the nearby high road with the car. At seven o'clock in the evening, Formis was sitting in the restaurant with the two friendly compatriots. Mueller later declared that he was very tired and going to his room ; but his " wife " continued her conversation with Formis. The innkeeper and the lonely waiter went to bed. Everybody was asleep at the hotel when Formis started upstairs with Edith Kersbach. During this time Hans Mueller let down a rope from his window and Schubert climbed up.

The woman succeeded in luring Formis to her room. Mueller and Schubert were already waiting and rushed at him. They wanted to chloroform him and drag him to the car.

But Formis fought desperately; he knew that he was struggling for his life. He succeeded in getting out his gun. But at this moment two shots were fired at him. Both were accurate.

By the time the waiter was awakened, the drama was almost finished. The trembling Bohemian youth must have thought it a nightmare when a man, revolver in hand, forced him to raise his arms. Mueller dragged back Formis' body to the engineer's room and then ordered the waiter to return to his bed and never move an inch. A few moments later there was a detonation; a bomb destroyed the bed and the sender which was hidden in it. The room caught fire and the head of the body was also damaged.

At last the waiter and the owner of the hotel found some courage and tiptoed up from the basement. But by that time everything was ended. The murderers were flying towards the frontier. By the time the gendarmes were notified, they had passed the danger line. At five o'clock in the morning the big Mercedes car arrived at Schneeberg, the Czech-German frontier, with only two male passengers. The barrier was closed. The two men jumped from the car, left it, and hurried on foot across the border. They were safe; friends waited and swift cars took them to Berlin.

What happened to Edith Kersbach?

About seven o'clock in the morning, two men carried a gravely injured woman across the frontier at Rosenthal. A military ambulance was waiting on the German side; the wounded woman was taken at once to the nearby Koenigstein hospital where she received first-aid and was transported to Dresden.

Formis had defended himself with the strength of a desperate man. He had fired his gun—once—and hit Edith Kersbach. The unexpected resistance forced his attackers to finish him. Mueller and Schubert dragged the unconscious woman to the car and drove off. But on their way they hurriedly discussed the matter. The severely wounded Edith Kersbach might prove a difficulty with the Czech authorities. So they stopped near the frontier and put her down by the roadside, close to a village in which some confederates of theirs were waiting.

They notified them and drove on. The other agents took care of getting Edith Kersbach into Germany.

The only clue left behind was the Mercedes. Even this might prove uncomfortable, as the Czech police were certain to investigate the murder with every means at their disposal.

The S.S. group waiting at Rosenthal was wakened at dawn. In a few minutes they were on their way towards the German-Czech frontier. They stopped. Only Group Leader Kreibisch crossed to the Czech side. He had the necessary papers ready to claim the abandoned car. The Czechs did not raise any difficulty and the Mercedes was driven into Germany.

It was lucky for the Czech customs officers that they did not make any difficulty. The S.S. group had been instructed to get the Mercedes at any cost—by force, if necessary.

For the Black Front the death of Formis and the destruction of his secret sender was a heavy blow. In the subsequent weeks a great many German refugees left Prague and Czecho-slovakia as they did not feel safe any longer. Otto Strasser himself changed his headquarters. Formis and his sender were not replaced; the activity of the Black Front was so diminished that Goebbels could be satisfied with the result.

The Gestapo had done its job efficiently.

Another " case " of the " death brigade " ended in failure, but, even so, caused a world-wide sensation.

This was the famous Strasser affair.

Dr. Otto Strasser had been for years Hitler's most efficient collaborator with his brother, Gregor Strasser. Their organiz-ing talent was of immense importance to the Nazi movement.

But at the beginning of 1930 great controversies arose between Hitler and Otto Strasser. The Fuehrer wanted to settle the matter amicably. He offered 90,000 marks for Otto Strasser's newspaper, the *Berliner Arbeiterzeitung*, the post of the Party's Press chief with a monthly salary of 1200 marks and emoluments. But Otto Strasser did not accept the offer; he broke with Hitler and founded the Black Front which kept the original Socialist points of the Nazi programme. His brother, Gregor Strasser, stayed with Hitler and was still an important member of the Party. Yet in December, 1932, he also left it. He thought that if he just kept quiet and did not meddle in politics he could live in peace. But on the 30th June, 1934, he also fell a victim to the German St. Bartholomew's Night—chiefly because General von Schleicher had wanted to make him Chancellor. . . .

Otto Strasser combatted Hitler till the Nazis came to power. Then he fled from Germany and continued his campaign abroad. Nobody in the world has caused so many uncomfortable hours to the Nazi overlords as Otto Strasser. Naturally, he was doomed. But Otto Strasser knew his former comrades too well to run into any trap. He moved to Prague and carried on his attacks.

Schultze and Sohst dogged Strasser's steps, but did not succeed in " eliminating " him. Just before the 30th June it became highly important again to silence the dangerous opponent. They knew in Berlin what a terrible weapon Otto Strasser would forge from the German St. Bartholomew's Night. A plan was evolved to kidnap him and, if possible, bring him alive to Germany.

Several Gestapo agents had succeeded in gaining entrance to the organization of the Black Front. " Refugees " came to Strasser and offered their services. Some of them even showed a newspaper containing his photograph as a man urgently wanted by the Nazi Police. Such a newspaper cutting was the best recommendation in exile. Two of them, Hildebrandt and Dr. Mahr, succeeded in getting into Strasser's most intimate circle.

In April, 1934, after Strasser had delivered an anti-Hitler lecture at Prague University, some Czech acquaintances of his called his attention to a Dutch manufacturer called Frank who wanted to be introduced to him. Strasser saw Frank, who told him that he was trying to get in contact with him on behalf of his English friends. These friends maintained an office in London which also wanted to make anti-Hitler propaganda, and they would be willing not only to co-operate, but to support Strasser with money. In principle Strasser agreed to the offer, whereupon Frank left promising to send news soon.

P

A week later Frank rang up Strasser from Amsterdam, telling him that everything was settled and he would return soon to discuss the details. A week later he reappeared. During the conferences he demanded details of the Black Front's organization so that he could inform his friends ; but Strasser refused to betray anything at such an early stage. Frank also pressed the request of his " friends " that Strasser should employ as leader of the organization either Hildebrandt or Mahr. Strasser again said that he would decide about this later.

The discussions had to be broken off because Strasser had to go to Paris, and from there to the Saar District where his organization was working strongly (he co-operated for a time with Max Braun). Frank at once offered to accompany him. But Strasser must have smelt a rat, for he did not accept the offer ; he only promised to visit Frank in Paris.

At this meeting Frank proposed that they should go together to Saarbruecken. Strasser again found some excuse to refuse, but he made an appointment to meet Frank at the Hotel Reichsadler in the Saar capital.

On the 23rd June they met there. It was very hot, and Frank offered the use of his bathroom to Strasser, who accepted gratefully.

This would be the end of the story, but fate intervened. Strasser had taken off his coat and put his watch on a table when he saw that it was almost noon, and he had to hurry to meet a friend. He gave up the idea of a shower and rushed away—to Frank's keen disappointment. But before Strasser went they agreed to meet again at five o'clock.

Around the hotel a number of broad-shouldered, strong-armed young men had been gathering. Hand-picked men ; a little farther off, a car waited. These people, who were all unprepared for Strasser's rushing away, glanced startled after their vanishing quarry. Two of them followed him cautiously when he went to lunch with his friend. In the meantime feverish planning went on in the hotel.

After lunch Strasser and his friend went to the Café Kiefer. The car which had been waiting near the Hotel Reichsadler glided now close to the café; the sturdy young men walked up and down waiting for Strasser, whom they expected to return to the hotel.

Fate intervened again. The café was crowded; Strasser's friend proposed that they should go to his lodgings to have coffee and a chat. They took a short cut through the back-door of the café. Time passed quickly in discussion and Strasser noticed suddenly that his train was leaving in a few seconds. He had only time to write a short note of apology to Frank and then hurry to the station.

And yet the whole plan had been to make him helpless in the hotel room, put him into a big trunk, and take him across the frontier in the waiting car. Strasser did not even suspect the series of lucky escapes he had had. The Gestapo agents sent from Germany had received orders to use force if necessary. The " Dutch manufacturer," Frank, was one of the most skilful members of the " death brigade."

It would be wrong to suppose that the failure caused them to abandon the plan. As Strasser did not suspect anything, Frank could continue his work.

A little later he appeared again in Prague, telling him that his " friends " were expecting Strasser in London to have personal discussions. An aeroplane was waiting to take him there. Strasser was afraid that the plane might have to land in Germany and refused the offer. Then Frank proposed that Dr. Mahr, Strasser's collaborator, who had been a pilot, should fly him over. Strasser still refused. Dr. Mahr was also in Frank's pay. Strasser was willing to go to London by way of Paris; but Frank objected to that. This roused Strasser's suspicions and he would not have anything to do with the cunning agent after that.

A little later he discovered that his " loyal " men, Hildebrandt and Mahr, received regularly large sums from Frank whereupon he expelled them from his Party.

The Gestapo did not succeed in kidnapping Otto Strasser, but in most cases they " finished their job."

Another sensational affair was the kidnapping of the German refugee journalist, Berthold Jakobs. (One of the greatest living English novelists based some provocative chapters of his latest novel on it.) One of its main actors was Dr. Hans Wesemann, who broke his neck over this case.

Berthold Jakobs was writing fulminant articles against Nazi Germany. He had succeeded with great difficulty in escaping with his wife from the Third Reich before the Gestapo could arrest him. He had no passport, but he was able to settle in Strasbourg. He figured prominently on Schultze's list because he published a series of sensational articles about German armaments. He was an expert in these questions, which was an uncomfortable fact for Berlin.

Hans Wesemann visited Berthold Jakobs. He introduced himself as a German journalist working for English newspapers. Jakobs lived with his wife in very modest circumstances, and Wesemann's plan was based on this. Wesemann first bought the English rights of Jakobs' articles which had been already published elsewhere. Of course, Jakobs and his wife were overjoyed at this unexpected income. Their acquaintance became more intimate. The rest went according to plan.

Wesemann intimated that he hated Nazi Germany. He knew very well that Jakobs had much trouble with the French authorities as he had no passport. He skilfully alluded to the fact that he could get him one. Jakobs was overjoyed, as he wanted to leave France. His happiness was increased when Wesemann told him later that through him Jakobs could place his articles in well-paying English papers.

After preparing the ground, Wesemann and his companions, Manz, Becker, and Krause—all members of the " Alarm Command "—or more vulgarly, the " death brigade "—made the last preparations for the kidnapping.

Wesemann wrote and telephoned to his new friend from Paris ; on the first of March he visited him again and told him that through his friends at Basle he could get a forged passport, and at the same time sign his agreement with the English newspapers. Jakobs was happy to go to Basle with his unselfish friend. He would only pass through Switzerland ; he did not think how near the German frontier was to his destination.

On the 9th of March he and Wesemann arrived at the

restaurant " Zum schiefen Eck " in Basle. They were waiting for a man from Liechtenstein who was supposed to bring the forged passport. At seven o'clock this man appeared—he was Manz, the member of Sohst's and Schultze's brigade—he showed an empty passport form ; then he advised them to go to the nearby village, Riehen, where he lived and where they could fill up the form and put the necessary stamps on it. Jakobs was dazed by his unexpected luck, he forgot all his mistrust and accepted the proposition.

The three men started in a car driven by Krause, another Gestapo agent. In this district the Swiss-German border runs in a zigzag. Some of the highroads cross German soil and return again to Swiss territory. The road on which Jakobs and his " friends " were driving was sometimes only thirty or forty yards from the frontier.

Near Kleinhueningen a short road leads to the customs shed. Here the car, which had been proceeding at a great speed, accelerated suddenly and, hooting wildly, drove towards the frontier. The unsuspecting Swiss frontier guards jumped away quickly while the car passed under the German barrier— which was standing open by a convenient " accident."

Beyond the barrier the car slowed down ; a few hundred yards farther it stopped in front of a group of uniformed men who had signalled to it with a lantern.

Poor Berthold Jakobs was still dazed when he was dragged from the car and saw that he was the prisoner of German policemen.

The play-acting was not yet finished. In order to retain Jakobs' confidence, Wesemann and the others began to protest. They had crossed into Germany only by mistake. They thought they were still in Switzerland. Of course, this was no use . . . Jakobs was a prisoner, as he believed, together with his " friends." But he sat alone in a cell, still incredulous of his plight.

As the frontier law had been violated and a kidnapping committed, Mrs. Jakobs had to be pacified in the first place so that she should not raise the alarm. She received a telegram the same day, signed by her husband, which told her that everything was all right, but Jakobs had to stay away for some time. A few days later another wire was sent which announced an unexpected trip; later, a money order for two hundred francs followed for the anxious woman, but even this did not reassure her. She found the matter more and more suspicious and turned to the authorities. The Swiss police quickly finished their investigations; the kidnapping was discovered.

Wesemann thought that the whole affair was finished. He had received a new appointment which took him to Italy; he returned through Switzerland. But when he wanted to leave this country at Basle, he was arrested and charged with kidnapping.

The proofs were incontrovertible; he had to confess his guilt, although he still maintained it was a mistake which took them to Germany.

The Swiss Foreign Office demanded the extradition of Berthold Jakobs. Under the pressure of universal indignation, the Third Reich was forced to grant the request. After spending six months in prison, Jakobs was delivered to the Swiss authorities. But at the same time the representatives of Nazi Germany accused him of being an accomplice in trying to procure a forged passport. The Swiss had to accept this charge and expel Jakobs from Swiss territory.

The Gestapo had certainly " lost face " before the world. The official report denounced Wesemann and pointed out that he had acted on his own initiative without any official appointment. But this was the usual way of disowning a secret agent who had failed. . . .

And yet Wesemann was one of the most efficient members of the " death brigade " who had a great many successes on his " merit-list." One of his most important achievements was connected with the so-called Balling case.

Karl Balling had been the secretary of a Trade Union in pre-Nazi Germany. He had succeeded in escaping to Copenhagen with his wife. Here they pursued strong anti-Hitler activities, keeping in touch with the illegal organization in Germany. The kidnapping of Balling seemed to be of paramount importance; not only to stop his own activity, but in the hope that if he should be captured he would betray his associates inside Germany.

In the autumn of 1934 Balling made the acquaintance of an amiable German exile. He found out that the young man who hated Hitler with all his heart had been for long years a member of the German Socialist Party. He had a membership card in the name of Paul Schroeder. Schroeder was supposed to be a collaborator of a London newspaper and to have come to Copenhagen to interview different politicians. In the beginning he was rather reserved, but later took Balling into his confidence, telling him about his anti-Nazi activities in London and in other places. Later, the " journalist " returned to London, but did not forget his new friend ; he wrote several letters to Balling.

In the course of this correspondence he succeeded in making Balling believe that with his help he could obtain a good position in England and continue his political work much more efficiently. He told Balling that he had prepared the ground for him ; when he came to Denmark the next time he would take his friend back to London with him.

At the beginning of January, 1935, Schroeder again arrived at Copenhagen. Balling said good-bye to his wife and friends ; Mrs. Balling was to follow him later to London. Then he set out on his way with Schroeder. They were travelling in a car with two friends of Schroeder's to whom it belonged.

The rest was easy. For some reason the car stopped in a lonely spot. Next moment Balling faced three guns, and a few minutes later he lay unconscious under a chloroformed cloth. The car drove on towards the frontier. The Danes did not make any difficulty about the " invalid " being taken to Germany for an urgent operation.

At the end of January Mrs. Balling—to her great surprise— received a letter from Germany. Her husband asked her to come to Berlin ; she had nothing to fear, everything was safe and settled.

Mrs. Balling did not hesitate for long. She left Denmark, arrived at the German frontier—and was immediately arrested.

Nobody will ever find out what means the Gestapo used to force Balling into setting such a cruel trap for his own wife.

But a few days later a gentleman appeared at Balling's Copenhagen flat who had a bunch of keys and Balling's letter as authority. He went up to the flat, packed every scrap of paper found there, and took them away.

"Schroeder," of course, had never been the correspondent of any English paper—he was no else but Dr. Hans Wesemann, one of the cunning members of the Special Service in the Gestapo.

To gain success the "death brigade" would do everything to protect its agents. It supplied them with men and money; every official, consulate, travel bureau, was at their disposal if necessary. But if a member got into hot water, if he was clumsy enough to be unmasked by foreign authorities and caused unpleasant notice, harmful to the prestige of the Third Reich, he would be dropped like a hot coal.

This was the fate of Dr. Hans Wesemann when he had failed after triumphing so often. And yet he had never displayed such skill as in the case which cost him his job and freedom. He failed because he trusted too much in his own cunning and the protection of the German authorities.

Franz Kruschwitz, another Gestapo agent, was much more lucky in another kidnapping which also failed. Kruschwitz was saved at the last moment by his superiors.

He had received instructions in January, 1935, to kidnap Johann Gutzeit, a German refugee worker who was employed in the Dutch Mengelo. Gutzeit, who had been a member of a Trade Union for a long time, continued his activities in exile and took an active part in smuggling "illegal" propaganda material into the Third Reich.

Kruschwitz and his companions arrived in Holland, and first of all tried to find out everything about Gutzeit's habits. After that one of them made his acquaintance. He told him that he could get him a very good job in Haarlem; he was even willing to take him there in his car and present him to his prospective employer. Gutzeit accepted gratefully. A few days later—in the meantime Kruschwitz had settled everything for the transport of his victim to Germany—the Gestapo agent appeared in his car and started with Gutzeit. The latter did not even notice the detour which the car was making until it suddenly began to race and rushed through the

Dutch frontier at Gronau. Here again the barrier was open on the German side and Gutzeit was on the territory of the Third Reich.

Kruschwitz had thought that the matter was finished and the job well done. But the Dutch were of a different opinion. A few weeks later Kruschwitz was sent with a new appointment to Holland and there he was arrested on a charge of kidnapping.

I have said before that Kruschwitz had important patrons who did everything to. save him. The Gestapo offered to return Gutzeit in exchange for its agent.

On the 18th May there was a dramatic scene at Glamerburg on the Dutch-German frontier. The Dutch police appeared with an acquaintance of Gutzeit, whose task it was to prove his identity. Soon the German police arrived with their prisoner. They told the Dutchmen that Gutzeit was free to go wherever he wanted. But Gutzeit listened with bowed head to this magnanimous declaration. Suddenly he began to speak and said that he wanted to stay in Germany. He even repeated this strange statement. The Dutch were forced to leave without him, and Gutzeit returned in deep distress to Germany.

This refuted every proof against Kruschwitz and the Dutch authorities were forced to release him.

The Gestapo had used a simple and brutal method. They arrested Gutzeit's family. He met them and saw their plight. Then he was told what they expected of him ; if he did not agree to it his brothers and aged mother would never regain their freedom. And Gutzeit sacrificed himself for their sakes.

Very often it was said in the world Press that this or that German exile had become the victim of unknown or escaped murderers. The Gestapo took good care to organize the retreat of its agents with all possible circumspection. In the first place it assures thereby the strong *morale* of its agents. It would be very disheartening for agents working abroad to hear of the arrest or execution of their colleagues. No job was ever tackled before the line of escape had been worked out.

Even if the foreign police found out the name of the

criminals, it did not matter. Months later they received a reply from Germany : the man in question could not be found.

In such a case the " wanted " agent received a new appointment, and naturally new identification papers, so that he could continue his work in another country.

To render German exiles harmless has always been one of the main tasks of the Gestapo. Their agents often use fantastic methods to attain their aims.

The most frequent was that these agents reported as exiles in the cities where genuine refugees lived in large numbers.

It was easy to get the necessary papers for them. The forms and seals of the old Trade Unions were all in the hands of the Gestapo ; they had also free access to all the documents and files of the labour organizations.

After the first groups of refugees, soon the hordes of pseudo-exiles arrived. Often the tragi-comic situation arose that the real refugee who had escaped across the border without carrying any dangerous papers on him was received with suspicion ; while the men of the Gestapo, whose pockets were full of letters and documents, were greeted with open arms. Thus they could do their jobs easily.

The pseudo-refugees organized themselves with real German thoroughness wherever they settled, and soon rendered harmless a good many members of anti-Nazi communities.

Such masqueraders had a great many weapons for their campaign.

The Dutch police expelled a large number of refugees till they found out by accident that it was not the " real " criminals whom they had put across the frontier ; not those whom they believed to be the secret agents of the Gestapo. The latter denounced the more dangerous anti-Hitler exiles as Gestapo-men. For a long time the police fell for this trick. Of course, these denouncers could always supply the best credentials.

There are, of course, various methods to be used against the members of refugee-groups, all depending on the circumstances. The skilful agent of the " death brigade " always finds the best ways and means to approach his victim.

In the editorial office of a German anti-Nazi newspaper,

published in Paris, a telephone mechanic appeared just before the lunch-hour. He said that the lines would have to be repaired. But he behaved a little suspiciously and so he was watched. The staff acted as if they were leaving the office, asking the mechanic to give the key to the janitor when he had finished.

As soon as the " workman " felt himself to be alone and unobserved, he forced open a drawer and started to investigate the documents in it. But this time his stratagem failed and he was arrested.

But a similar trick is almost always successful. A Gestapo agent can always gain entrance as a telephone mechanic, a gas company collector, or a plumber. Nobody minds having repairs done—free.

It may be a salesman or an insurance broker who visits the refugee. When he " notices " that he is calling on an exile, he sets about recounting the terrible sufferings he has had to endure before escaping from hated Nazi-land. He has all his credentials and papers handy, showing that he has belonged for a long time to some worker's union. The unsuspecting exile very often takes him into his confidence.

Another frequent method : two immaculately dressed gentlemen appear in the flat or house of the refugee ; they discreetly communicate the fact that they are detectives and asks him to accompany them. His fate is sealed if he does . . . and very few people have the pluck to verify such a demand by telephoning the police.

Many are the ways and devious the methods, but they all aim at the same thing : to get rid of the enemies of the Third Reich, by hook or by crook—preferably by " crook "—and silence the critics outside Germany. Sohst and Schultze are still working to the satisfaction of Heydrich and the still higher chief : Adolf Hitler.

Let me add a word of advice to the political refugee.

Always keep some handy weapon—and be careful to have the necessary licence for it. Don't open your door to strangers —even if you find this uncomfortable. Never go out alone in the evening ; and even if you walk in company, avoid deserted streets. If you can do so, buy your food yourself and prepare it alone. You may be considered a crazy eccentric, but life is sweet, and if you don't want to end it abruptly, guard yourself against emergencies. The tentacles of the Gestapo are very long—let's hope you and I both escape them. . . .

CHAPTER XV

★

THE GESTAPO IN SPAIN

I<small>T IS FAR FROM</small> my intention to maintain that my activities in Spain from the second half of 1934 to 1936 had an essential importance in preparing the Spanish insurrection. I had been acting on behalf of the Gestapo as usual, holding a special appointment from Heydrich himself. But I think that the following pages offer a true sketch, a series of irrefutable episodes, facts, and personalities which may help to prove that the idea of the Spanish Civil War was first conceived in Berlin and directed for years from Germany. Perhaps some later historian will find some useful data in this chapter if he wants to write an unbiased account of the tragedy in the Spanish arena. . . .

When in 1934 I sent my first report about my experiences in Spain I viewed the situation of the German organization on the Iberian peninsula rather pessimistically.

The different German institutions and agencies were in a very bad state. Gil Robles, who came to power in 1933, had helped the German interests, as he was a dyed-in-the-wool Fascist. Their leaders had an easy time and earned huge sums. But for this very reason they intrigued against each other and fought like wolves. For every good job there were dozens of self-appointed candidates who schemed against each other. The man who had good connections progressed rapidly. Hardly had he filled some job, when he flew out again, however —unless he had had the necessary pull *and* skill.

To cite an example : Consul Rehmann lost his job in San Sebastian through the intrigues of Group Leader Beisel

238   INSIDE THE GESTAPO

because the latter was a friend of Zuchristian, chief of the whole organization. Rehmann was followed by Leistert—and the first act of the new consul was to dismiss the man (Beisel) who had intrigued against his predecessor and whom, after all, he had to thank for his own promotion. A similar fight-for-all-comers was going on everywhere.

For clever men such a confusion was simply an advantage. Herr Steffin, for instance, who conducted the German secret group in Madrid, embezzled huge amounts, whereupon an investigation was started against him. But he simply bribed the investigators and was—promoted and transferred to the Madrid Labour Front. Here he again embezzled some money, another investigation followed ; and the result ? He was again promoted and transferred to an important post of the South-American organization.

Even dirtier and more scandalous things happened in Barcelona, Madrid, Malaga, and Saragossa. The leaders denounced each other secretly. If they did not succeed in blackening their rival's character in Germany, they turned to the Spanish authorities. There was hardly one among them who had not something to hide and this method of intrigue and counter-intrigue proved very effective. In the worst cases the Nazis, in order to avoid scandal, were forced to shield or help the victim to escape. Naturally all this damaged the work of German penetration and propaganda.

The German organizations in Spain were—up to 1936— under the authority of the Hamburg Political Police. The agents of the Gestapo were placed everywhere in offices and agencies, working under the cover of the " Harbour Service."

Now the foreign organization of this " Harbour Service " demanded the right to conduct the whole work as the Spanish representative of the Nazi Party, supervising all activities ; even tried to claim the right of appointments and promotions for those Gestapo agents who were detailed for duty within its territory.

In Madrid I found a number of Gestapo agents who were almost desperate ; they felt they were only puppets of the

"Harbour Service." Of course Himmler and Heydrich were far away in Berlin, while this organization was on the spot. Whether it was the kidnapping of a Communist worker or espionage against some factory, everything had to be reported to the " Harbour Service " and its instructions taken into consideration. Koerner, the leader of the Madrid branch of the Gestapo, did not know what to do.

We had to go about the thing cautiously. I visited the leaders of this rival organization and explained my anxiety about the dangers of double correspondence. All the secret letters went on two different routes to Germany, through the " Harbour Service's " foreign organization to Hamburg and through the Gestapo to Berlin. They accepted my objections and offered to simplify matters. All correspondence should go through the diplomatic couriers and they would send on the copies from Hamburg to the Berlin Gestapo centre. I avoided giving a decision, saying that this was Koerner's business. Next day Koerner received a polite note demanding that all correspondence should be thereafter sent to the " Auslandsorganisation." Koerner asked my advice. I told him that I would not interfere with administrative matters, but it was better not to provoke the anger of the Party—and the " Harbour Service " did represent the Party. This was Koerner's opinion too and he acted according to it. But only for a short time. Heydrich became furious when a few days later he noticed the meddling of the " Auslandsorganisation " and that it was remitting the correspondence of the Gestapo. The first victim was Koerner, who was dismissed at once. But his successor received strict orders that the only instructions which he was to follow must come from the Gestapo.

I was sorry to have sacrificed Koerner, but there was no alternative. But thereafter work went on smoothly. At last the Gestapo became independent in Spain.

This was the situation in 1934—but it changed suddenly.

All the organizations were headed by energetic, efficient men who had the full confidence of the Party. Nobody could suspect the things which were brewing ; but everybody knew that these large-scale preparations were not inspired by purely commercial reasons.

It was no longer our task to cover the Spanish market and to silence a few meddlesome refugees ; all of us felt that it was something bigger, something more important.

Yes, something was brewing. . . .

About this time—it was my second trip to Spain—the Gestapo sent a whole " general staff " to the Iberian peninsula to organize the well-tried network of the Gestapo in the country.

The main task was to hide the Secret State Police in the different organizations, firms, associations, were it could not be discovered.

The most important institution was the so-called " Harbour Service." There was hardly a German merchant, firm, of enterprise in Spain which had not something to do with shipping, and a German organization serving this purpose could not raise any objection among the Spanish authorities.

This was an excellent method not only in Spain, but in many other countries. The chief of all these " Harbour Services " was Kurt Wermke, highly valued collaborator of Himmler and Heydrich. His Berlin office was the centre for the activity of the Gestapo in Spain. Our organization was under his administrative authority except the special branches.

The outward structure of the " Harbour Service " was very complicated. Only the main departments figured in it, because there was no serious danger even if they were unmasked. But the most important work was done in the sub-departments which were independent units and belonged to the territory of the local " Harbour Service " centres.

These sub-departments which did all the dangerous jobs (espionage, etc.) were masked by private firms or innocent associations. One of the most important was the *Academic Exchange Service (Akademischer Austauschdienst)* which, under the cover of scientific exchanges, conducted part of the industrial espionage. Military espionage was pursued by an engineering firm called " Windkraft Centrale " (Aircraft Centre) which had branches and representatives all over the country. But our men worked in a great many other private firms.

The five main departments of the " Harbour Service " did the supervision, the observation of its own association, refugees, suspected persons, and that of the Spanish political parties. Even our highest party members, the consuls and the members of the legation had to be watched. The rest of the work consisted in spying at the postal communications and the supervision of the S.A. men who had already been introduced secretly. The real espionage was the task of a special sub-department.

The most important fighting organization was the so-called Public Security Branch, whose members were the toughest and strongest S.A. men. I might almost call it also the " terror-brigade."

Often rebellious or suspicious people had to be sent to Germany. Sometimes dangerous refugees had to be dealt with who could have easily demoralized the Germans in Spain by describing the situation at home. Again sometimes from here German smugglers directed the illegal removal of currency and property still locked up in Germany.

Sometimes the withdrawal of a passport sufficed. At other times we had to use stronger methods, as, for instance, in the case of Ludwig Felsenstein.

Felsenstein had got into hot water in Berlin where he commanded an S.A. group. But he succeeded in escaping to Switzerland and from there to Spain. The Gestapo ordered his return. But this man was possessed of devilish cunning ; we did not succeed in luring him to a German ship. Then two Gestapo men became acquainted with him in Barcelona. They went to a harbour inn and began to drink. A nearby motor boat was waiting to take him to a German ship. But Felsenstein could carry his drink very well; in the end the two Gestapo agents " passed out," while their victim remained more or less sober. But even he felt the effect of alcohol : he paid for the drinks from the money in the wallet of one of the Gestapo men and replaced it by an ironical note stating the fact. Then he left in high spirits.

Next day the Spanish police arrested him—for theft. The

Q

two Gestapo men had denounced him for felony and slander because he had called them German agents. Felsenstein was sentenced to six weeks' imprisonment. But while he was sitting in a Barcelona prison, an employee of the consulate appeared and demanded his extradition, proving with documents that Felsenstein had embezzled seven hundred and fifty marks in Berlin from the firm where he was employed. In truth Felsenstein had never worked for the firm. But he protested in vain; the court believed the well-dressed and suave attorney of the consulate and not the ragged tramp who hardly knew any Spanish and who was also proved to have been an S.A. man in Berlin. He was extradited and Spanish gendarmes took him to a German ship. . . .

Sometimes a man had to be taken on shipboard by force. There were innumerable methods for this. A dangerous refugee would roam the harbour trying to find work. A Spanish boat which was unloading would offer him a job. He would go on deck where he was hit with a rubber truncheon; he lost consciousness. Charitable Germans put the "poor sick man" into a motor boat and hurried to the German ship waiting in the outer harbour. Nobody ever asked for him.

Another refugee met a jovial Portuguese gentleman who on a Sunday afternoon invited him to a little sailing trip. When they were far enough from shore a motor boat appeared and gunmen forced him to follow them. . . .

Next day the Spanish building firm which employed him received a letter in his handwriting; his affairs had called him unexpectedly to Norway. There could be no doubt about the authenticity of the letter. His Spanish chief had no reason to run to the police.

Of course sometimes a kidnapped man never arrived in Germany. If scandal had to be avoided, he vanished silently somewhere in the Bay of Biscay, weighted with a sack of coal or some scrap iron; and if the log had to contain his name he was accounted for as a victim of appendicitis who had died suddenly. . . .

Observation and supervision work was much simpler. I have always found that most people are too comfortable to be cautious and they trust everybody—or at least suspect very few strangers.

Let us take a well-frequented café. Nobody could imagine how much information the lady who sits in the telephone exchange, or even the guardian of the cloakrooms, could supply. . . . Not to mention an alert waiter !

In families we often succeeded in " planting " a modest, quiet, diligent German nurse who had wonderful references and took care of the children for a ridiculously small sum. After a few weeks she proved herself so loyal that she was trusted completely. The master of the house did not hide his letters or business papers as the nurse " didn't know any Spanish," except the little she had picked up during her short stay. It was so much better for the children ; they were certain to learn German.

But three months was quite enough ; the reports of the " nurse " gave an exact picture of the whole life and secrets of the Spanish business-man, industrialist, or politician. He would be most amazed to see it. The report included every-thing : sometimes even his wife's lover, with all the proofs and photos which might force the lady to serve the Gestapo if necessary.

And now the " nurse " suddenly receives news of urgent and tragic family affairs. With tears in her eyes she asks permission to leave. She is certain to receive the very best references and will have no difficulty in getting another position in a different city with a distinguished Spanish family to whom some rich German friend, priest, or the Consul himself recommends her independently.

The Gestapo was interested in every confidential matter and secret ; not only among the German subjects, but also among the Spanish.

Several thousand workmen, business employees, engineers, agents, and other people, had found jobs in Spain. All of them were members of some German association : the German Labour Front or the League of German Business Employees : at other times it was the Association of German Engineers, some insurance club, cultural league, scientific corporation, or the German church.

The Gestapo had one or two men in every such institution. These gave the different members the necessary instructions and drew up questionnaires to which the German employees in Spain had to supply answers. Very few masters could have secrets from their bookkeepers, shop assistants, or engineers. Often such an employee was even able to give information of rival or associated firms.

All these clubs and associations collected thousands of such questionnaires, followed by the preparation of extracts and graphs which gave a precise picture of economic life in Spain.

The same work was done by the German business-men and the branches of big German firms who were in contact with hundreds of Spanish enterprises and factories. All the branches of the great electrical, chemical, hardware factories of Germany became a highly efficient source of industrial espionage for the Gestapo.

Then there were the German banks which could ask and receive information unobtrusively just like the chambers of commerce.

Soon in the files of the "Harbour Service" everything was collected which was worth knowing about Spain. Our work began on the basis of these details.

The first organization I must mention was the Foreign Trade Post (*Auslandshandelstelle*) which was founded to help German exports and kill the rivalry of foreigners, rob them of big orders, and chase them off the market. But this Foreign Trade Post could be useful in betraying the secrets of rivals. The selected victim began to notice that strange rumours were being spread about him, destroying his credit; his offers were refused; when he went bankrupt nobody suspected that he was not a victim of depression, but that of the German economic war. He had been "eliminated" so that a German firm or one with overwhelmingly German control could take his place.

In 1935 and 1936 there were several business failures in Spain which attracted attention even abroad. Huge concerns closed their doors on account of the "economic crisis." Out of the nineteen large bankruptcies, twelve were the immediate result of German activity, while in the case of the rest it sufficed to "help a bit" by secretly destroying credit and exercising unfair competition. Their places were taken by firms well under German control.

During these months the German organization was completely finished in Spain and had stood its trial.

Almost every German in Spain led a double life, his peaceful private existence and his work for the Nazi Party. If someone was not a member either because he was a Jew or unreliable he was exposed to the most tenacious persecution, expelling, kidnapping, etc. Every German and Germanophile door was closed to him. But most of the Spanish doors, too, because if such a man found work, he was soon slandered, his name blackened ; reduced to the direst poverty he either committed suicide or left the country.

Every German association, club, or league, whether official or not, worked feverishly and collected all necessary data.

At the same time the most stubborn propaganda went on against any Communist, Socialist, Liberal, or Freemason movement, and for the right-wing, loyalist, and monarchist parties. Everybody was labelled a Jew, Freemason, or Communist if he was not a friend of the Spanish Fascist Parties. The German Ministry of Propaganda sent millions of pamphlets to Spain ; the agents of the " Harbour Service " smuggled these papers from German boats into the country. The handbills and pamphlets were distributed by German workers and clerks everywhere : on trams, in cafés, restaurants, streets. Every right-wing Spanish Party received as much of this material as it wanted. There were unselfish German gentlemen who even covered the cost of distribution. There was no post box, open window, or door, into which such a printed sheet was not slipped ; slowly they poisoned the minds of the Spaniards, making them hate their own Government, their own Liberal and Labour Parties. Slowly they were recruited for the Fascist Parties, and these gratefully accepted the " unselfish help " of the Germans in their campaign against the " Reds " and were willing to return the service. This service was only " information " about the " Jewish-Communist-Freemasonic " Spanish enterprises. The most patriotic Spanish firms rivalled each other in industrial espionage for Germany—without suspecting it.

At the same time various other activities were pursued, but in the first place military espionage. As I said, there was a separate department for this in the " Harbour Service," and the German General Staff sent a great many secret agents to Spain.

I belonged to the very few who had been told quite early what Germany was doing in Spain ; but I must confess that I had no idea of any object beyond the enlarging of German commercial influence.

It was only later that I understood : military espionage was needed on the distant Iberian peninsula for the purpose of helping insurrection to a swift victory.

The special centre for military espionage was in Barcelona, under the cover of an engineering firm, the Aircraft Centre (Windkraft Zentrale). The Barcelona branch of the Berlin Wilhelm Teubert firm worked here under the name of *Central de Fuerza Motric Aerea W. Teubert*, its leader was the former Lieutenant Hans Gunz. In parallel Captain Konrad Heerdt pursued his activities ; if anything should happen to Gunz he would take charge. The Madrid branch was headed by Wilhelm Gefaell, in Alicante Joachim Knobloch, in Malaga ship-chandler Petersen, in Morocco Heinrich Hoffman (the latter at Ceuta) was responsible for the work.

The leaders of the different centres had all some more or less important position in the Nazi Party. They did not know anything about each other's secret work, and could not betray each other in a tight spot. This method had the advantage that Gunz and Heerdt could give the same task to two different groups who supervised each other unconsciously.

Every group formed several small " cells." The chiefs and members of these cells did not know each other. If the Spaniards caught an agent it did not matter much. The other groups could continue their work without danger.

Two independent sections of the " Aircraft Centre " pursued naval and aerial espionage ; these two were connected not only with the Barcelona centre but directly with Berlin.

Of course we were not satisfied with the work of German agents only; we had a great many Spaniards and South Americans employed.

The " Windkraft Zentrale " worked most efficiently. But it had another important task which made its activity even easier: it supplied war material to the Spaniards, took part in every important State order, and did immense service for the German armament industry.

Captain Heerdt, the deputy chief of the " Aircraft Centre " in Barcelona, had married the daughter of a Spanish general whose father was the leader of the artillery section in the Ministry of War. His father-in-law took good care that his son-in-law's firm should be given a fat share of State orders and notified him of every movement of his rivals. But even he did not suspect that his daughter's husband thus acquired the most important military and engineering secrets.

Lieutenant Gunz also succeeded in getting into the Ministry of War through distinguished patrons, where he formed his connections under title of a supplier of armaments. A well-known Barcelona lawyer, Juan Salvo, helped Gunz not only to obtain important orders, but also essential military secrets. Even more useful was the friendship which Gunz formed with Alvares Malibran and his brother, a very distinguished member of the Spanish General Staff. The two brothers were familiar in the highest circles of Spain.

Through them Gunz was always notified of the changes in the Spanish garrisons, of every manœuvre, of the exact placing of war materials and munitions.

As for naval secrets, Enrico Fricke did the good work. He had a huge export and import business in Carthagene. During the war Fricke had served in the Naval Intelligence Service of Germany; for a time he worked in the Kiel Admiralty. Carthagene was one of the most important Spanish naval bases. The naval officers sent from Berlin were all employed by Fricke and in his office was collected the necessary data. Fricke took over the Carthagene agency of the Bremen " Neptune " shipping line and this made his work very easy. Fricke knew Spain very well, having worked there for part of the World War. His dangerous job had been to plant bombs in the ships of the Allied Powers which arrive in the neutral ports.

It is an interesting addition to Fricke's portrait that during the war he had been imprisoned by the Spaniards for espionage. When they released him, he returned to Germany and demanded his pay. As he was refused, he simply sued the German Republic. This was the first case of which I know when a spy dared to do this. The German War Office was forced to pay as Fricke proved his services. When he got his money he found it advisable to vanish from Germany. He returned to Carthagene, and when Hitler came to power Fricke was one of the first who offered his services to the Nazis in Spain.

Fricke used extremely simple methods. In and around Carthagene lived a great many high naval officers. Politically they were all rather " right wing." They were almost swamped with Nazi propaganda. Everybody was glad to receive a finely bound volume as a gift; was glad to read how thoroughly the " Reds," the common enemy, had been routed in Germany. Fricke, who in the meantime became German Consul, was naturally invited to every social function and *fiesta*; his acquaintance with the leading officers slowly developed into friendship; the great, ornate German ladies and gentlemen were often invited to the lavish banquets. Few Spanish naval officers could withstand a " distinguished " and pretty lady. These women agents of the Gestapo procured a large number of naval secrets; they looked over the coastal defences and were shown whatever they wanted to see.

The Spanish Civil War showed what a thorough work Fricke and his men had done in the navy; the Government was practically left without naval officers. All of them joined Franco right at the beginning and made possible his rule in Morocco.

Among the preparations we had to draw up the plans of army movements. This was a much more difficult thing than to worm out secrets of unsuspecting Spaniards. At the beginning of our work we had little connection with the local military authorities of the country. But there was also nothing to spy out as in other matters. The Spanish Army had never evolved a plan which would serve it against an internal enemy.

Therefore we had to create these plans ourselves. But here we met an unexpected obstacle. For every such plan, manœuvres were necessary to try out the different theories.

We were sitting in Madrid with the officers of the General Staff sent from Berlin, discussing the problem. Major von Hinze was rather gloomy; bursting out at last, he said:

"Damn it all, I can't ask the Spanish Army to lend me a few regiments."

"Perhaps some of the S.A. men. . . ." someone offered, but I protested. The Spanish authorities would have swooped down on us at once if they had found out about the S.A. in their country and its military manœuvres.

Captain Guertler then had a brain-wave. The S.A. could not hold open-air manœuvres—but what about the Hitler Youth? Could not they " play soldiers "? This plan was soon realized. On Sundays and holidays—of which there were many in Spain—the officers of the General Staff took part in the " outings " of the Hitler Youth organized from the German boys in Spain. As they were not very numerous, we soon recruited a number of Spanish children; in the first place those who were pupils of German schools. These received a decorative uniform cheaply and were happy about the excursions.

Thus we could try out every military movement, the isolation of barracks, the occupation of important strategical points; we could examine every point without raising the suspicion of Spanish authorities.

Later on General Franco received these plans which he executed with small variations and which for the most part brought swift success.

How we had to ascertain the strength of armaments and spy out the equipment of the future enemy. . . .

The largest Spanish munitions factory, the *Sociedad Española de Armas y Municiones*, was the biggest contractor of the Spanish State. There were some Germans among the proprietors and shareholders of the company, among them the most important Adolf Thieme who was also a prominent member of the Nazi Party. Through him it was easy to get the most important data about the arms possessed by the Spanish Government ; a great many of the storage places were also betrayed. The rest was procured by the agents of the " Harbour Service," and later the Spanish officers supplied data when they joined General Franco.

Spanish aviation was a difficult problem. Most of the young flyers were loyal to the Government. Therefore the Madrid branch of the Lufthansa and the Junkers Company were appointed to train new pilots. Junkers were especially glad to do this because they hoped that the rich young Spaniards would not only take part in the training, but later buy Junkers planes for private use and thus patriotism could be combined with a little business.

The propaganda for aviation started on a large scale, trying to recruit enthusiasts for civil aviation. Junkers had their connections with the Spanish private aero-clubs, these they tried to enlarge and develop. It was comparatively simple : a few members had to be selected to whom Junkers made a discreet offer of a very cheap plane which could be bought on long credit ; they only had to find new followers for flying and put their machine at the club's disposal for training purposes. Most of them were happy to accept.

In this way a great many young men—of course all scions of " right-wing " families—were gathered together and taught flying on Junkers planes by German instructors. All of them became great friends of Germany and were easy prey to well-conducted propaganda.

When General Franco started his revolts, these young men were almost without exception ready to join him ; they sat in the cockpits of the planes which Junkers supplied and which bombed Spanish cities and villages.

The Spanish Government was not suspicious ; they were even glad that youth was becoming interested in aviation. In Saragossa and later in Barcelona private airfields were built ; it was not at all difficult for the German instructors to work out plans from these bases which later were used by the insurgents. Of course we could not hope to train all the pilots whom Franco would need. Most of these young

Spanish amateurs would probably perish in aerial battles fought with the superior pilots of the Government; especially as there was no way to teach them bombing and machine-gunning.

This was a point we had to take into consideration and therefore we had to count on German flyers who would have to be added to the rebel air force. Therefore it was highly important to smuggle as many German pilots into Spain as possible. They were exchanged for others after a few weeks. We also prepared photographs from the air of every possible strip of territory.

A photographic study was installed in the office of the Madrid Siemens branch where the aerial photos were copied and filed. Work went on very diligently; thousands of shots had to be taken, not only from the vicinity of barracks, but of harbours, more important factories, and different cities. We had to prepare for regular air-raids against the cities where Government resistance would be especially strong. In the possession of photographs it was not difficult to fix the objectives for bombing.

The most trusted Spanish youths were sent to Germany where their training was completed. Here, of course, they could learn freely the handling of bombs and machine-guns. But their number was necessarily limited because we had to take great care.

The young Spaniards were delighted at this German generosity. Of course they had no idea that they would be able to use their knowledge against their own countrymen.

Frankly, the naïvety with which the Spaniards viewed all these problems was almost amazing. They believed and accepted everything with childish gullibility. We could hardly avoid the young Spanish aviators talking about the large-scale photography. Sometimes even the original prints came into their hands, but nothing happened.

At the beginning of 1936 the Barcelona " Harbour Service " sent us two photos of the Barcelona port. These pictures had been taken by the German aviation experts. The " Harbour Service " started to investigate at once. We found out that the photos had been procured by Spanish sporting flyers.

One of these gentlemen who took part in such an aerial survey, received two prints which he had reproduced by a Barcelona photographer.

An agent of the "Harbour Service" visited the photographer, had some pictures taken, and began to talk to him. It was easy to steer the conversation around to photography and aerial photos. The photographer soon showed the prints he had made. Our agent asked him what purpose they served.

"The pilots must know the lay of the city," the photographer replied with perfect seriousness, "otherwise they would easily lose their way. After all, you can't put signposts or traffic policemen into the air."

This reassured us. The Spaniards apparently did not think of suspecting us of any serious purpose. Nor did they have any good reason to fear any danger. They were living at peace with their neighbours. They did not dream that distant countries had designs on their land. For centuries they had become used not to fearing any external enemy and if a scaremonger spoke of such a possibility he was rewarded with mockery. I remember the article of a newspaper discussing the question just before the insurrection. There was nothing to fear, the journalist wrote, not only because there was no great power which would have territorial aspirations in Spain. It was the paramount interest of both France and Great Britain that no other power outside Spain and Portugal should have a foothold on the Iberian peninsula. That was the reason for Portugal being Great Britain's oldest ally. Even if Spain had no such agreement with England, a silent appreciation of common interests and the knowledge of Great Britain's protection was just the same. That knowledge compensated Spain for Gibraltar which Great Britain had to guard—and on account of which she could not let foreign soldiers invade Spanish soil.

This great feeling of security was shown everywhere. The Spanish Government gave all its attention to the internal enemy which threatened its home policy from the monarchists and the extreme left. This occupied them too much to notice any foreign threat.

To return to the problem of aviation, we had to know what air fleet the Government possessed and its capacity.

In this question the chief of the Madrid branch of Junkers offered us the greatest help. Carlo Rodatz played an important part in von Bohle's " Auslandsorganisation " and was entrusted with confidential tasks right from the beginning. Rodatz had himself been a flyer whom Junkers trusted implicitly. He was one of the best armament " salesmen," and whoever knew these gentlemen knew that they would stop at nothing. It was Rodatz's doing that for a long time the Italians were unable to compete in Spain with Junkers. He always found some way to annihilate his rivals. He knew perfectly well what the other firm wanted and offered. When " Fiat " or another company had a new model, keeping its details strictly secret, Rodatz had the exact plans in his drawer.

Once the English Handley firm demonstrated a plane to a Spanish commission of which they wanted to supply a whole series. During the trial the plane crashed and its crew of four were killed. Of course no orders were placed. During the investigation some clues pointed to the fact that an unknown *saboteur* had placed powdered sugar into the petrol tank, which ruined the engine. This was only a suspicion because both the engine and the tank had burned to cinders and there was no evidence. But suspicion pointed to Madrid —to Herr Rodatz. Nobody, however, could prove anything and of course Rodatz could not be accused.

We could trust Rodatz and were never disappointed. He supplied us with comparative ease with the most important data. Through him we found out the precise details of the Government's air bases. Later he got for us the data on tanks and the description of the anti-aircraft guns at Minorca.

I had met this brilliant man and was surprised at the simplicity of his methods. If one of us wanted to get some plan we had to work amidst a thousand dangers, often risking our lives. Rodatz did it in another way, although nobody could have imitated him.

Of course he had free access to the Ministry of War ; he was often the contractor for State orders and so he knew the ropes and the men to whom he could turn. If he wanted to get the plans of some tank or other instrument of war he simply went to the Ministry of War and visited the chief of the competent technical department in whose drawer or safe the plans were kept.

" You can do a service to your country, señor," he said.

" I'm always glad to serve my country, but how ? " the Spaniard replied.

" Give me the plans. The firm which I represent can make you a much cheaper and better offer if it can study them."

If anyone else had made such an offer, he would have to start with a bribe of a hundred thousand pesos—or run the danger of being arrested at once. But Rodatz was in a different position. They were sure that he did not want to spy ; he was simply out for business. And the War Ministry officials believed him that he, the Spaniard, would serve his country.

Rodatz knew how to select his men ; after all, he could not turn to everybody with such an offer. He never had any trouble, even if he was refused, because he was considered to be a rather energetic business man, willing to use any method to land an order—but at the same time an unimpeachable patriot. . . .

It would be difficult to enumerate the work of all the German organizations, but a few examples might serve just as well.

Some time ago a scientific exchange had been installed, sending young students and scientists from Spain to Germany and vice versa. In Berlin its centre was in the Neue Friedrich-strasse, called " Deutscher Akademischer Austauschdienst " (German Academic Exchange Service), while in Spain its headquarters were at 18 Calle Aribau in Barcelona. This office sent young Spanish students and engineers to Germany where they could study at the universities, were shown the German industrial plants. The Spanish Government was always grateful for this help and supported it in every way. The German students and engineers were welcome in Spanish universities and factories.

We sent only picked men. The official chief of the exchange was Karl Supprian, Professor at Barcelona University, but its real direction was in the hands of General Faupal who later figured as official German Ambassador to General Franco.

Faupal had had an amazing career in Spain. At the end of the war he was a Brevet-Captain, and as many others of his comrades, he fought in a Free Corps against left-wing movements and took part in the punishment of " traitors." He joined the Nazi movement fairly early and proved to be a very useful man in the brawls which the S.A. men had during and after the Nazi meetings. He also turned out to be a good organizer. Himmler became his patron. I noticed this man ; his suave, brilliant manners did not betray the incredible energy which moved him.

Brevet-Captain Faupal did such brilliant work in this " scientific exchange " that he soon became a general. But his achievement was in a distinct relation to his quick promotion. His men did excellent work in every aspect. His young engineers visited the Spanish factories and mines, showing keen interest. If there was some especially difficult job in industrial espionage, Faupal and Supprian could always manage it. The collection of data on the organization of armament plants was wholly Faupal's work.

When revolution started in Spain, a great many important plants had to stop work. A series of acts of sabotage incapacitated them. Often a bomb exploded at a cardinal point ; sometimes the electric centre, the factory's heart was destroyed by powdered iron which had been put into the turbines. All this damage could not be repaired for weeks, sometimes even months. Causing short-circuits, they burned cables and set fire to whole factories.

The preparation, planning, and execution of all this was carried out by Faupal's and Supprian's men. If they had failed, Franco could not have attained his success in spite of systematic military preparations. But this prevented the Government from getting quick supplies of armaments while Franco received plenty of whatever he needed.

Faupal's organizations, co-operating with the espionage departments of the " Harbour Service," obtained valuable

military information. There were some territories to which
he could not send his men without attracting attention ; for
instance they had nothing to seek in the military garrisons.

But Faupal had his brain-waves. He got into touch in
Berlin and had the Hagenbeck Circus sent to Spain. For
months it roamed the country.

Such a circus had hundreds of employees and the agents
of the Gestapo could easily be placed among them. Before
the circus arrived in some garrison, its pioneer workers and
publicity men could be sent ahead ; they could gain access
to almost any place. On the lorries of the circus they could
drive across districts which were important from a military
point of view and could take measurements and photos.

The propaganda which the circus made must not be overlooked. They took tons of pamphlets with them and distributed them chiefly in the south into which part the other
German organizations had some difficulty in penetrating.
The purely Spanish landed class which would have been
susceptible to Nazi propaganda, was very difficult to approach.
Of course our salesmen of agricultural implements and
artificial manure worked diligently. But for mass-propaganda
Hagenbeck's Circus was the most suitable and fulfilled its
task amazingly well.

About the end of 1936 the Gestapo had cleared Spain
almost completely of dangerous or harmful German elements.
The Party controlled all the German subjects through the
Secret State Police ; they were willing to fulfil any command.
The counter-espionage departments of the Gestapo had
acquired through their agents and the German associations
all the important data on Spanish economic and industrial
units and were able to influence them strongly. The main
details of the navy, army, aviation, railways, high roads,
and shipping were all in our hands. The Gestapo not only
watched closely its own Nazi members, but had its men
planted in every important place of both friendly and inimical
Spanish Parties who reported every movement.

The winning of Spanish middle-class and right-wing public
opinion was well on its way with the help of propaganda.
The right-wing Parties worked for us, with our weapons. The

split between right and left had become so wide that only a single touch was needed to disrupt the whole peninsula.

We had a decisive influence on the most important newspapers. The huge advertisements of great German firms were handled by the German chambers of commerce. If news, uncomplimentary to Germany, was printed, advertisements were withdrawn at once. Thus we were assured that they would be wary of printing anything detrimental; they were even ready to do us any favour.

I must mention that the Germans living in Spain did not put themselves at the Party's disposal so easily as might be imagined. We had to overcome considerable resistance in many cases. But the Gestapo and the Nazi Party were well experienced in such matters. A very important and simple method was that the Party members were made to believe that almost a hundred per cent of Germans in Spain were in their ranks. Thus nobody dared to lag. Every organization was forbidden to give information about its roll of members. if some doubting soul wanted to have a look at it, they gave him a list containing the names of all the Germans living in the district, whether members or not. If two non-members met, each of them believed that the other was denying his membership on purpose; he became suspicious, afraid of some trap and hastened to join. I could not say that the German colony in Spain joined the Nazi Party through conviction. But I can safely state that practically everybody became a member, sometimes in spite of his convictions, being afraid of consequences and for the sake of his own interests.

This belief and this fear welded the Party into a single, huge machine which worked obediently under the touch of its masters, just as in Germany. But I found that people slowly became used to the situation and excused themselves by believing that they were following the Fuehrer out of conviction and faith.

At the end of 1935 I had to prepare a detailed report about the progress of our work in Spain. I returned to Berlin. During one of my discussions at the Gestapo Rudolf Hess, the Fuehrer's Deputy, was also present. He seemed to be much

R

interested in all I had to say. He put a great many questions
to me, then took a list from his pocket and followed them
up with other enquiries to which I tried to give answers
according to my best knowledge.

Hess, in spite of his frail physique, was an extremely
thorough man. I saw from his notes that he had already
put the same questions to someone else. He had the answers
noted ; but it was no news to me that my work was supervised by secret, watchful eyes, although I had the fullest
confidence of my superiors. My replies seemed to give
satisfaction.

One of the most important enquiries was whether we could
count on the Spanish Parties of the right and what they would
be prepared to undertake against the Government ?

Before I could reply to this question of Hess, he interrupted :
" Consider well before you answer. I'm willing to wait
a little."

There was no need for consideration.

" The Spanish right wing isn't united, it's divided into four
parties and they hate each other more than they hate their
opponents . . . this is the only reason why Spain has a
left-wing Government."

And now the word " revolution " was mentioned for the
first time.

" What would they do in case of an armed revolution ? "
Hess asked.

Without waiting for my reply, he began to talk, like a
man possessed.

A revolution was being prepared in Spain.

I felt a cold thrill ; to be quite frank, I did not think of
the dead and wounded of a probable rising, nor about the
flames which such a rebellion would cause to break out in
peaceful Spain ; I was thinking of myself. . . .

Drawing all the necessary conclusions from my past
experiences, I took good care not to know too much about
the plans of my employers. I tried to remain the self-effacing,
unsuspecting instrument even when I saw everything clearly.
That was the reason why I was able to serve the Gestapo
for such a long time.

In the moment when I was "officially" told such an important secret I felt that the "beginning of the end" had arrived for me. I knew too much to be safe. I had two courses open to me : either I must make myself useful, or begin the inexorable fight for the favour of the "boss," betray and stab in the back everyone whom I had reason to fear; to be on my guard day and night that they should not be able to intrigue against me.

If I could carry on this game, I could attain anything. But even then I could not live in safety, just as there was no safety for anyone in the Third Reich. Goering, Goebbels, Himmler, Heydrich, even the Fuehrer himself were constantly walking on a very tight rope. The number of great men I saw smiling while there was death in their hearts ! I thought of General von Epp and Kaufmann, the Hamburg Gau Leader, whom I have seen trembling for their lives, weeping maudlin tears, half intoxicated. . . .

I knew that I was unable to play this game, even if my nerves were strong. One must be born for it, and I wasn't.

In this case I had only one road, just as Hanfstaengl and the most skilful of the others had done. To continue the gamble with my whole soul and in the opportune moment— jump out of the line, vanish, hide, try to find a refuge somewhere abroad. . . .

It only depended on whether I should succeed. Hanfstaengl had escaped in time although he knew everything about the Reichstag Fire. He knew that this secret could be fatal. But Edmund Heines and Karl Ernst died—for the same secret. Von Alvensleben also died although he had opened the first financial resources for Hitler. All those who had brought Hitler foreign money were killed. Rummler and Stein had risked their lives a thousand times in Russia to contact the General Staff, but when they had done their work, Heydrich considered them too dangerous. Both died, for "dead men tell no tales."

But now I had no other choice. From the moment when I became a recipient of this secret, I did not cease to seek for the road of escape, because I knew that every achievement was another step towards my grave, while failure meant quick death.

I wanted to explain all this because it might shed light on a great many things I did; on the other hand it was this realization which has enabled me to set down my memories—instead of rotting in a nameless grave.

I now understood the gigantic gamble. Germany was preparing the armed revolt of the Spanish right wing. A Spanish politician or soldier had to be selected who was willing to defy—under German guidance—the Liberal Government and proclaim a dictatorship. This Spanish politician would grant any concession to Germany for the help he received. He would also form a military alliance with the Third Reich.

About this time discussions had been proceeding well with Italy in this matter. Germany had to be assured of the Duce's consent; alone she would not be strong enough to defy English and French opposition. Mussolini was prepared to offer support, but he demanded a heavy share of the spoils. Not only Germany, but Italy as well needed the raw materials of Spain, especially copper and quicksilver. Mussolini asked too much. In the first place he protested that no other country except Italy should get a foothold on the Spanish islands of the Mediterranean; he raised no objection to Germany taking anything from the Spaniards west of Gibraltar. Bargaining went on slowly and for a long time.

There was another big controversy between Italy and Nazi Germany. The Third Reich wanted to develop industrial and agricultural Spain under German direction. This was highly necessary in order to import agricultural products into starving Germany. But Mussolini wanted just the opposite. He demanded the cessation of any economic activity which meant rivalry for Italy. Spanish oranges and table oil must no longer be marketed abroad.

General Franco's name had not yet been mentioned. The first man on whom Germany and Italy agreed with was a Spanish admiral whom they had won for their purpose. This man figured in our correspondence as " Admiral Juan." He hated Socialists and was prepared to do anything in order to harm them. Count Beroldingen, the Spanish representative of the Luft-hansa and leader of the German Labour Front, was

appointed to discuss an agreement with "Admiral Juan."
The latter was willing to fulfil most of the German demands,
but he must have found out slowly that not only concessions,
but the whole of Spain would have to be delivered to Nazidom. Thereupon, he announced that he had reconsidered the
matter and would rather withdraw from the whole plan.

For a few days there was almost a panic in our offices (just as
in Rome) because we were fearful that "Admiral Juan"
would place difficulties in the way of our work and perhaps
even betray our scheme. This panic was only quieted when
the news arrived that "Admiral Juan" had suddenly died—
from a heart-attack. At that time I considered his death a
"lucky coincidence" for Italo-German interests. I still have
no grounds for changing my opinion, except the knowledge
that "coincidence" always helps the Gestapo when it is
necessary. . . .

The next man selected was General Franco. He was willing
to give large economic concessions to Germany and Italy.
Nothing more was demanded from him, but nothing more
was promised except moral support. He could have rifles
and tanks, guns and aeroplanes, but not *gratis*. He would have
to pay for them.

Franco looked around to find a financier and discovered
the banker, Juan March, who was willing to risk money in the
hope of good business. For the capital he was putting up he
demanded the most important concessions which Franco
granted gladly. It was easy to agree with March, he was no
politician, but a business man, and was willing to pass on the
concessions to Germany. He could calmly accept large
advances for the products to be supplied, but he received these
advances only partly in cash ; most of them were settled in war
material ; these he sold to Franco, who paid in cash. So
everything was "fine," and March certainly did not lose on
the deal.

And if Franco started, this was the German plan—it would
not be difficult to blackmail him into granting the political
concessions which Germany and Italy wanted. (This was
exactly what happened later.) But for the time being Franco

had to be kept under the impression that as a Spanish patriot he was fighting only for his country. . . .

The plan showed devilish cunning and was a masterpiece of diplomacy.

But at the beginning Franco had doubts. What if some foreign power should intervene ? He received guarantees that Italy and Germany would back him up with all their might in such a case. The Italians did not think that France would remain neutral. In French right-wing circles, where Fascism had won a great many friends, the Italians went to work. It was not difficult to strengthen the movement against the Communists. The French branches of the " Auslandsorgani-zation " and the Gestapo were entrusted with the task, and succeeded comparatively easily in creating an organization in France called the C.S.A.R. This underground league was discovered only at the last moment by the French police and a huge store of German and Italian arms collected. The C.S.A.R. prepared for an armed attack against the " Communists." Well provided with cars and arms, they could easily provoke riots in Paris and in the French provinces if France should decide to help Government Spain. . . .

So every preparation was made for Franco's defence. He also received guarantees that during the whole campaign German and Italian warships and airplanes would be kept ready for himself and his staff in Spanish ports should the Putsch fail.

After that the final work began, now with the co-operation of Franco. He was very popular in aristocratic circles, he had many friends in the army and the middle-class parties. Juan March's money was at his disposal, and the whole German propaganda organization which worked miracles. In a few months Franco's friends and followers had been placed at every important military post. They all worked for a single aim. It was also a minor miracle to make these people under-stand how important was secrecy. To the very last only half a dozen people knew what Franco really wanted. Tension and excitement increased, fanned by propaganda. The slogan was given to Spanish right-wing circles : the Germans are our friends, should anything happen we could count on them ;

but apart from Franco, Juan March and a few of their followers, nobody knew what was going to happen.

In April, 1936, there was a decisive conference in Berlin. Hess, Himmler, Heydrich, Bohle, Goebbels, Nielland, Wemke, and the deputies discussed the situation. Everything was ready for an armed rising. Only the Italian envoys were reluctant, probably because they found that they would have comparatively small part in the direction of affairs and were afraid of being cheated of the spoils. But Germany managed to convince the Duce that this was the best time for action.

Now it only remained to summon Franco's confidential men to Berlin and to discuss the final details. But the General still protested that he was not well enough prepared. His doubts were only silenced when he was told that he would have everything settled for him; his only task was to head the movement—to lend his name.

When he received our plans of attack, he raised new objections. According to his conception, the revolt was built on the South of Spain which he was sure to occupy quickly as the inhabitants were " right wing." But he was afraid that in the mining districts and industrial centres where workers were strongly organized, his men would be literally beaten to death by them—if they had no weapons, then with their naked fists.

The Reichswehr experts shared Franco's doubts only to some extent, but they advised him to try and strengthen the garrisons in the mining districts. The German conception was in favour of a general rising even if this cost more blood. The " Reds " must have no time nor place to organize themselves. If the Putsch failed in the industrial centres, the reserves of the Government must be destroyed or disorganized to cause general confusion.

Franco was forced to accept everything, and the last throw in the big gamble began.

Now it was proved how good had been the organization of years. Everything went with clockwork precision.

At the end of April all our organizations began to destroy secret documents and hide all traces. The most important papers which would be needed were sent to the consulates.

The envoys of the Reichswehr left for Spain and started to discuss the battle plans with Franco's staff. The generals Mola, Queipo de Llana, Hillan-Astray, and Goded began to organize their troops under the direction of the German experts.

And now the German fighting organization was enlarged. The selected representatives received their instructions according to the previously prepared plans. Our men were ready in every town to start the recruiting of insurgent troops at the given moment and to proceed with their equipment, provision of food and shelter, and military training.

At the same time the smuggling of arms and munitions began. Franco's men helped us greatly in this work. They built roads for us in a number of places ; a whole army of customs officers and railway-men shut their eyes at a given sign, and the consignments of " potatoes " passed the Spanish frontier without difficulty.

The influence of Franco's followers proved very useful when they forced the Spanish Ministry of War to order a large quantity of infantry and artillery ammunition just before the war, which for the most part we succeeded in delivering to Franco—but at the cost of the Government.

In June I was in Spain for the last time. I took extremely important orders with me about the organizations which would remain working under the cover of the consulates after the revolt had been started. These organizations had to keep in touch with the neutral German consulates at all costs and to remit information to Franco from the territory held by the Government. We had to organize this network of spies in a very short time, but all of Franco's trusted men helped us. In every town there was a list of names of the " loyal " Spanish men and women who would give us the necessary support.

When I boarded my ship I knew that one or two watchers were behind me. Often I amused myself by trying to discover who these secret companions of mine were. There were many passengers on board, and my task was difficult. But I knew I was being watched. There were probably many others on the ship who were also supervised. If I walked on deck late at night I could seldom stay alone more than a few moments. Other men or perambulating couples appeared and I could not know who was watching whom.

I have very little to add. San Sebastian, Barcelona, Madrid, Saragossa, Alicante, Malaga, again received the diligent travelling salesman who had offers, plans, estimates in his brief-case for all sorts of machines. I have played the part myself. According to my instructions I was to wire from Lisbon on 14th July whether everything was ready. But Spanish laziness and indifference kept me longer. I received desperate urgent messages every day from Madrid. But only on the 16th could I report on my way to Lisbon. I know to-day what great troubles this delay caused. In several places Franco's men were notified too late that they were to wait another two days, and in several places on the 17th the officers ordered their troops to move. This attracted the attention of the Government and caused unrest; in Minorca, Barcleona, and Alicante it prevented Franco from making a surprise attack.

In Lisbon I delivered to the German consulate all the papers which I had to take there from the different centres of the " Harbour Service," then I rested a day and boarded another ship.

In Rotterdam, where we put into port, I bought a newspaper. I glanced at the first page. Huge head-lines screamed :

" GREAT MILITARY REVOLT IN SPAIN."

What more is there to add ?

There was a people of twenty-two millions on the Iberian peninsula which had not the slightest intention of rebelling. It was blessed with all the good things in the world ; in the first place with raw materials which Germany needed badly and had to buy for foreign currency : quicksilver, copper, iron ore. . . . And this country could also serve as an excellent market, almost a colony, not to mention the important strategic position if German guns could be established in the South of Europe.

This country had to be possessed. It did not seem to be a serious opponent ; it did not belong to any group of European powers, it was improbable that any one of them would expose itself for Spain. It was an easy prey, especially since it had driven away its king.

Systematic, stubborn work had been going on in this country, and its fruits fell easily into the German lap.

The German talent for organization has always been appreciated all over the world. But it has never achieved anything greater than this revolution. A revolution unparalleled in history.

Who knows which country is the next on the list ? Holland ? Switzerland ? Tanganyika ? Poland ? Ukraine ?

Only the lords of Nazi Germany know. And they keep silent.

CHAPTER XVI

★

I GUARD HITLER

IT WAS A SIGNAL honour to be selected for the branch of the Special Service of the Reich Fuehrer S.S. which was detailed to guard the life and safety of Adolf Hitler. The man who was elected to this select group had to be reliable from every point of view ; before anyone was detailed for such duty he was subjected to the most searching examination, his past, his friends, his relations, his connections were scrutinized with equal care. These were the men who were in daily contact with Hitler and who had the difficult task of guarding the Fuehrer's " Berghof " in the mountains of Obersalzberg, nine kilometres from the nearest human community.

More than five years had passed since I had been in Berchtesgaden, and when I arrived I hardly recognized the small Alpine village. A large modern health resort had developed during the last few years. It had an airfield ; the mountain paths became wide and excellent motor-roads ; everywhere new villas had been built ; it seemed as if they had grown out of the mountain-side. A new railway track was laid, the station enlarged ; buses brought hundreds of tourists every day. They did not come to enjoy the panorama of the Obersazlberg—they wanted to see the Fuehrer . . . or at least the house in which he lived.

But the motor-buses stop on the highroad to Berchtesgaden and the disappointed tourists are shown only the side-road which winds upwards leading to the " Berghof "—only open to privileged and invited persons. The road is closed by a barrier and the barrier guarded by two armed men.

It is here that the work of the Security Service begins.

At the barrier I was stopped ; one guard reported me to the next by telephone.

" Are you armed ? "

" Of course," I said.

" Give it up."

In vain I explained that I was, myself, a member of the SD.RFSS, and it was my duty to carry a gun ; that I was his superior officer—he would not listen.

" You must give it up."

The winding road rose steeply. Its length is about nine kilometres, and the higher it rises, so the guards increase. They are connected by telephone and pass the visitor almost from hand to hand.

Practically this is the only road by which you can get to the Fuehrer's residence. It would be difficult to climb the steep, almost vertical wall of rock. But in spite of this I soon found out that the " Berghof " was surrounded with a defensive system of six-miles' radius which turned this mountain into an almost impregnable fortress.

A concrete guard's hut was hidden on every tenth jutting rock ; the guard huddles there beside an electric fire and a machine-gun ; every ten minutes he has to report to the central guard in the " Berghof " by telephone :

" Nichts neues " (" Nothing new ").

At night, excellently trained hounds keep up the connection between the outposts ; the tourist who might lose his way and meet such a dog would have a very bad time of it.

But if someone should succeed in outwitting the guard and the bloodhounds, he could hardly avoid the high-tension wire stretched between the trees which surround the domain of Adolf Hitler like a spider's web.

Why did the Fuehrer retire to these mountains which were so far from general routes and connected with such a complicated way with the capital ? It is an old story.

It was at the beginning of the Nazi movement when Hitler did not let himself be photographed. The German news-papers did not know anything about him beyond his name. The Berlin dailies offered a high reward to the photographer who would succeed in taking a picture of Hitler. But every effort was in vain ; the spotlights were so placed around the Fuehrer's rostrum that no photo could be taken. Afterwards, the S.A. took care to prevent any such attempt.

Hitler was afraid of Communists' attempts on his life. That was the reason why he did not want to have his photo published. About this time the different reporters were sitting in a Munich beer-garden, complaining about their failure. In the same place, at a neighbouring table, sat Hitler with his friends, laughing at their plight.

The Fuehrer wanted to find a secure hiding-place where he could escape if anything should happen in Munich. He inquired about some secluded mountain house in the Bavarian Alps. Thus the idyllic retreat near Berchtesgaden was discovered. It seemed to be especially convenient because a skilled mountain guard could lead one in a few hours across the frontier into Austria.

In the little mountain house called Platterhof, on top of the Obersalzberg, a former German Colonial officer, Bruno Buchner, lived with his wife. They let their four guest-rooms to tourists. The house had some literary tradition—Richard Voss, the well-known German author of the novel *Zwei Menschen* (*Two Human Beings*), described it, and his heroine, Judith Platter, had lived in this very house.

Early in the 1920's, a friend of Buchner, a member of the Munich City council called Weber, arrived in the Platterhof with a companion whom he introduced as Dr. Wolf.

" Dr. Wolf," who said he was a writer, rented a room and lived there with few interruptions for a year. A year later when near the Platterhof, the owners of the little mountain villa " Wachenfeld " moved away, Dr. Wolf bought the small house and furnished it for himself.

It was only in 1923, when Hitler became known through the Munich Putsch, that Buchner recognized his guest, " Dr. Wolf " . . . his guest and the new owner of " Wachenfeld."

Thereafter it was in this mountain retreat that Hitler could stay with a few friends. So he had lived for almost twenty years in this district. Here he was also safe, surrounded by his trusted men.   He could live here as he wanted, without bothering about the masses and publicity . . . it was easy to understand that after he came to power he did not want to give up this peaceful haven.

Of course, the small mountain villa became almost a palace. The original building was left standing, but it was surrounded by new wings and new houses, re-christened "Berghof." Here the Chancellery of Berlin could find room and the Special Service was installed.

The head of this special guard was Captain Brueckner, a young man who was responsible for the whole organization which watches over the Fuehrer's safety.

The Special Service group consisted of three hundred men. Their discipline was perhaps even stricter than that of the Reichswehr.   The slightest carelessness was followed by severe punishment and immediate transfer.   There could be no errors in this service ; should a guard let a single suspicious visitor through the triple defence, that single man might be the assassin who would kill Hitler.

During my work for the Gestapo I knew of four attempts on Hitler's life which, of course, all failed.   One of them was here in the "Berghof."   An S.A. group leader, called Krause, had been allowed to present a petition personally to the Fuehrer, and he was the would-be assassin.   If the unfortunate man had waited patiently for another five minutes until he could face Hitler—the history of the Third Reich would probably have been changed.   But, sitting among the others waiting to be received by Hitler, he fired at him when the Fuehrer came down the stairs and passed through the hall to enter his study.   And he missed. . . .

Now it was proved how well the defence apparatus worked. The unlucky S.A. leader was killed in half a minute.   Five guns fired at the same time. . . .

It can only be surmised why he had committed his desperate deed.   He wanted to present a petition for pardon of an S.A. man who had been sentenced to three years in prison for homosexuality.

This might have been Krause's reason.   On the other hand

another theory maintained that he had attempted the assassination because he was hired by the well-known Niekisch group.

But after this attempt new defensive measures were taken in the mountain palace. Even before that every visitor had had to submit to a search; no revolvers or daggers could be taken into the "Berghof." Now Krause's case had proved that all this was highly necessary.

Lately arms and munitions have to be deposited at the beginning of the branch road to the "Berghof"; often it happens that the car driving up is searched again on its way.

Every letter or parcel addressed to the Fuehrer is examined first in a special room of the Berchtesgaden post office and only after the examination is it taken to the mountain-top. If someone succeeded in mailing a bomb (although all post offices have to examine suspicious parcels at the time of accepting them) it would explode down in the village, and not in the mountain retreat of the Fuehrer.

As for my work, it carried much responsibility, but was rather easy. When I reported to Captain Brueckner, he told me my duties.

By some mysterious method details of the famous Hitler-Schuschnigg encounter had leaked out. The traitor must have been among the Special Service men. The group which was on duty at that time had been questioned, but it could not be ascertained which of the fourteen men was the guilty one. Captain Brueckner solved the matter simply: he sent all the fourteen to Dachau, the concentration camp. They would be released only when the guilty man had confessed or been found out.

My duty was to watch the members of the bodyguard, to control their correspondence, listen to their telephone conversations, try to involve them in argument—supervise their every movement. . . .

Most of my time was spent in just idling about. My only amusement was to try and find out which member of the staff had been entrusted with—my control.

Adolf Hitler is the sort of man who likes to stretch himself in his bed when he wakes in the morning, to have his breakfast brought in on a tray, and if his whim so demands, to stay in bed till noon to finish a novel. Hitler is a great reader and belongs to that omniverous class who cannot do anything before they have turned the last page.

What does he read?

Every book published in Germany is brought to his bedroom; he looks into every one, reads a few pages, and if he likes it, finishes the whole thing. If he doesn't find it to his taste, he throws it on the shelf near his bed, and it is taken away by his attendants.

It is an open secret that in his hours of leisure he prefers adventure and detective stories. After the Nazis took over the government, one of the well-known Berlin publishers of thrillers stopped his series in the belief that such books would not be welcome in the Third Reich. But he was soon told that the Fuehrer did not object to them, on the contrary. . . . For Hitler reads only German, and so, being unable to enjoy foreign literature in the original, must confine himself to German works.

If he stays in bed in the forenoon, Captain Schreck, who prepares his daily schedule, knows that this will be a *faulenztag*, (lazy day), and all the different items of the programme are changed.

On such days Hitler eats his second breakfast, composed of cakes, milk, and fruit, also in bed. In a warm dressing-gown he appears at noon in the dining-room, where Captain Brueckner, perhaps his deputy, Lieutenant Schaub, and Captain Schreck, share his meal.

The next " event " on such a *faulenztag* is a little game of dominoes. In the meantime, without waiting for a special order, the small theatre, the Fuehrer's private cinema, has been warmed. It looks exactly like the private projection-room of a film studio, and just as the Fuehrer receives every new book, so also every new film is shown to him here.

Everybody knows that Adolf Hitler is a film-fan of old standing. He was still a struggling political agitator, but he did not miss any opportunity in Munich, or later in Berlin, to go to the cinema. If he liked a film especially, he saw it twice or even three times. And on some gloomy winter days, when time lagged on his hands, he went from one movie to

the other and watched till midnight three full-length
programmes.

In his private cinema at the "Berghof" German, English,
Italian, and American pictures are presented. There is a little
table in front of him with a bell; he can give a sign if he
wants to see a sequence a second time.

The little cinema is equipped with all the achievements of
modern cinematography; a wonderful sound apparatus and
excellent operators ensure the smoothness of the performance.

Adolf Hitler knows only German and is unable to enjoy
French, English, or American films in full measure. To
help him, special German sub-titles are made for him.

Sometimes these "movie-orgies" last till late at night;
they would last even longer, but the Fuehrer's eyes are none
too strong and he has to keep within reasonable limits.

So much is sure that the immense amount of reading and
watching of moving pictures has made it necessary for Hitler
to use his spectacles more or less continuously. Goebbels
has given strict orders that he is never to be photographed
with them; there is no German paper which would print
such a photo.

Such a "lazy day" mostly ends with early retirement.
The Fuehrer returns to his bedroom and turns to the books
waiting at his bedside. He turns the pages of this or that
till at last one of them attracts his interest—then he settles
down in earnest to reading. There is always fruit, a glass of
milk, and some cake at his bedside.

He reads and nibbles and sips till he gets sleepy and the
book falls from his hands.

And outside, among the high-tension wire, in the concrete
huts, near the machine-guns, every ten minutes the guards
call into the telephone:

"Nichts neues . . . nothing new. . . ."

Another characteristic diversion of the Fuehrer consists
of the "evenings of discussion" which sometimes last till
early in the morning. These take place in the huge study and
all the visitors to the "Berghof" are present.

Sometimes Hitler sends at once for Goebbels, Ribbentrop,
or Captain Wiedemann, commanding them to fly to Berchtes-

gaden at once. He likes them because they dare to contradict him. During these discussions almost every subject on earth can be mentioned, a lively argument may start around a political problem, a book, or a film. But the evening mostly ends with Hitler taking the word and talking . . . talking . . . sometimes such an argument finishes with a speech by the Fuehrer lasting one or two hours . . . just as in the Munich beer-hall so many years ago.

And then Hitler returns exhausted to his bedroom.

Nobody knows how long such a "lazy period" lasts; sometimes a single day, sometimes four or five. Captain Schreck cancels schedules nonchalantly, preparing a programme for next day only to cancel that too if necessary. He notifies Berlin, Munich, Karinhall (Goering's residence) and in a few hours the whole of official Germany knows that the Fuehrer must be left in peace till further notification, which means that no affairs should be submitted which may disturb his peace and quiet.

Such long periods of "*faulenzen*" are mostly followed by days of feverish activity. The Fuehrer, as if he felt remorse for the idleness in which he has indulged, wakes at seven o'clock in the morning.

Until recently he always dressed alone; he even objected to his personal valet being in his room. But slowly he relented, and now he permits his servant to offer him his garments one by one. He even condescends to allow the valet to help him with his boots. . . .

The next person to enter Hitler's room is Otto.

Otto is a strange fellow.

A typical, loquacious, amiable German barber. The Fuehrer has known him ever since Otto worked in the Berlin Kaiserhof where Hitler lived with his staff and Otto shaved him. When Hitler became Chancellor, Otto was promoted to "court barber."

Otto did not change a bit. He is the only man who tells the Fuehrer the same atrocious puns which he offers to his other clients. His position resembles greatly that of a court clown. He is allowed to say anything. He collects and tells all the jokes—against Hitler. He is an amusing fool—and a dangerous man.

Otto has his own connections and slowly has become an important person in Hitler's entourage. With a single pun, a single allusion he can break careers and ruin men. . . .

Ten minutes later the freshly shaven Fuehrer briskly leaves the "Berghof." There is a stout stick in his hand. Brueckner accompanies him for a little mountain walk. He stops on top of a hillock and looks round. He is alone with Brueckner.

But this solitude is deceptive.

The guards posted among the mountains report every minute where the Fuehrer is and what direction he is taking.

Half an hour later he is at home. The table is laid with all kinds of meat, cheese ; there is even a flagon of beer.

But the Fuehrer is on a strict diet. He eats bread and butter and cheese, drinks beer very seldom as alcohol has been forbidden to him by his doctors. His aides-de-camp, however, can have their fill of everything.

It is only recently that food has been served at the Fuehrer's table of which he does not eat. It was Captain Wiedemann's skill which helped the members of Hitler's court to be relieved from the necessity of sharing the Fuehrer's diet.

During the forenoon, Spieler, the architect of the Chancellery, reports. And if he has a bulging brief-case, the aides of the Chancellery are resigned to a totally ruined schedule of the day.

Apart from reading and the cinema the Fuehrer has a third ruling passion—architecture.

When the young Hitler wanted to enrol on the Vienna Academy of Art, he presented a few rather clumsy drawings. The committee refused to accept him, saying that his drawings showed aptitude for architecture and not for painting. This decision started Hitler on a hobby ; his dream of becoming an architect has remained with him during his whole career. He, himself, designed the symbol and coat of arms of his Party ; he planned the concrete and steel mountain palace which grew from the modest "Berghof." He designs his own furniture. Everything is rectangular and of severely modern lines.

It was Spieler's fault that Hitler has stuck to such a strict and uncompromising style of architecture. Spieler had been a follower of the " Moderne Baukunst "—but he forgot that this style would be all right in a huge flat-block, but rather ridiculous if applied to a mountain retreat, or . . . a bedroom.

Spieler and Hitler spend hours over the detailed plans, discussing singular points ; then Spieler takes the plans away to revise them according to the Fuehrer's tastes.

In Spieler's brief-case a new Berlin is born. Some people are rather horrified that the ancient city of Prussian culture will be completely changed according to the plans of two rather amateurish architects. If ancient buildings have to be demolished, they do not worry about them. Most German cities resemble a shambles ; part of them is being broken down while the other part has not yet been finished. Hitler does not care for statues for himself—but he wants to leave his mark on German architecture ; a mark which it will be difficult to erase in future decades. . . .

If the Fuehrer moves from the " Berghof " to the Berlin Chancellery the members of his entourage continue their work exactly in the same way. He has his own cinema in the Chancellery, his self-designed bedroom, his books ; the Special Service guards him in the same way as among the mountains. The only difference is that here the Special Commissariat for special purposes (Sonderkommissariat zur besonderen Verwendung) has a centre. I have mentioned this branch in Chapter II. Its task is to prevent any attempts against the lives of Nazi dignitaries.

The branch recently discovered the so-called Niekisch plot and brought about a hundred men and women to trial. It works under the direct instructions of Heydrich ; the Gestapo remits to it every scrap of paper which can have even the remotest bearing to such an attempt at assassination. Every country has its cases in " high treason." But this term covers a great variety of offences in Germany. If anyone makes Hitler responsible, for instance, for some mistake or blunder, or involves his person in any criticism—that constitutes high treason.

The idea is very simple : the man who criticises Hitler to-day may be ready to attempt his assassination to-morrow.

The same special branch made almost every plot impossible by a simple expedient. Every S.S. and S.A. man knows of the curt announcement in connection with this problem.

Whoever denounces a conspiracy against Hitler, leading to the arrest of a single individual, receives a reward of a million marks and a passport enabling him to leave Germany whenever he wants.

The same reward is offered to those persons who have taken part in such conspiracy, but have reconsidered their standing and denounced their fellow-conspirators.

This simple edict makes almost every plot against Hitler impossible. The man who can resist such a sum, coupled with complete freedom, must be an exceptional fanatic. . . . And there are very few such men or women in history.

I guarded Hitler . . . and then I left Germany, although without such a reward or a free passport. In my opinion the Fuehrer is one of the happiest men in the world. He is the " small citizen " who has been crowned king and now that his most daring dream has been realized he can set out to realize his other, lesser dreams. He behaves and lives as an English, French, or even Rumanian " little man " would behave if he had been raised to the same power and the same place to which the co-operation of so many different and curious circumstances have raised the " Bohemian corporal."

This was the last job which I held in the Gestapo. Soon I realized that my misgivings in connection with Spain were all too true ; I was initiated in too many dangerous secrets to stay alive in Nazi Germany.

And so I left it. Without regret and without looking back. If fate—and " Heydrich's Killers "—grant me a little respite, I will do my best to impart my knowledge to the world. God knows how badly such knowledge is needed to shake up Democracies from their inertia and make the world safe again—not for Democracy—but for humanity, an existence in which there are no persecutions, purges, drives, " movements " and in which Man again can be Man.

★

CHAPTER XVII

ODDS—AND THE END

W HEN I LEFT GERMANY and arrived in France I had two little notebooks in my pocket. They were filled with closely scribbled script—but nobody could read it but myself. I had been circumspect enough to evolve a shorthand for my own, very private use which must defy even the most skilful code readers of the Gestapo. The notebooks have given me the material for this book where my memory has failed—I have kept them for more than six years.

I am looking them over now to see what is left. Oh, quite a lot, both in these notes and in my head. Material for another book—but there are chapters in the history of the Gestapo and Nazidom which are either too dull or too dark to recount. I have drawn two diagonals over the pages with which I had finished. Yet there are odds and ends to be cleared up, like rummaging in the attic before moving to another house. I have chosen a few at random, marginal notes, short summaries as I made them for my own use.

The Gestapo had much trouble with the Bureau of Race Research. These stubborn scientists would not knuckle under and we had to take several to a concentration camp. The greatest anxiety was about two prominent Nazis : Dr. Paul Goebbels and—Leni Riefenstahl.

In some circles it was whispered about Dr. Goebbels that he was a Jew. We took five bearded gentlemen into custody till five others could be found who declared our Minister of Propaganda " a post-darked wizened German type." Not that anybody had ever heard of such an ethnological species, but the authority of the Research Bureau sufficed. Leni Riefenstahl, who made the huge film of the German Olympic Games and was one of the Fuehrer's very few lady friends, was accused of having had a Jewish grandmother. But see, the Bureau of Race Research proclaimed her a " perfect German type." Only we of the Gestapo know how Miss Riefenstahl came to acquire this flattering verdict. . . .

There was an astonishing document circulated around the European chancelleries just after the *Anschluss*. It gave amazing figures about war materials which the Third Reich had acquired with the foreign currency sequestrated in Austria. We of the Gestapo knew that this " secret " had been betrayed on purpose—just as was the menacing lecture of General von Reichenau in which he spoke of Germany's Spanish and Portuguese aims. This got into French and English papers, but not by accident. Such " leaks " are arranged on purpose —and are called by Heydrich and his associates " blackmail propaganda." Useful to frighten the Democracies and at the same time to make them believe they had made an essential discovery, whereas the truth lies somewhere else. . . .

I have spoken about Buchenwald and its " hell on earth." But from December, 1937, to April, 1938, it achieved a new record. During this time a hundred and forty-five men died of beating or shooting—or committed suicide. And Buchenwald is still being enlarged. . . .

German commercial and political penetration, of which I have spoken in connection with the Gestapo's work, has recently had two main aims. One is Central and South-eastern Europe, the other, Latin America. High-collared Dr. Schacht, who can look so benevolent, has devised an extremely simple and efficient method. He buys raw materials on credit. He refuses to pay in cash—he offers German merchandise which his creditor can sell to other countries, or keep for his own use. The rather peculiar situation ensures that the Hungarian farmer gets eyeglasses and mouth-organs for his wheat, not to speak of typewriters and gramophones.

This is one of the minor results of this procedure. With German goods German propaganda enters, followed by the agents of the Gestapo. In this case it is the debtor who calls the tune, even if his creditor pays the piper—and pays heavily. Yugoslavia, Hungary, Greece, Rumania, Turkey, have all to suffer from this downright robbery. The Gestapo has to see to it that they don't complain, that they even welcome German " co-operation." The " unruly " elements are eliminated, a few politicians assassinated, journalists muzzled—if there is no Jewish problem in the country, one is created by force . . . and Germany profits while Dr. Schacht smiles benevolently behind his tall collar. . . .

The Gestapo also works overseas. German propaganda was started several years ago in the United States—but it seems that transatlantic air dulls the cunning of Nazi agents. At least it was their clumsiness which—coupled with the atrocities committed against Jews and Gentiles alike with ever-increasing force—caused the serious diplomatic break between U.S.A. and the Third Reich ; a break which may have more important consequences than anyone can suspect at the moment.

The Gestapo masquerades in America as the " Volksbund." American newspapers and magazines—Ernest Hemingway's and Paul de Kruif's *Ken* is more or less their leader—have denounced the activity of these Bunds for a long time. The American Fascists are called " Silver Shirts," and Sinclair Lewis' *It Can't Happen Here* is turning out to be a rather grim prophecy since the book refutes its title. To characterize their work it suffices to quote a " blurb " from *Ken* which precedes an article by William Miller : " It happened here last summer in Ohio when a professor, an ex-German spinster, a clergyman, a Volksbund Fuehrer, some Silver Shirts, a tear-gas merchant, the local Chamber of Commerce, a steel-master, a sheriff, a police chief, an ex-prosecutor, a German consul, and a complaisant National Guard combined to break a strike against ' Little Steel.' Here is a pattern for the Shape of Things to Come."

But not even *Ken*, not even the Washington Foreign

Office, knows all the widespread plans of the Gestapo in America. They may have been checked for the moment— but sooner or later there will be a " show-down " and the great American democracy will have to defend itself against its inner enemies.

In the same hemisphere the Dominican Republic has a pocket-Hitler at its head. " President Generalissimo Doctor The Illustrious Rafael Leonidas Trujillo y Molina, Benefactory of the Fatherland," has retired officially, but is still pulling the strings behind the scenes. Or rather, he follows the instructions of his distant but revered model and hero, Adolf Hitler. It is only a slight modification of the German methods that Trujillo's son, Ramfis, aged seven, has been a colonel in the Dominican army since he was three ; that his mother is a State Minister and Trujillo's brothers are high officers of the army. After all, a man has to look after his family. But should America get involved in a war with Nazi Germany, Dominica would prove a useful base for German warships. Trujillo has also given full economic support to the Third Reich ; German imports have increased seven hundred per cent ; and the agents of the Gestapo have a merry time in Trujillo's " Paradise on earth," in which massacres, executions, embezzlements, and tortures are more frequent that the apples on the tree of Original Sin. . . .

I have written about the tragic end of Engineer Formis, who was killed by Gestapo agents on Czechoslovak soil. Even if his short-wave sender was destroyed with him, there were others, even more courageous, who took up his work where he had left it off. There is a short-wave sender in the Reich itself, operated, as the Gestapo has reason to believe, on a lorry continually moving. It operates on 10.51 mega-cycles and can be heard abroad. It broadcasts anti-Hitler news and propaganda of the " German Freedom Front." . . . But I would not like to be in the boots of those plucky men who are working it—when, as they must be sooner or later, they are found out.

Sosnovsky was sent to Germany to spy out everything that

could be ferreted out.   George Blessmer was sent to Poland
to do the same and to direct the Nazi propaganda in the
country.   But he was called back to Berlin on some pretext
and was stupid enough to obey the summons.   A few days
later a short notice appeared in the papers announcing
Blessmer's suicide.   He had been " eliminated " by " Heydrich's Killers " as he was suspected of double-crossing the
Third Reich and working for another foreign power at the
same time.   Blessmer was an efficient man—but he was not
cunning enough to escape Heydrich's watch-dogs.

He had made one bad slip.   Having many friends in former
German colonies, he corresponded with some of them.
Quite a few wrote to him quite openly about their fears of
Germany regaining the colonies in which they lived.   They
also protested against Nazi propaganda which had been
organized in these territories.   Blessmer was careless enough
to receive these letters without denouncing their writers to
the Gestapo.   This was enough for Heydrich—coupled with
the other suspicion it served to seal Blessmer's doom.

There are about four hundred other " odds and ends " in
my note-books.   Let me save them perhaps for another
" report " on the Gestapo.   I am quite aware that some of
my readers will doubt all that is contained in this book.
They may be entitled to do so.   They will ask themselves :
are these leaders of the Third Reich human ?   Can there be
such depths of human baseness, cruelty, treachery ?

Yes, they are certainly human.   And most of them have
one or two qualities which raise them above average humanity.
Goering has personal courage, Goebbels cunning, Hitler a
great power of propaganda and oratory, Himmler a grasp of
details, and Hess enthusiasm.   But they also represent all
human failings ; only in their case these failings have full
play and complete freedom.   They are like sadistic children
who are allowed to do as they like.   Only a whole great nation
is at their mercy, a nation of mathematicians and musicians,
of great poets and brilliant inventors.   The evil they do is only
temporary—but its effects will be felt for centuries.

As for the genuineness of my data, the truth of my descriptions, let me end this book by quoting an article. It was written by William E. Dodd, the former ambassador of the United States to Germany and published by *The Nation*, a magazine of, as I believe, considerable standing in America. Mr. Dodd is neither a Jew nor a left-wing politician. His matter-of-fact report, inclining to understatement, might give the best support to all I have said in this book.

This is what Mr. Dodd writes :

" The black tide of anti-Semitism sweeps east and south : Nazi Vienna now vies with Berlin in terrorizing its native citizens who happen to be Jews. According to Vincent Sheean, not less than twenty thousand Jews have been thrown into concentration camps since the Nazis vaulted into the Austrian saddle. Their property has been confiscated, their persons subjected to the grossest physical indignities.

" Unless one has been an eye-witness, it is almost impossible to realize the horrors of this persecution. Never in modern times has a sovereign power bent itself so savagely upon the extinction of its own inhabitants, or so deliberately transgressed every tradition of culture and humanity.

"I cannot undertake to explain these transgressions ; I merely wish to set down some of the shocking incidents which took place in Germany during my ambassadorship. Many of them came to my personal attention ; some of them have documentary support, while others were gathered from unimpeachable sources.

" The keynote to the whirlwind of persecution which now thunders over Mittel-Europe is struck by Julius Streicher's newspaper, *Der Stuermer*. Across the front page of this journal snarls a fixed headline : THE JEWS ARE OUR DESTRUCTION. Beneath this sensational streamer the news columns reek with stories of atrocious Jew-baiting, ranging from the castration of a Jewish clerk who sought to ' defile ' the Aryan race by marrying a Christian girl, to the latest arrests of prominent Jewish scientists and scholars in Vienna and Bucharest. The whole journal daily spits *Judenhass* (Jew-hatred).

" Anyone who dissents from the Nazi programme—every class or creed that nurses a dream of liberty—is labelled a ' tool of international Jewry.' Streicher sneers at our Western democracy as ' Jewish decadence.' According to him the Dawes Plan was a Jewish plot : Dawes' real name is Davidsohn. Because J. P. Morgan helped finance Germany's enemies, his name is ' proved to be Morgenstern,' Streicher has even demonstrated that the Pope is a Jew and that his real name is Finkelstein.

" In every German city to-day large signs hang in café and shop windows : ' Only traitors talk or deal with Jews ' ; ' Jews visit this place at the risk of their lives.' Last year, during the height of anti-Semitic fury, Storm Troopers marched into cafés, seized Jews without any pretext and dragged them to jail. Aged men were beaten by the mobs ; one Jewish lady of high social position was dragged from her limousine and forced to scrub the streets, ' in order to demonstrate to the world that no Jew is beyond the power of the German Government.' Jews are thrown from moving trains, are whipped or shot down in front of their children ; they are molested with taunts and physical violence when they appear in the streets.

" Jewish men and women of all ages are frequently summoned to police headquarters for questioning and search. The ' questioning ' is accompanied by brutal beating ; the ' search ' is a pretext for stripping the Jews of whatever valuables they have on their persons. While awaiting their ordeal they must stand facing a blank wall for hours at a time, often until they collapse. For the slightest ' offence '—such as speaking to Aryans, or for ' touching food that an Aryan afterward ate '—they are heavily fined or imprisoned.

" The courts offer little or no redress; one merchant, whose store was looted by Storm Troopers of goods worth 1600 marks, was given a verdict of twelve pfennigs. In Magdeburg a Jewish youth was sentenced to four weeks' imprisonment for inviting an Aryan girl to a motion-picture show. A Jewish lawyer, seeking refuge in a police station from attackers, was forced to walk barefooted and trouserless through the streets of Breslau bearing a placard : ' I will never ask for police protection any more.' It was in protest against this type of atrocity that Stefan Lux, exiled German writer, shot himself before the League of Nations Assembly in 1936.

" The persecutions are not confined to powerful leaders of Jewry, or to persons who might be dangerous to the Hitler regime. No child, no aged or infirm person is spared. On April 22nd, 1937, the Gestapo evicted hundreds of inmates from thirty-three Jewish orphanages, sanatoriums and homes for the aged. Several hundred children were turned into the streets utterly homeless. Two hundred aged Jews, who had contracted with a society for support during the rest of their lives, were reduced to wandering beggary. At the same time, two hundred and fifty Jewish working girls were ousted from the Krugerheim Home, taken over as sleeping quarters for Storm Troopers ; no provision was made for the evicted young women.

" Ghetto benches, painted yellow, are placed in parks all over Germany ' for the use of Jews only.' Only the children of Jewish war veterans are allowed to attend the public schools ; these also sit in Ghetto benches and are shamefully addressed as ' Du, Jude ' (' You, Jew '). To-day by law all the learned professions are closed to Jews. Musical compositions by Mendelssohn and others of Jewish blood may not be played anywhere in Germany ; books by Jewish writers are burned in public bonfires.

" In provincial towns of Germany and Poland the shops and homes of Jews are stoned, robbed and burned. They are numbed with cold and emaciated by hunger. These persons are wholly dependent upon money received from relatives or friends in America, yet unless rigid technicalities are observed in transmitting such funds, the amount actually retained by the recipients is greatly reduced.

" A far-flung and systematic ' cold pogrom ' is being waged against Jewish business men from the Reich. In Nuremberg, signs are affixed in front of every Jewish store : ' Whoever puts his foot in a Jewish shop is no decent German, but a Jewish knave.' Deposits of Jewish money amounting to $500,000 were confiscated from banks last November by the Danzig police ' to prevent the flight of Jewish capital abroad.'

" Another device of the ' cold pogrom ' is the ' tax examination.' Nazi agents are empowered to enter a business and examine it for tax-determination purposes. This

' examination ' may easily last several weeks or months, during which time no merchandise under ' inspection ' can be sold. If a business is ' examined ' long enough, the merchant will be ruined.

" Trains to the border are packed with fugitive Jews who must pay a ' flight tax.' In everyday practice these fugitives are taken to police headquarters *en masse* and searched to the skin for contraband currency. Nazi searchers at the former Austrian borders claimed a haul of 20,000,000 schillings in one day.

" Refugee Jews who have expressed opposition to the Hitler regime are not safe even in another country. Professor Theodore Lessing of Hanover, one of the outstanding philosophers of Germany, was forced to take refuge in Czechoslovakia. There he was hunted down and murdered by Nazis. In 1935, one Rudolf Formis, a radio official, fled to Prague ; the Nazis attempted five times to abduct him, and finally shot him dead.

" When Hitler came to power there were only 500,000 Jews in Germany ; less than one per cent of the population. Of this number nearly 100,000 had fought in the World War ; 35,000 had been decorated for bravery. In the face of Junker military tradition, 2000 Jews had won commissions as officers. Baron Manfred von Richthofen, Germany's famed air-ace, had Jewish blood in his veins.

" I mention these facts to prove that there can be no truth in the Nazi claim that Jews are a race of unpatriotic traitors, ' overwhelming ' the Aryan element. To-day there are less than 40,000 Jews in Germany, a very small part of the population. Further, the Jews are not foreigners ; they have lived in Germany for hundreds of years.

" The fact is that anti-Semitism in Germany to-day is not a rational movement ; nor has it the unanimous consent of the entire German people. This mass persecution all springs from Hitler himself. He saw a prostrate and humiliated post-war Germany, bewildered by defeat. He needed an internal scapegoat to drain off thwarted nationalistic emotions.

" So he tossed in the oldest political trump-card, the Jews. He revived the old but almost extinguished Ghetto hatreds, and used *Judenhass* both as a lubricant and fuel for his Nazi machine. He predicts that by 1950 no Jews will be living within German boundaries, that they will all have been killed or driven into exile."

This is what William E. Dodd has to say—and I have very little more to add. If the people of the world would understand what menace Nazi Germany and its Gestapo means, they would certainly try some concerted action. Not war, for war would only unite Germany against a common enemy. But there are other methods—even if we exclude those of the Gestapo. We may or may not live to see the fall of this regime of hatred and blackmail ; but we must see its true face clearly.